I0168137

WISDOM, GLORY AND THE NAME

A BOOK OF WISDOM CHAPTERS IN TWO CENTURIES

PRIEST-MONK SILOUAN

SOPHIA INSTITUTE THEOTOKOS PRESS

NEW YORK

2014

COPYRIGHT 2014 Priest-monk Silouan.

ISBN   978-0-9835867-4-6

The right of Priest-monk Silouan to be identified as the author of this book has been asserted by him in accordance with the Copyright, Designs and Patents Act 1988.

All rights reserved. No part of this book may be reproduced, stored in a retrieval system or transmitted in any form or by any means, electronic, mechanical, photocopying, recording or otherwise, without written permission of the Publisher.

First published by the Sophia Institute in 2013, using their imprint: Theotokos Press, The Sophia Institute, Suite 416, 3041 Broadway, New York, NY 10027, USA. Tel. 212-280-1592.

Available from the Printer, Lulu.com. www.lulu.com

And from the Monastery of Saint Antony and Saint Cuthbert, Gatten, Pontesbury, Shropshire, SY5 0SJ UK.

Monastery website: www.orthodoxmonastery.co.uk

Email: Silouan@orthodoxmonastery.co.uk

Telephone: 44 (0) 1588 650571.

The icon of Holy Pentecost on the front cover, and the icons of the Feasts on the rear cover, are the work of the iconographer, Elaine Waller, and are reproduced here with her permission. < www.theholyimage.co.uk >

CONTENTS

Foreword

Very Revd Dr John A. McGuckin

Father Silouan's elegant and poetically lyrical new book continues an ancient Biblical Tradition in a modern age: that of the 'glorification of the Name.' The concept may be unfamiliar to many Christians today, but upon this tradition stand the very foundations of our faith. In order to approach to the heart of Jesus' message in the New Testament, we need to understand this basic context of the Lord's own thinking.

In order to understand the New Testament's own glorification of Jesus we need to be able to comprehend this theology or else we could never begin to understand what Scripture means by its acclamation (Mt. 21.9): 'Blessed is He who comes in the Name of the Lord.' In ancient thought the name 'stood for' the person it signified, and accordingly, immense reverence was given to the divine Name. The Name of the God of Israel was held to be so holy that the Israelite was forbidden to utter it aloud. Only the High priest spoke it out vocally as a great invocation on the Day of Atonement (Yom Kippur) and only then after he had filled the Holy of Holies in the temple with thick incense so as to 'mask the glory,' as he stepped inside the great curtain to offer the sprinkling of blood on the Mercy Seat of the Ark.

The Name of God, as biblically conceived, contained great power: it invoked the very presence (Shekinah) of God on earth. Of course, the Hebrew Bible had many other titles for God, and they are scattered over many pages – just as the word 'God' is used so often today that it drops off people's lips without thought many a time – even as a careless exclamation of surprise with little regard for meaning. But the titles are not the Name: to invoke the Name of God is something else, before which angels tremble.

The titles for God, such as El, or Adonai (what we might call the modern equivalents of God, Lord, Divinity) were a class apart from the sacred Tetragrammaton: YHWH. It was so important, for the later scribes, that this Holy Name should not be sullied by careless speech, that the vocal sounds (the marks within Hebrew writing that supplied what English writes in to its words as 'vowels') were deliberately written in to it from a different title altogether – thus leading to the common European misconception that the term was pronounced 'Jehovah.' The Jerusalem Bible scholars of more recent times were insistent on supplying the correct vowels and this has resulted in the anomaly, today, of hearing the Name read out aloud in many churches with original vocalizations – to the profound shock, I imagine, of any rabbinic hearer present: indeed to the dismay of any listener conversant with (and sensitive to) ancient theology.

Jesus glorifies the Name with a deliberate new and radical dimension. He speaks it out, but not as the Hebrew Tetragrammaton, but in his 'I AM' sayings and in the Aramaic vernacular of the people, it sounds out in his teachings as 'Abba, Father'. This is the burden of his message to his disciples about prayer: Pray as you would to your father (Mt. 6. 9-13), not as if begging a great Lord, but as if speaking to your father who loves you. In this case, our very prayer testifies to our love and trust in the power of God. Saint Paul summarized the whole essence of the apostolic teaching received from Christ, as a matter of shouting out that same message received as the Divine Spirit's illumination. Paul synopsizes the Gospel in simplest terms: Once we were enslaved in dark ignorance: then we were liberated by the Saviour, who reconciled us to God and put the Spirit into our hearts. Now it is this Holy Spirit that makes our hearts cry out: 'Abba. Father.'

There it all is in simplicity: the redemptive work of Jesus; the ineffable mercy of God; the overwhelming joy of the mystery of prayer. It is prayer of the illumined heart that thus becomes the act of glorification, revealing what mere mortal creatures make of that immense power, which renders angels speechless when they see it face to face. The Byzantine poets used to refer to this paradox with phrases such as: 'singing with our tongues of clay.' Our prayer rises up in great simplicity of vision: we only see enough; only what is necessary. As Moses himself learned when he was given the Name at Sinai (Ex. 3:14; 10.28; 33.20) to see too much would be a fatal overload for us. And so we glorify this little Name, Father, with the sense that we are skating over ice that is poised over a fathomless ocean beneath.

The invocation of the Name is an awesome thing nonetheless, despite God's clothing it in mercy. Even to invoke the Name gives proof of our obedience, our discipleship: for it is the primary reason that a human being stands on earth – so as to articulate the glory of the creation to its maker. How sad a world it would be (how contradictory to its own purposes of existence) if the praise of the glory ceased to emanate from the beauty of the earth. This will never happen: the world will turn as long as the creatures give glory. And if the human race falters, the natural world will sing on regardless. But what a glory it is when human hearts and minds sing the glory of the Name in harmony with the angels. Then glory shines radiantly and articulately: then love is nurtured, charity exalted, communion established; then the forces of darkness are pushed back and communion once more becomes the charter of humanity.

All this deep theology is put much better and more simply by the great teacher who phrased it so elegantly (Mt. 6. 9-10): 'Our Father in heaven, may your Name be reverenced; may your Kingdom come; may your will be done on earth as it is done (by the angels) in heaven.' Clearly, the hallowing of the Name is a matter of entering into the very heart of God's presence and being drawn up into his own compassionate plan for the cosmos. It is not a quiet mysticism at all: rather it is a fierce energy of life.

Father Silouan once again shows us in this book of deep mysteries, that contemplative prayer remains no escape from the world, or from that ever-active Spirit of Life. This is a book for those dedicated to learning wisdom in quietness. It is not a treatise: it is rather an artisan's manual. It offers the sparks to set the flame, which God himself will provide if we leave our hearts open to the divine descent through the ascetical exercise of prayer. This is a book that will lead us into the desert: where we shall find simplicity without distraction and wisdom enough here to deepen our understanding of the inconceivable beauty of God.

Father John Antony McGuckin.

Professor of Byzantine Christian Studies, Columbia University.

President of the Sophia Institute, New York.

Feast of Saint Macarius the Great of Egypt.

Sunday January 19th 2014.

Introduction

'Wisdom, Glory and the Name,' is a book of Wisdom Chapters in two 'Centuries,' the fourth and final book of a Wisdom Tetralogy of twelve Centuries, five entitled 'Wisdom Songs,' two, 'Wisdom and Wonder,' and three, 'Wisdom, Prophecy and Prayer.' It deals with the mysteries of Wisdom, Glory and the Name, which are hidden with Christ in the Holy of Holies. The mysteries are ineffable, and so inaccessible to the senses and to rational investigation, but wisdom discerns the ineffable and transmits what is discerned. Wisdom discerns the glory of the Name, and awakens the 'eye' of the heart in uncreated light.

The genre of a 'Century' of Wisdom Chapters apparently first appeared in the Orthodox Christian world between 382 and 399, possibly with the gnomic Centuries of Evagrius Ponticus, such as his *Praktikos*. The wisdom genre of Byzantine *kephalia* was gnomic, transmitting wisdom to unveil spiritual knowledge of the mysteries, through purification, illumination and deification, which Biblical wisdom calls glorification. It was highly valued in the desert because it renewed illumination and union at the heart of the tradition of stillness, *hesychia*, and does so to this day. It was employed in the desert for a thousand years, from approximately 380 to 1380, and was revered in monastic libraries but not reused since then.

It is brought out again in this cycle of twelve 'Centuries' in order to impart the integral Christian wisdom of the Name, challenging the current view that Christian wisdom is shallow and narrow, even null and void. At a time when all the world's wisdoms are flooding our cultural shores, Christian wisdom is obliged to break silence, without profaning the ineffable mysteries of the Holy of Holies.

Five Centuries of 'Wisdom Songs,' on the Name, the Song of Songs, Holy Wisdom, the Mysteries of Glory, and the Wisdom of Stillness, impart again the wisdom of the glory of the Name. Two Centuries on 'Wisdom and Wonder,' reflect a wondrous openness that sustains wisdom, whilst three Centuries on 'Wisdom, Prophecy and Prayer,' impart the wisdom that is renewed through prophecy, and sustained by prayer. Two Centuries on 'Wisdom, Glory and the Name,' complete the Centuries on 'Wisdom, Prophecy and Prayer,' together with the whole cycle of twelve Centuries, where it began, with the ineffable glory of the Holy Name.

Archimandrite Sophrony imparted the Name 'I AM,' without referring to controversies over the Name or wisdom, and Saint Silouan preferred silence on these matters, even though he lived through the Name crisis on Mount Athos that saw the exile of hundreds of his contemporaries. The Onomoclast and Sophiaclast Synods of the Twentieth Century intended to affirm Orthodoxy against what they called the heresies of Name worshipping and Sophiology, but managed to affirm, instead, little more than shallow nominalism and narrow Trinitarian formalism. Shallow controversy tends to spawn narrow extremes, falling fatally short of ineffable wholeness, the Spirit and Truth of Holy Orthodoxy.

The nominalism of Onomoclasm is not cured by sophisticated philosophies of the Name, such as we find in the circles of *Imyaslavi,* but by wholesome Name hallowing, such as we find in the Lord's Prayer and the Magnificat. The external formalism of Sophiaclasm successfully condemned the heresy of a fourth hypostasis, which Father Sergei Bulgakov insisted he never taught, but fell short of the ineffable mysteries which Biblical and Patristic wisdom transmit through Hesychasm.

The Name of God is God's self-revelation in his uncreated energy, but not God in his essence. The wisdom of God is God in his uncreated energy of illumination, but neither God in his essence, nor a fourth divine person. The Name, as a word of human language, is created, but as the self-revelation of God, is uncreated. Chalcedonian wisdom imparts the Name as communion without confusion, and wisdom as union without division. To condemn love of wisdom is unwittingly to condemn Christ. To be condemned for love of his Name is to be condemned for his Name's sake, which Jesus said is inevitable, since that is why they condemned him. But there is no divine condemnation for those who are in him, which gives strength to those who are condemned by men, for his wisdom or his Name's sake.

Long ago, iconoclasts intended to affirm Orthodoxy, but produced a serious heresy, which the Seventh Ecumenical Council eventually corrected. Onomoclasts intended to condemn what they saw as Name divinization, but unintentionally produced Onomoclasm, which is shallow nominalism. Sophiaclasts intended to condemn what they saw as the heresy of Sophiology, but failed to do justice to the luminous depths of Biblical and Patristic wisdom. The cure of both Onomoclasm and Sophiaclasm lies in the Biblical revelation of wisdom and the glory of the Name, which Patristic wisdom prescribes to heal extremism in the uncreated fires of hallowing vision.

The recent Orthodox witness of Archmandrite Sophrony to the central significance of the Name of God, 'I AM,' throws a profound and searching light on the whole Patristic Tradition, especially as it is lived in the desert. His writings present this as a vision of the person or *hypostasis*, addressing the Patristic theologies of the person, as well as the world of French existentialism and personalism in the Paris of his time. But more than half a century later, the vision of the Name now has to address wisdom in the light of a global meeting of cultures, and to bring out the treasures of Patristic wisdom and the Name for this encounter.

There is no Orthodoxy, right glorification, without glorification of God through his self-revelatory Name, which deeply questions names and naming, as well as the function of language in deification, in the light of the revelation of the Name and wisdom. Both Testaments bear witness to the Name, and so it is no surprise to find the Fathers interpreting Baptism in the Name, Chrismation in the Name and Communion in the Name, in their teaching on the Eucharist. The wisdom that discerns the glory of the Name is not an optional extra, but the very heart of Biblical and Patristic wisdom.

Patristic wisdom is endless renewal, reinterpretation, and regeneration, in the light of wisdom and the Name. Since the ultimate Name is above all names, it has a logic that opens directly into the *Logos*, which is exactly what the logic of 'I AM' does when it transcends predication. The Name is saying, ' I AM who I AM,' or 'I AM the One who is,' or 'I AM He who is.' (Exodus 3:14). 'I am I AM, that is my Name, and I do not give my glory to another.' (Isaiah 42:8). 'I am I AM and there is no other. There is no God but I AM alone.' (Isaiah 45:5). 'Before Abraham was, I AM.' (John 8:58).

The name Jesus means 'I AM saves,' *'Yah shuah.'* (Mt 1:20f). It is evident that the Name 'I AM' is ineffable and so says nothing that defines the indefinable, yet somehow says everything that can be said, for the Name defines God to be beyond definition. The Name, as 'word' of the Word, is saving, liberating, healing prophecy. As prayer of the heart, it releases into freedom. It self-liberates God in all and all in God. The Name, beyond predication, communicates ineffable openness as consummate completeness. When Christian prophecy speaks of a new Name, (Rev 3:12), it is not saying that another name will supersede the ultimate, saving Name above all names, but that the imparted Name is a renewing Name, the Name that, when invoked by prayer, makes all things new.

Saint Ephrem the Syrian says God clothes himself in our language so that he might clothe us in his mode of life. (Hymns of Faith 31). From the standpoint of convention, our language is the construct and the product of convention, and so is created. But when God clothes himself in 'words' of the Word, our language becomes charged with uncreated energy, and so becomes the expression of God in act, and so in a certain sense uncreated, being God's Word clothed in our words as his 'words,' his *logoi*. When the Word says '*Abba*, Father,' our word father is filled with uncreated revelatory energy, unveiling the glory of the Name.

When 'words' of the Word unveil the 'I AM' of God, God is encountered in his self-revelation, received through profound recognition of 'I AM' by 'I AM,' which imparts deification. It is passed on as transmission of the remembrance of God from heart to heart. The divine mode of life is deification, *theosis*, and it transcends our ways and means to approach God, our talk of God, and all conventional rites and practices that are means to an end. 'Words' of the Word are *theologia mystica*, not to be confused with our words about God in conventional theology.

Wisdom has an ineffable capacity to unveil the Name and awaken hearts, because it is the enlightening energy of the Spirit's insight into the mutual reciprocal recognition of the Father and the Son. Such wisdom is the wisdom of the Father invested in the Son, discerned by the Spirit, one 'I AM' in three persons, each of whom bears witness in a unique and different way to oneness of glory in the Name. When wisdom discerns 'words' of the Word, in creation and in God, it is not a conventional wisdom that knows nothing of deep turning. It sees with God's 'eye' in the heart, not as the world sees. It communicates the wisdom that inspires the divine-human language of prophecy and prayer.

The Name *YHWH* names God, 'HE WHO IS,' but the Name *EHYEH* reveals who he is, 'I AM.' The Name of God is God's 'I' awareness and 'AM' presence in act, actualizing his essence as uncreated creative energy in us, as purifying fire, uncreated light and deifying glory. The Name Jesus, '*Yah shuah,*' imparts the saving energy of God's 'I AM,' as in the 'I AM' sayings in the Gospel of John, with and without predicates. The name of Jesus mediates the saving energy of the Name, to embrace all in his healing energy of glory.

To the Onomoclast, words are just words and names are not God, but for Orthodox seers, the Name is not just a word or sound, but expresses the uncreated energy of God by means of which God is signified and recognized. God is really present in his Name, a real presence that is shared with us, as in the Holy Mysteries. In this sense, as mystery, the Name is God, indivisibly one with his saving energies, whilst remaining unconfused with his essence.

When God reveals on Sinai his Name 'I AM,' the Word is God's self-revelation, not information about the divine. When Jesus transmits the Name, in the Gospel of John, he uses signs and 'I AM' sayings, unveiling ineffable openness. As essence or substance, God infinitely transcends his Name, but as energy, his Name includes us in his uncreated life as way and truth. (John 14:6). The dialectical antinomy of essence and energy in the Name is at the heart of this mystery, so for the reader who is unfamiliar with Patristic wisdom, it helps to see the difference between seeing from without and seeing from within.

Looked at from outside, the mystery of the Name appears to confuse the uncreated and the created, which is why stones were thrown when Jesus said, 'Before Abraham was, I AM,' (John 8:58). Onomoclasm springs from this external objectification, for it seeks to challenge what it sees as confusion, only to fall into division. Its intention is to preserve Orthodoxy in the only way open to it, from without, only to fall short of indivisibility, which is the mystery of union and communion.

From within, wisdom holds paradoxical antinomy steady, without confusion or division, saying, 'Turn and see!' The *praxis* of *theoria* in the awakened heart discerns what every external perception misses, leading to the decisive conclusion that there is no Orthodoxy of the illumined heart outside the state of *theoria*, which is wisdom.

From within the Name, not only is God unveiled as ineffable openness in everything, everything is unveiled as ineffable openness in God. *Theoria* not only transforms *praxis* into an expression of illumination, it opens the veil of the Holy of Holies and transmits the mysteries of *theosis*. Within *theosis*, the ineffability of God permeates everything.

Predication undergoes a profound paradigm shift when illumination opens onto the ineffable glory of the Kingdom to come. Revelation of the Name 'I AM,' beyond predication, unveils the ineffable openness of God beyond conventional predication. Saint Denys' negation of the negation, so crucial for Saint Maximus, now informs every perception. The senses perceive everything with the 'eye' of wisdom, spiritually, not materialistically. Wisdom sees ineffable glory unveiled in everything, ineffably. Christ is wisdom imparting the Spirit's ineffable Chrism of glory, unveiling God in our midst through his Name. He reveals his presence so that, with the Apostle Paul, we awaken not to ourselves, but to Christ in our midst.

Wisdom's vision is unfamiliar in a technological and scientific age, but this is only because she turns and sees the glory the objectifying mind overlooks. There is no inherent conflict between wisdom and science, and science and technology have their legitimate job to do. It is only when wisdom is usurped that delusion reigns. It is when confusion replaces communion that division parodies paradox.

Chapters on 'Wisdom, Glory and the Name' are not giving us information, nor are they expressing religious, moral or aesthetic opinions. Desert wisdom imparts the injunction to turn and see, freeing recognition to flourish as the remembrance of God. It transmits the wisdom of a neglected, very ancient tradition. It bears witness to the wisdom of the Paraclete, which is why an icon of the Feast of Pentecost adorns the front cover of this book. Christ the *Logos* is the shepherd of wisdom, whose function is to unveil the glory of the Name. The senses fall short of what the mind overlooks, the wisdom of glory revealing God in his Name.

Priest-monk Silouan.

Monastery of Saint Antony and Saint Cuthbert.

Feast of Holy Theophany, January 6th 2014.

WISDOM, GLORY

AND THE NAME

FIRST CENTURY

1.

Wisdom discerns the mysteries of resurrection, ascension and glorification descending from heaven to wed earth to heaven in the Kingdom of the Holy of Holies. Wisdom's sevenfold completeness embraces a threefold ascent to God by purification in the Spirit, illumination through Christ's Name, and glorification of the Father, and a fourfold descent of his Kingdom of wisdom and glory in the Paraclete, as tongues of fire, the fire of fire, fire of water, fire of earth and fire of air.

Wisdom and glory descend as tongues of fire at Pentecost. Fire of fire separates out satanic confusion and burns off its impurities. Fire of water dissolves diabolic division so that divisive fixations melt, leaving the heart purified. Fire of earth coagulates what was dissolved and congeals it into translucence. Fire of air integrates all translucent fires by glorifying God in his Name, which is glorification in God through his Name.

Descending glorification in wisdom is the radiant blessing of God, which is so pure that no impurity can intrude between wisdom and God. The wisdom of the Paraclete is the agent of resurrection and the energy of ascension, bride of the Lamb in the Kingdom of immortality. Wisdom's reign is uncreated light creating all things anew.

Wisdom is sight to the spiritually blind, hearing to the spiritually deaf and understanding to hardened hearts, curing spiritual sclerosis. She descends in glory to undo all falls, and empty all hells, so as to turn the 'powers' back from corrosive confusion to communion, from dislocating division to deifying union. Her mysterious descent in glory is described in the Book of Revelation as the appearance of a likeness to a heavenly city and a tree of life, a gift of wisdom as bride, mother of eternal life.

Wisdom returns from exile, as glorification of God on earth, as God is glorified in heaven. Wisdom is witness to Christ's return of all things to God in glory, earth wedded to heaven, in God, through God.

2.

Wisdom's return is paradise regained, a tree of life and a throne of glory in the midst, from which living waters of eternal life never cease to flow. The fountain of life is hid beneath the shadow of very ancient wings. The light in which light is seen is a river whose streams make glad the dwelling of wisdom in the glory of God Most High. The place of glory in the midst is a place of broad rivers and many streams, waters of immortality renewing creation. It is the place of wisdom and glory hid with Christ in God in the inmost heart.

The waters of wisdom satisfy, so that we do not thirst, for whoever drinks Christ, drinks wisdom welling up to eternal life. Whoever drinks wisdom becomes Christ by grace, deified by grace in his Kingdom of light. Living waters of wisdom flow from hearts purified and illumined by wisdom in the midst. In the light of such fountains of wisdom, light sees light. The seed is too small to objectify, but the tree has branches that embrace all that there is.

Wisdom shares the glory she had at the beginning with the Father, through the Son, that all might see, in the Spirit. She prays with Christ that the glory she sees in the age to come be shared with us, in this 'place' of the Name, where end and beginning meet. Here all worlds end, where all worlds begin again anew in every instant. Here, God ends this world to welcome the world to come, making all things new.

The unceasing openness of wisdom and glory is enshrined in the blessed purity of the heart that sees God. The pure in heart are purified and illumined by love. They see God, not in essence, but in energy of glory, and glory is the uncreated energy of unselfish love. To be washed in the blood of the lamb is to be infused with the life-blood of unselfish love.

When wisdom returns, she brings love's glory descending from above, to hallow the Name in all, and to hallow all in the Name. To suffer love's glory is to enter into the glory of love. Blessed is the pure heart of wise and glorious love.

3.

Wisdom descends as the bride of Christ unveiling love's glory as a garden of paradise. The paradise garden is a symbol of the Holy of Holies, which is no place in space nor moment in time, but the 'place' of the Name 'I AM,' that leaps right over space and cuts right through time. The garden of the Name is a one-pointed flash of illumination born of deep ecstatic turning. Such turning turns us out of ourselves and into God. It turns confusion out so that God is in, for we were never really at centre, but only thought we were, when we were caught in the delusion of self-centred self-obsession. In which case, God in Eden was always at centre and we can enter the garden if we spiral out of time and space, by spiralling into God, through Christ, in the Spirit.

Glorification in love's glory is God's descending initiative not ours. Wisdom knows what he originally intends, intimate as she is with the heart of the Word, communicating the Name, and of the Paraclete, unveiling its uncreated light in the heart.

We ascend with Christ in illumination, whilst the Paraclete descends as glorification. We live between the moment of illumination and the moment of glorification, sometimes in one, sometimes in the other.

There is a critical tension between the timeless moments of light and glory. There is no argument, because both lie beyond what the conceptual mind can grasp or argue about.

We turn and see, entering profound *metanoia* that generates profound *theoria*, but it is God who works the holy mysteries of *theosis*.

4.

Wisdom counsels us to receive the grace of illumination, which purifies and enlightens the heart, so that we might partake of the blessing of glorification, which deifies the world with great peace. Wisdom stands steadfast as the peace in which we pray for peace in the Litany. Wisdom is herself the garden of peace, the *unio mystica*, which is immaculate and pure. Wisdom is mother and bride of all her peace making children, whilst remaining ever virgin.

Hermas, in his 'Shepherd,' says he loves his Lady Rose, *Kyria Rhoda*, but his love and her peace are not of this world. She is his spiritual bride and guides him into paths of peace, as later Beatrice was to do for Dante, and the *Madonna Intelligenza* for her *fedeli d'amore*. She is not subject to him as his possession, but is an icon of the peace and grace of illumination.

Wisdom's symbol is sometimes the lily and sometimes the rose, the rose of Sharon or narcissus rose. Wisdom's lily is symbol of purification, of illumination and ascent. Wisdom's rose is God's descending blessing of glorification and deification, inspiring a rosary that opens to mysteries of glorification. The complete dispensation of wisdom is lily and rose, transcending ascent and immanent descent, grace of illumination and blessing of glorification.

Wisdom's garden of great peace is a symbol of the perfection for which love longs, the wholeness, which love seeks, and the sevenfold completeness love desires here in the midst, *in medio mundi,* at the centre of the world. Gregory Nyssa, Denys and Maximus know of no division between love as *agape,* and love as *eros,* for both are the grace of love's glory that illumines, and both are love's glory blessing the deified.

The key to the Kingdom of Christ in the midst is the Name. Recognition of 'I AM' imparts illuminating grace and deifying blessing when we turn and see who sees at centre, permitting wisdom to wed the Name in the depths of the heart. Wisdom weds glory, beauty of the Name. Illumination is their spiritual betrothal as the lily. Glorification is their spiritual marriage as the rose.

5.

Desert wisdom bears witness to the oneness of *praxis* and *theoria,* unveiled when both are integrated in *theosis.* To turn is to see, and to see is to be turned, unveiling glory for which turning and seeing are one. Wisdom reveals what the Name does, which is to discern the unconditioned 'I AM,' so that the conditioned body-mind no longer usurps God in the midst. The uncreated is no longer confused with the created at centre. The Name is the ground of illumination, whilst wisdom is its indispensible condition.

Christ says, 'Before Abraham was, I AM,' but this does not impinge on us at all until we turn and see. We do not actually awaken to the Name except through illumination. To turn is to see what he means. Illumination grounds the practice of seeing. But when reification creeps in, turning and seeing are objectified. They are grasped by the binary mind and reduced to abstractions like opposing rivals in a court of law. Uncreated grace and created free will are locked into a courtroom of juridical abstractions. Reifications of the uncreated and the created, which fall short of the glory of things as they are, can become fixated extremes. Extremism is a symptom of subtle separation that calls for healing and hallowing.

Practice of timeless *theoria* dissolves abstracted extremes and the unreal confusions and divisions they engender. For *theosis, praxis* and *theoria* are one, though not confused, in a reciprocal union. Christ is God's self-revelation of his Name, and his indivisibility is love's glory, lived as integral wisdom, for which turning and seeing are one. Glorification requires oneness of *praxis* and *theoria,* hallowing the Name in the Kingdom of wisdom, where means and ends are reversed anew in every moment.

The vertical axis of uncreated light is unveiled by the Name, whilst the horizontal resolution of confusion and division is revealed by wisdom. The Name is the ground of original illumination, whereas wisdom is its precondition. Wisdom is the awakened state of *theoria,* whilst turning is the *praxis* that actualizes the revelatory Name.

6.

Purification seeks God in the midst. Illumination embraces God in the midst. Glorification embraces all things in the midst, as the self-emptying of Christ, who is the self-emptying of God and the self-emptying of Man. Glory fills heaven and earth and glorifies all that there is. It is not anthropocentric, like purification, nor theocentric like illumination, but turns both kinds of centrism inside out so that what was outside comes in. Both purification and illumination have their scope and way of seeing things. Purification has illumination in view and so sees itself as a means to that end. Illumination sees purification not as means but as expression of itself as end, but since it has glorification in view, it does not transcend a subtle separation, which lasts until it is dissolved in glorification. Glorification is our destiny from the beginning and it is our destiny in the end, but being timeless, glory has no beginning and no end.

Illumination is the self-emptying of man into unconfused union with God, whereas glorification is the self-emptying of God into unconfused communion with all that there is. It is the integral divine-human mystery of the Eucharist lived as deification of all in all. When glorification is discerned by wisdom in the Spirit, purification is the glory of illumination in the Word, and illumination is the glory of the Father, origin of all glories. The turn that transmutes light into glory is the mystery of deifying descent, which finally empties us of everything exclusively anthropocentric or narrowly theocentric and embraces everything in God for God without trace of separation. The Name communicates deification of all in all, which the Eucharist empowers, raising purification and illumination to the frequencies of glorification. These frequencies are ineffable but wisdom discerns them and transmits them as mysteries of union and communion.

Once the Eucharist is truly operative, glorification integrates purification and illumination into its higher frequency as purifying union and illumining communion. Just as every earthly Eucharist is an icon of the Heavenly Feast in the age to come, so its mysteries of the heart are foretastes of purifying union and illumining communion.

7.

Christ reveals that 'I and the Father are one.' (John 10:30). He tells us that when we see who he is, we see the Father who sent him. For 'I AM' is one as God is one. Filial 'I AM,' is one with paternal 'I AM,' and this grace of recognition is given in 'I AM,' the Holy Spirit, whose presence is freedom. The Spirit does not proceed outside God when he proceeds from the Father to abide in the Son. Rather, he embraces all that there is in his abiding, so nothing is outside God in the Son.

When God releases God to be Father, Son and Holy Spirit, embracing all in all, we let God be God in his image, giving glory to God the Father, through God the Son, in God the Holy Spirit. When we hallow God's Name and let his Kingdom come and his will be done, we let God be God in us rather than get God to do our will.

Christ comes to us saying, 'Fear not, peace be with you.' He grants us great peace, not the false peace that deludes and deceives. The Spirit prays without ceasing in our midst, so that confusion and division cannot come nigh our dwelling place, which is wisdom. Wisdom is herself in the image of God when she prays unceasingly for the enlightenment of all in the Holy Spirit. Such prayer is God's prayer, through the Son, in the Spirit. It is the unceasing prayer of glorification, from the Father, through the Son, in the Spirit.

No one knows what God is, but elders and saints concur with angels that they are certain that *'He is who he is,'* and that his Name, 'I AM,' is his revelation of who he is. This consensus in heaven is ours on earth in the hallowed Name and the Kingdom come. The Spirit frees by releasing us from all confusion that divides. It follows that there are no fallen powers that can separate us from God or one another anymore. All such powers of delusion dissolve like mist in morning sun when glory comes. The Spirit frees by disempowering all subtle powers of separation. Wisdom empowers us to live in freedom from all powers of division, which spring from the confusions of vainglory. She empties vanity of vanity so that glory no longer falls short of glory, but hits the mark. This undoes falls in heavenly realms, which confuse and divide what God unites and differentiates.

8.

Myth pictures the mysteries of the heart as heavenly realms until the single eye of the heart awakens. Mythic imagery falls away when wisdom sees, yet the moment she turns back to speak, her words use imagery without which the invisible could never be clothed as symbol or her mysteries conveyed. Mythic imagination is not wisdom, but wisdom weaves her myths to tell of the ineffable. Myth and symbol are wisdom's gradual unveiling of the Name.

We sometimes talk as if it was up to us to make the Kingdom come, whereas it is God's unifying energy not ours that saves. Our co-operation is crucial, but when we react by over reacting, the mystery of synergy is overlooked. Wisdom teaches us to go beyond every fixation and reification, so that separation is dismantled even as it arises. We lose God when we let the symbolic image usurp God. We bind ourselves in knots until we loose God from our grasp and let God be God. Divine power to bind and to loose comes to help us loose our double binds and release God's glory to be glory in the Kingdom come.

God is 'I AM,' revealing God in our midst. God is 'He who is,' eternally. It is not what we do but 'Who he is,' that saves. He is always already the glory that he is, but our free co-operation is called for. It is a subtle synergy that does not usurp God at centre. Release looses God's glory from our knots so that his Kingdom within can come. Releasing glory releases us in God to be who we are originally meant to be. We return to the origin, which is the Father, who generates the Son in us eternally.

We are released in the Father to be sons by grace in the Son, sealed by the Holy Spirit. Body and mind are released to be a temple for wisdom when they no longer usurp God's throne of the heart. Grace is enough and can be trusted, for God alone saves. One with God at the beginning, we are one with his energy of glory. 'Let there be light,' and there is light. To let there be light is to be light, enlightening the world. Light in abundance arises in the midst, and the uncreated creative light is without bounds.

9.

The *praxis* of *theoria* is wisdom lived as glory through the Name. It calls for tradition, which offers a mystagogical phenomenology of divine human perception to disclose the mysteries of union and communion in the Spirit. It speaks only when God inspires speech to transmit the Name in wisdom, and is silent when gossip seeks to objectify the mysteries. It refuses to cultivate reifications that replicate the mysteries as parody. It stays with the void of the uncreated in the midst, as the uncreated reveals its indivisibility with created form, arising in timeless presence as the glory of the Name. It does not avoid the void but abides at the point of timeless presence, letting God be God in the midst, letting created form arise in union with God without interfering.

Lived wisdom and glory are inseparable, but a phenomenology of inseparability is possible only when gossipy objectification is avoided. This is no mere philosophical posture but a demanding *praxis* of turning, *metanoia,* which allows *theoria* to purify the heart and illumine the mind. It suspends the fixations of the binary mind in order that the mind and the heart unite in uncreated light, which is the uncreated glory of the Name. The irruptions of uncreated grace rupture the hardened heart so that its addictions can begin to dissolve.

Uncreated light is fire at first, then light, before glory is revealed. The tradition of Christian wisdom does not speak about itself in ways that harden hearts, but transmits the Name in wisdom by communicating the injunction to turn and see. Archimandrite Sophrony loved to speak of the mysteries of the Name 'I AM.' What he had received in freedom, he passed on freely and without reserve.

The Day of the Name is time for wisdom to return and turn hearts, so that all that there is can return to God, which is called *theosis* by monastic wisdom, and glorification by the Bible. Wisdom's scope is cosmic like the Holy Liturgy, for her enlightened intent is the glorification of one and all.

The *praxis* of *theoria* opens the heart to glory in the Name, and is the best remedy for reification, because it purifies the heart for freedom.

10.

Wisdom discerns the glory of the Name, revealed by the Father, through the Son, in the Holy Spirit. Wisdom severs confusion and heals division, so that all falls are undone by love's mysteries of glorification. Without wisdom in love's glory, purification, illumination and glorification remain hidden with Christ in God, yearning to be made known. With wisdom, God is with us, Emmanuel, purifying and illumining all. Hearts open to God's destiny of glory, hidden in Christ with God from before the foundation of the world. The Name inspires glorification when God's uncreated creative energies of grace awaken the eye of the heart, so that what sight and hearing missed, spiritual vision sees and illumined hearts hear and understand. There is no end to the mysteries of revelation and glory, once wisdom is unveiling them in the Holy of Holies.

Wisdom is witness to the Name when confusion dies in the midst and union rises in its stead to heal division, which separates the soul from God. The witness of wisdom is spiritual martyrdom, dying to delusion, dying into glory, which is illumined glorification. The timeless presence of 'I AM' unveils the timeless wisdom of glorification. We die before we die by hallowing the Holy Name of God. We die before we die so that death has no dominion over us. We die to confusion to live mysteries of union, dead to separation in hallowed communion. We live the wisdom of the cross, alive to glory in resurrection.

Wisdom loves the Name, reciprocating the Name's love of wisdom. The lost meaning of philosophy is restored. For centuries, the word philosophy has been bandied about without love and without wisdom, with no awareness of the Holy Name. When the Name is lost, love of wisdom dies, and the Kingdom is left dangling in mid air, vulnerable to every passing ideology. When love of wisdom is lost, philosophy becomes talk about talk, then reason reasoning about reason, in the University. It is left to the desert to revere love of wisdom and to hallow the Name so the Kingdom comes.

Philosophy is restored in the desert when love of wisdom is lived as noetic turning, as illumination, and as glorification in the reign of the Name.

11.

Wisdom discerns the glory of the Kingdom of the Holy Trinity, not as a presumptuous scrutiny of the divine Essence but as direct revelation of the uncreated energy, or activity, of the originating Father, communicated by the revelatory Word, accessible in the radiant clarity of the Holy Spirit. The Kingdom of glory is wisdom's realm in which all phenomena arise, abide, and finally return. It is the original place of uncreated grace, in the eternal personhood of Christ, which unveils the mind of the Spirit at the heart of creation and revelation.

Glory transforms everything, but nothing transforms glory, which wisdom discerns in the glory of the age to come, which is primordial glory in the beginning. 'I AM' is not opposed to anything, passing over into freedom, in perfect wholeness. Uncreated light empties out heavy conditioning in every situation. Once the saints step back and turn right round, a halo of light sees through every temptation of the enemy to usurp God in the midst. Seers do not dither and doubt, because they do not fall into temptation to play God in place of God at centre. Christ points to the Kingdom of God in the midst. He does not trust thoughts about externals. He restores us to the glory of his coming Kingdom. He frees us from delusion in the hallowed Name.

The way of 'I AM' is truth and life, the same yesterday, today and forever. True as timeless life, the way of the Name frees everything everywhere without strain or stress. The Spirit seals all moments with the sign of the cross, severing dissipating thoughts, so that in God nothing separates God from God anymore. All glory is to God, whatever arises, so nothing can separate us from Christ in the primordial ground, which is God the Father.

True personhood is transcendent and unconditioned. The Spirit of wisdom frees. It is ineffable, and utterly indefinable, so nobody can get a grip on it from outside. It is called the Great Peace because it is free of knotted conflicts and warring obsessions. It is life eternal because time past and time future fall away. Christ is in our midst and ever shall be without end. Death has no dominion in the Kingdom of God.

12.

When we awaken to Christ in the midst, the wholeness of God is revealed in his ineffable completeness. We begin to live according to the whole, *katholon,* which is what Catholic really means. We give glory to God aright, which is what Orthodox really means. The teaching of the Fathers was transmitting this. The Saints were not trapped in their own words and formulations, all of which point to the Kingdom. They revered the mind of Christ, which says, 'Not I, but the Father!'

The Kingdom of God is not something that can be grasped by an unenlightened mind, nor can the sacred tradition, which hands it on in age after age, be understood by a mentality that is not awake to God, through God, in God's Name. Possessing a correct opinion on the Holy Trinity is not to be confused with *theoria* of the Holy Trinity. Right opinion is not right glorifying Orthodoxy, which is hidden with Christ in God's glorification of God. Doxological *theosis* is not an optional extra but the living heart of the sacred tradition. The Kingdom of glory is not acquired but is unveiled when what obscures it is emptied out through *theoria* by *theosis.* Illumination is sudden but its assimilation takes time, and calls for the practice of wisdom and purification of the heart. Glory and wisdom work together in co-operation as purification and illumination, consummated in glorification.

The Kingdom of God comes when God's Name is hallowed and his will done, not when we just repeat the Lord's Prayer by rote. God wills his Kingdom of wisdom and the Name because it is the direct, living expression of 'Who He Is,' 'I AM' from 'I AM,' causing to be all that there is. He inspires hallowing of the Name because it undoes the separation at the root of the fall. It cures the narcissism that insinuates itself when 'I AM' is confused with 'me.' It heals neuroses, which arise when confusion spawns division, reducing us to shattered fragments of who we are. Wisdom discerns the glory of the Name and so unveils the Kingdom in our midst. The Name is hallowed, revealing the glory of the age to come, raising the living dead and healing the dolorous wound.

13.

The Name is wondrous in the Kingdom of uncreated light. 'I AM' is all that it knows, but is not confined to anything. When body and mind fall away off-centre, 'I AM' liberates into the freedom and the glory of the age to come. Sorrow and sadness flee away in the uncreated energy of unconditional love. The Name opens the heart to its uncreated ground when wisdom discerns the glory of the Kingdom come. The Name awakens us from separation in time and space, but embraces all in its eternal presence. 'I AM' is release and freedom from attachment, expanding and contracting with ease, one without confusion with everyone and everything. Awesome joy, arising as love, explodes to embrace all that there is. There is nothing narcissistic about this selfless 'I AM' or its radiance. Narcissism arises when the egocentric contraction is superimposed, and like a virus, infects every perception. Wisdom sees through this confusion and heals the heart with uninfected freedom. We turn and see the 'I AM' of Christ omniscient and omnipresent in our midst.

For 'I AM who is, who was and who is to come,' past, present and future are ever-present, simultaneous, and timeless. Wisdom unveils the eternal glory of the Name, which eternally enshrines the mysteries of wisdom. Orthodox right glorification of God's Name awakens the eye of the heart and gradually opens it to prayer for the whole world as for oneself. Love is the real meaning of Orthodoxy, not the narrow trammels of fear.

Saint Silouan sings of this love, which inspired him to break the silence of humility. This is not understood by fear, which tries to overcome pride by ascetic effort. Love cures fear so as to rise into the fullness of glory, which wisdom unveils in the hallowed Name. Archimandrite Sophrony, schooled in this love, on the Holy Mountain, awoke to the 'I AM,' which became his song, imparting the wisdom of the Name to broken souls, so it becomes their song too. Thus it is that sacred tradition is transmitted and handed on, where salt marshes and mud flats bequeath the translucent air of the Holy Mountain, and the Name unveils its glory to wisdom on a hill.

14.

Wisdom opens the eye of the heart to the Great Peace of the Holy of Holies, by unveiling the glory of the Kingdom in the hallowed Name. Wisdom dawns to illumine the dark night of our spirit, one spirit with the uncreated light of the Holy Spirit, curing the confusion and division that characterize the fallen state. The ancients transmitted this wisdom in the desert, in the Name of Christ, not themselves, so that they remain living springs of wisdom in every age. With this ancient wisdom, the desert can address the pathologies of modernity as well as the narcissism and nihilism of post-modernity.

Wisdom's timeless origin in the Father of lights is the Word's primordial revelation in the Spirit of Truth. There is perennial uncreated energy in wisdom's transmission, which is none other than the revelatory energy of the Holy Trinity. Christ is both the revealer of this energy and the revelation itself. Wisdom Chapters transmitted his mysteries in the desert, not with cold logic but with symbolic power, not with mere repetition of traditional formulas but uncreated creative energy awakening direct vision.

Wisdom initiates the heart so that the glory of the Name is unveiled. Initiatory symbols serve this formless transmission by transcending their external form, renewing the heart of the tradition. There is no trace of anything created in the limpid purity and transparent clarity of this wisdom, yet it is wisdom that renews creation in every moment, with capacity to cleanse the prisms of perception and intuition. The clear light of wisdom is not something special. It is the Spirit of Truth, everywhere present and filling all things.

Wisdom does not impose something conditioned from elsewhere, but unveils unconditioned awareness, which is primordially present, as 'I AM,' always already what the Name reveals it to be. The impact of wisdom transmission cannot be grasped. The magic of her poetry remains ineffable. Wisdom is light uncreated, unveiling the glory of God's Name.

15.

Wisdom renews tradition when she inspires prophecy and prayer, which hallow God's Name to awaken hearts. Prophecy is alive and well when the Word is heard revealing the Name so that the Kingdom comes. Prayer is living when the heart is awake and inspired to trust in God's Name completely, so that the Completeness of the Name begins to permeate the incompleteness of our wounded brokenness.

The vision of wisdom is infinitely great, inspiring whole-hearted trust in God's Name to save us. Scripture bears witness that all who trust in the Name like this, with their whole heart, shall be saved. Thoughts come and go, but 'I AM' stands steadfast. There remains nothing but 'I AM,' penetrating right through directly with unconditioned clarity. Revelation of the Holy Name is from the Father, through the Son, in the Holy Spirit. This unveiling of the Name in wisdom is without end, the same yesterday, today and forever.

To cleave to the Name in all circumstances is to experience liberation even in this life. When things arise in the uncreated light of 'I AM,' they liberate freely, unveiling glory spontaneously as glory, in the uncreated energy of God. In glory, there is no trace of confusion or division. Name hallowing frees delusions so that errors unravel and passions are cured. Prayer assimilates what prophecy reveals. Wisdom makes all things new, as at the beginning.

The mysteries of wisdom, prophecy and prayer spring from the hidden treasures of wisdom, glory and the Name. There is no end to the completeness of uncreated perfection when the Holy Trinity interpenetrates created wholeness as wondrous openness, unveiling the sevenfold completeness of wisdom. Elders bear witness to Christ in their midst, unveiling the mysteries of Holy Trinity. They are shepherds of wisdom when they fulfil the function of angels, initiating prophecy of the Name and prayer in glory.

16.

Wisdom is in search of hearts in which to dwell. So the desert offers opportunities to turn and see, to deepen wise insight in order to welcome wisdom back from exile. Wisdom dwells where the Name illumines. The Kingdom comes in glory when the Name is glorified. There is ineffable openness whenever hearts turn and see. There is unconditioned oneness wherever uncreated presence is aware and uncreated awareness is present. The Name does not waver nor is wisdom hesitant in her Kingdom of uncreated light.

Wisdom is pure from the beginning. That is why Christ invites us to his Eucharistic Feast. Wisdom does not need to be purified by conditioned ways and means. In our fallen state, when we are caught up in impurity, we try to purify ourselves. But Christ is wisdom whose purity stands steadfast from the beginning. He bestows this wisdom as gift, as uncreated grace. He resurrects us in her light. He purifies us by turning us right round so that turning we may see.

Seeing is restoration of the primordial state. It is illumination in uncreated light. Wisdom is everywhere present and filling all things. We overlook this when we fail to hallow the Name and so fall short of the glory, which is filling all in all. We may have changed our opinion but if not the heart, the result will be that the 'eye' of the heart will still be closed and the heart still hard. The Kingdom still appears to us as if it has not come and we seek it in the future, trusting in our own ascetic efforts.

Wisdom comes to hallow the Name and make the Kingdom come. She dispels confusion and dissolves separation so as to cure the divisions that cut us off from glory. Hallowing the Name is the practice of seeing, the *praxis* of *theoria*. The Orthodox Tradition imparts the injunctions to turn and see. Glory does the rest. *Theosis* refers to the deification intended by wisdom when God becomes man, so that by grace we might become as he is, because he has become as we are. It refers to union and communion, which are the enlightened intent of the Eucharistic Liturgy

17.

All things arise from the Father, exist through the Son and return in the Holy Spirit, in the Kingdom of God, the Holy Trinity. Experiences come and go. The reason we attach no importance to passing experiences is that we put our trust in the Name, which reveals the way things are, and practice seeing, which unveils what the Name reveals. Wisdom is our home and the Name is our birthplace and our dwelling place, not concepts of these, but the reality. Everything is as it is at the beginning, when wisdom is present, making all things new. Visualization without wisdom is blind.

Hallowing the Name becomes recognition of God in his Name through the practice of wisdom. Repentance purifies the heart when it is sincere and genuine, transmuting recognition into glorification. When the Name unites crown and root in the heart, rainbow mysteries begin to unfold their secrets in the midst. Cessation of binary thought is not blank blackout but revelation of 'I AM.' *Metanoia* is transformation of mind and heart, from root to crown, neglecting nothing. The Name hallows everything when it is hallowed, leaving nothing out in the cold.

The Kingdom comes on earth as in heaven to the degree that God's will is done and the Name hallowed. When temptation arises, we are delivered from evil when the heart is awake to the Name. Wisdom stands steadfast in the midst, so delusion dissolves and passions flee. Wisdom abides in peace whatever happens. Temptation is wisdom's moment to rise into her peace. Trial is an opportunity to ascend into her glory. True blessing is glory and peace, fruit of the union of wisdom and the Name. The Great Peace of the Name should not be confused with a soporific pseudo-peace that is one of many obstacles to illumined vision.

Love of wisdom is never completed without wisdom's compassionate love for all as for one-self, which cures ascetic activity of self-interest. *Theosis* never neglects the deification of all, even down to the last sufferer in hell. The prisons of pride are opened and the poisons of hell cured, when wisdom awakens hearts to the hallowing Name, which harrows the hells of pride.

18.

When we turn and see, we ascribe all glory to God, because we find nothing created here in the midst but uncreated glory. Wisdom discerns the glory of God's Name, as in the beginning. Right glorification of God is recognition of the primordial origin of everything in the Father, through the uncreated light of the illumining Son, in the uncreated grace of the Holy Spirit. The luminous mind of Christ permeates Scripture and Tradition with wondrous openness, inspiring the Patristic mind to see all things in God and God in all things.

Wisdom lives in the eternal now, womb of every awakened heart. The Name unveils uncreated awareness, God's 'I,' to be the revelation of God's 'AM,' the uncreated presence of his unconditioned awareness. The radiance of wisdom rises like the morning star at dawn, to renew creation. The uncreated creativity of wisdom's glory makes the Kingdom come. It is the pinnacle of all her ways and means, the expansive firmament that communicates her limpid purity to every perception. This uncreated creativity is the ground of all that arises, ineffable in essence, generous in her unconditioned energy. Although not something created, wisdom is present in anything created, unveiling God in everything and everything in God.

Heaven and earth are one in wisdom's wondrous openness, never falling short of the glory, which is ever present here in the beginning. The Kingdom of glory is at first a luminous firmament, a lucid expanse eternally present and filling all things. Visible creation adorns this invisible expanse with translucent form, capable of being transparent, so that glory shines through with transfiguring light.

All sound resounds with wisdom's song, *Hallelu Yah*, giving glory to God on earth as it is in heaven. The Kingdom of heaven is nearer than near when wisdom unveils the saving Name, 'I AM.' Glory is heaven on earth and earth in heaven, a conjugal embrace that heals the dolorous wound.

19.

Wisdom unveils the generous scope of the Name by severing the confusion between the uncreated and the created, which heals the divisions of the fall. 'I AM' is 'I AM,' pure uncreated awareness ever present, timeless uncreated presence ever aware. In the immediacy of the awakened heart, nothing can separate the Father from the Son, in the uncreated light of the Holy Spirit. Nothing can impede the power of uncreated grace. Recognition of 'I AM' right hallows God's Name. The Kingdom comes and God's will is done. Wisdom searches out the mysteries of the Lord's Prayer.

Whatever happens, wisdom hallows the Name so that the Kingdom comes. We cleave to the Name, which reintegrates primordial awareness and original presence. The deifying union of the Father and the Son is eternally poured out as wisdom from the heart of God. To abide in this grace is to indwell the Son in union with the Father, in the light of the Holy Spirit. To hallow the Name by abiding in its saving grace is to rest in the peace that passes all understanding. It is to pray without ceasing so that there is no difference between times of prayer and anything else. It is to live wisdom's indivisibility as the air we breathe, which is to be one breath, one spirit with the Holy Spirit.

The moment prayer of the heart ceases, we begin with times of prayer again until unceasing prayer is restored. At all times, wisdom loves to hallow the Name, hallowing the earth as in heaven. It is a state of hallowing that abides as unceasing prayer, until the eye of the heart closes and we need times of prayer again. The Name saves by liberating whatever arises into glorification. Glory frees passions by releasing their energy from glory to glory. In the Kingdom, energy is once again the uncreated creativity of the glorious King, Christ in the midst. Angels and saints bear witness to the saving power of the hallowed Name to be glory that liberates glory into glory, rather than fall short of the Kingdom. The Kingdom is the treasure house of wisdom, full to the brim with uncreated grace and truth. It is the heart of the Old Covenant as well as the New, wisdom's testament in every heart, to which she bears eternal witness. Wisdom transmits her *praxis,* her *theoria* and her deifying *theosis* to all, in the glory of the Name.

20.

Praxis turns mind and heart into God that we may see. *Theoria* sees through delusion that we may be what seeing sees. *Theosis* is glory in action as deification of all. It is divine grace in act undoing all falls from grace. Wisdom transmits her injunctions to turn and see. The *praxis* of *theoria* opens the heart to glory, which undoes the fall. Glorification is uncreated glory of the Name in act, awakening the eye of the heart. It inspires doxological reciprocity, which is our co-operation with uncreated grace. We turn and see because glory woos our love and inspires our synergy. 'I AM' is way, truth and life when uncreated light opens the eye of the heart to the Son's primordial union with the Father of lights. Wisdom is recognition of God in his Name, which sees the uncreated light of the Son in the midst to be indivisibly one with the uncreated light of the Father, origin and ground. Wisdom's light is the uncreated light of the Holy Spirit, unveiling Christ as wisdom in the Father. In this way, the Name 'I AM' is lived as way, truth and life.

Trust is crucial because without confidence in the Name's power to save, remembrance is nominal and recognition shallow. Glory can truly liberate only if the Name is really permitted to save. Right hallowing is right glorification, which releases the Name to save. Nothing can bind when the Name frees. Passions find nothing to get hold of here at centre when wisdom finds nothing but God in the midst. 'I AM' purifies and sanctifies the moment it is recognized to be God's Name.

Thoughts, *logoismi,* liberate of themselves when they arise into the glory of the Name. Those who are determined to save themselves rather than trust in the Name to save, struggle to reject thoughts and so fall into their power. Wisdom transmits the Name so that the uncreated creativity of grace is allowed to do with ease what, without it, effort and struggle are unable to do. Uncreated light releases effort into trust and struggle into rest abiding in the peace of God. The blind energy of effort and self-interested struggle are freed when wisdom sees. Passions are liberated when the heart turns and hears. Their energy is purified in the illumined heart so that glory can glory in God, singing, 'Glory to thee.'

21.

Christ transmits his wisdom together with its uncreated glory, which unites all opposites such as male and female, active and passive, in paradise. Heaven and earth are united in paradise, but this is not noticed until wisdom opens the eye of the heart. The intelligible world is an invisible expanse that is ineffably one with the sensible world, but this is not evident unless wisdom is present. Both the intelligible and the sensible worlds are created, but their union with the uncreated is not apparent until it is unveiled by wisdom. When Christ transmits his wisdom at the heart of sacred tradition, all wisdom's mysteries of union begin to manifest. Nothing is left out from her integral embrace and nothing strays from his enlightened intent.

The Holy Trinity is not reified when the Name is revealed by wisdom. 'I AM' shines forth from his primordial origin in 'I AM,' unveiled to the eye of wisdom. 'I AM' is not something created. Nothing strays from this luminous ground. Nothing falls away from its revelatory lucidity and its liberating openness. There is no confusion between the Father, Son and Holy Spirit, and no confusion between the uncreated and the created here, in this dynamic integral completeness. The co-inherence interpenetrates all that there is without insinuating the least trace of confusion. It is beyond all division too, being without separation in its timeless ground.

The Kingdom of 'I AM' does not come or go, being uncreated awareness ever present, creative presence ever aware. It does not need improving nor does it fall away from completeness into incompleteness. 'I AM' is enthroned in the Kingdom of God served by uncreated creative energies in the Holy of Holies. Created incompleteness is the dynamic created energy of this uncreated completeness, revealing that in God, incompleteness does not waver from completeness, but contributes its relative dissonance as tension within consonance.

Wisdom abides in God's Kingdom, seeing everything in God and God in everything. Elders shepherd us with wisdom so that we awaken to the Kingdom. Heavenly hosts are one in God as God is one. Earth is glorified when wisdom hallows the Name.

22.

The Kingdom of God is not a place in space or time. It is wisdom's all-pervading realm of uncreated light, timelessly aware and ever present in glory. The uncreated creative energy of wisdom has no boundaries but embraces all that there is in the eternal now. As in the beginning, so at the end, wisdom is with God and is God, everywhere present and filling all things, without mass or volume. When the Kingdom of wisdom descends, it deifies everything in God and transfuses God into everything. It descends to undo confusion and heal division without reserve. It inspires trust in the Name to save and insight into glory to glorify all who turn and see.

Wisdom humbly trusts in the Name, whereas pride insists on effort and struggle, unable to hear the Word. Vain glory is determined to save itself, by its own strength, so it ignores the revelation of the Name and is deaf to uncreated grace. Effort and struggle put their trust in ascetic ways and means, as if grace was unheard of, whereas humble wisdom descends to transform ways and means into expressions of illumination, effort and struggle into humble synergy. When glorification descends to raise purification and illumination to its ascended uncreated frequencies, the narrows of fear and the shallows of self-obsession are transcended.

The metaphors of ascent and descent are not taken literally because what glory unveils is always actually the case, and the Name is simply ridding us of confusion between the uncreated and the created. The heights are really quite ordinary, once glory is come. The is-ness of glory has no beginning and no end, and its middle is free of reification. There is no trace of anything the binary mind can call 'eternal' here in this timeless now, which alone is. There is only what is arising spontaneously in glory right now. The Kingdom of timeless spontaneity pervades all in all. It is the reality of the glory of things as they are.

Nothing can usurp the throne of grace, except by delusion. Nothing intervenes between glory and wisdom. Nothing can separate God's 'AM' from his 'I.' Wisdom is revelation of the Name in glory. Christ is King in his Kingdom of wisdom. In God's Kingdom, everything gives glory to its King.

23.

Everything unveils glory, giving glory to God, in the realm of uncreated light. Glory is overlooked until wisdom dawns as illumination. Deification is a mystery enclosed in an inaccessible future until we turn and allow illumination to regenerate as glorification. Wherever we turn, the unveiled face of glory is all-inclusive, although it cannot be said to exist as something among other things, or not to exist at all, since it fills all in all. Glory is pure expanse like space, but is not spatial. Glory is immediate like the present moment, but is not temporal. Uncreated and unceasing, it is incommensurable, having no common measure with anything. The eye of the heart sees with wisdom's insight, but its vision is ineffable. There is no way wisdom can be grasped or glory conceived, yet the Name saves and glory frees without hindrance.

The uncreated 'I' is unconditioned uncreated awareness and the divine 'AM' is timeless uncreated presence, freeing all that arises to glorify the Name and to be glorified by the Name. Wisdom discerns the glory of the Name in everything and restores everything to glory in the Name. When 'I' and 'AM' are one, as in the Name, there is no separation between self and other, subject and object. There are not three kingdoms but one, in the radiant sphere of the Holy Trinity. There are no warring extremes in the Christly realm of luminous blessing.

Glory is the unconditioned ground of all that there is. Nothing falls away into confusion or strays into separation. The self-generating origin we call the Father is never cut off from the revelatory Word that names the Name. The only-begotten Son is never severed from the Holy Spirit, for wisdom and glory are one in the awakened heart. God's many names are one, for God is one, and his Name is one. The names do differ because God loves difference, but the indivisibility of the Name does not compound them.

Pure awareness and real presence are one in God's Name 'I AM,' but when we think this is obscured and that our obscuration calls for purification, we adopt ways and means to purify ourselves with a view to illumination. But wisdom knows that clouds do not stop the sun from shining, and that the Name always saves and never itself needs saving.

24.

Wisdom unfailingly transmits *metanoia*, which turns us right round in the deep heart. The eye of the heart is pure when seeing sees seer and seen in the revelatory Name, 'I AM.' The Name unifies perception by extinguishing confusion and healing division in Christ, in whom all pathological extremes are cured. Wisdom in him is a Kingdom of uncreated light transmitting light to the world. He is the light of the world opening the eye of our hearts that we may see. The glory of the Name is discerned by wisdom so that the veil is lifted without causing profanation. God is 'I AM' revealing himself to us, Emmanuel, who is God with us, in the glory of his Name. The Holy of Holies is unveiled without reification. Blessed is the one who comes in the Name of the 'I AM' of hosts, his angels and elders in the heavenly realms.

There is a wondrous openness whenever wisdom sees the glory of the age to come as God's Kingdom come, but no trace of narcissism if the left hand is not spying on what the right hand knows. The Name is not profaned because separation is seen right through. There is no one to be confused and nothing to divide. If the glory of the Name is really to be way, truth and life in Christ, then wisdom will be established with seeing as way, on the basis of prophecy as initiation into truth, and prayer as assimilation in life. If seeing is not the way, nominal Christianity is combined with endless postponement, and *theosis* then appears to be way over the horizon. The cross becomes a symbol of an endless crucifixion of Christ, not the revelation of his resurrection in glory. Such an icon may inspire unseeing devotion, but the real function of icons is to transmit resurrecting *theoria,* that we may see, for it is seeing that sustains *theosis.*

Theoria enlightens the eye of the heart with an immediacy that outruns intimacy, opening directly into the mysteries of *theosis*. The Name undoes objectification, distance, and endless postponement. Orthodoxy is not just right opinion but glory rightly ascribed to God, unveiling Christ right here in the midst, as elders and saints bear witness. Belief that Christ wrought miracles long ago should not be confused with trust in the miracle of his Name right now. Belief can distract from whole-hearted trust in the power of the Name to save, but such trust fulfils our beliefs beyond all reckoning.

25.

The *praxis* of *theoria* is wisdom's way, her method, which is noetic vision. Wisdom is recognition of God in the midst, opening the 'eye' of the heart. The Tradition discerns here the difference between wisdom and sophisticated sophistry. For *theosis,* glory dissolves confusion and resolves division naturally and spontaneously. The uncreated creativity of glory does with ease what, in our fallen state, we cannot do. But glory is ineffable. It transcends opposed opposites, their affirmation and denial. Glory arises beyond yes and no, in the Amen that gives all glory to God. [1] One reason why the tradition says little of glorification is that the binary structure of logical thought finds itself in difficulty, even impasse, when glory in the midst turns out to be its excluded middle. Neither its yes nor its no, nor both of them, nor neither, can grasp this glory in the midst. Wisdom indwells glory in the timeless uncreated presence and uncreated light of the Name. It is ineffably direct. The *theoria* and the *praxis* are indivisibly one. This is not hypothetical. It is immediate. *Theoria* is not theory that needs to be put in practice. Glory turns *theoria* into direct *praxis.*

What purification envisaged, illumination sees, what illumination sees, glorification actually already is. The theological tradition conceptualizes what wisdom sees non-conceptually, so offers its concepts as liberating precepts to transmit wisdom. Dogmatic concepts are not closed, but symbols opening out onto the mysteries that they symbolize. Glory transmits remembrance of God as radiance of recognition. Prophets, apostles and saints bear witness that illumination is the basis of glorification, and that the *praxis* of *theoria* purifies the heart by enlightening it. Prophecy transmits the Name to awaken prayer of the heart. Wisdom inspires prayer in spirit and truth, purifying the heart. Together, prophecy and prayer unveil glorification, when all else falls away, but to the extent that glory is still to come, prayer of the heart lives it as in a glass darkly.

---

[1] See 2 Cor 1:19-20.

26.

Prayer in spirit is prayer that the Holy Spirit inspires, in which the mind, illumined by God, turns and awakens to God present in the midst. The practice of spiritual vision, *theoria,* turns the mind right round, with a most profound *metanoia,* so that it unites with God in the inmost heart. That is why seeing is grounded in turning, and illumination is rooted in purification. The Patristic tradition often appeals to experience, *peira,* but it does not follow that it is empirical in the same sense that modern science is. For the Fathers, it is the experience of awakening that is crucial. It is revelation of the Name. Science reduces *theoria* to mere theory and *peira* to empirical observation, so that the vision of God in the awakened heart is overlooked.

The Spirit of Truth comes to open the Scriptures and Tradition, making all things new. In the modern era, the reputation of science can be so overwhelming that sometimes theology is tempted to see itself in the image of science, forgetting that the practice of science does not produce saints, or even seers. There are scientists who are seers, but not because the theory and practice of science purifies and illumines the heart. The desert does, however, regard the oratory as a laboratory, and the hallowing of the Name in the heart as a spiritual labour. The *praxis* of *theoria* is indeed a therapeutic theopathy, with capacity to diagnose and cure pathologies, which the desert called passions, *pathe.* The Patristic consensus is a humble submission to what heals. It bows before the facts, but it does not confuse physical with spiritual health. Saints may die of cancer, but hallowing illumination bears fruit in humble glorification of God.

The symbols of the faith are inherently open, overflowing with uncreated energy that empowers their realization. Glory sees *praxis* as the practice of *theoria,* no longer as the initial stage that eventually progresses to illumination. Glory is timeless in the age to come, but it is still to come unless wisdom descends to discern its timeless radiance. Glory flees objectification, but frees it the moment wisdom unveils her seraphic vision. Thinking grasps at glory and so loses it. Wisdom neither grasps nor fixates, leaving the spirit free. Fleeing objectification, wisdom frees.

27.

Christ is radiant luminous wisdom enlightening the world with vision. Effort and struggle miss the point. They fall short of the glory that wisdom discerns, abiding in freedom at the heart of the world. The uncreated light of wisdom has nothing to discard or espouse. The glory of God does not come or go, but shines like the sun even when clouds conceal it from view. The limpid purity of wisdom abides, neither arising nor subsiding. She neither wavers nor fixates, being free of the compulsions that cause strain and stress.

Revelation of glory in the unspeakable speech of the mysteries employs speech to transcend speech. It is impossible to say whether glory is in the body or out of the body, for God alone knows the glory that is ascribed to God alone. Speech desires completeness and wisdom completes speech. Speech as such is incomplete, but as prophecy and prayer, has the spiritual capacity to make completeness visible to awakened hearts. Completeness is accessible to incompleteness through wisdom, not as complete speech but as incompleteness bearing witness to completeness. *Logos* and *hesychia* come to the aid of each other, curing the pathologies that reduce one to the other. Speech and silence are not opposed, for both point to the completeness from which they arise.

Prophecy and prayer abide between speech and silence. Wisdom inspires a humble speech, which preserves the difference between the creature and God, without separating God from creation. It says enough to unveil glory without usurping the glory of God. Incompleteness points to difference, completeness to union, and it is wisdom that unites without confusion and distinguishes without division. Incompleteness is intrinsic to completeness, not its enemy.

Wisdom calls for prophecy that unveils completeness, and prayer that acknowledges incompleteness. Prophecy and prayer humbly reveal the glory of the Name, in the light of which the completeness of wisdom is unveiled in glory.

28.

Prophecy bears witness to the glory of God revealed in the Name, but glory is uncreated and so ineffable. The vision of God bears no resemblance to visual perception of anything created. There is no common measure or perceptible similarity between the uncreated and the created. The experience of glorification is not like the experience of something perceptible to the senses. The language of prayer is affirmative when it is symbolic, but every affirmation calls for a corresponding negation, and the negation of that negation, because the uncreated transcends both affirmation and negation. Prayer inspires theology to be doubly apophatic, because it addresses God, who differs from everything that language can conceive or describe, deny or negate.

The experience of *theoria* is indescribable because the vision of God is ineffable mystery, incomprehensible to the rational faculty, and inconceivable to the imagination, but seen with different degrees of spiritual intensity by the illumined heart. The experience of *theosis* is also ineffable but the energy of glory is creative as well as being uncreated, and so inspires prophecy that reveals the Name, and prayer that assimilates what is revealed. Seers bear witness to glory and so regenerate tradition to renew the world.

Glory unveils the difference between unseeing belief and faith that sees because it is illumined. When seeing comes, belief falls away, when glory comes, seeing rises into the fullness of its stature in Christ, and trusts this recognition with wholeness of heart. The experience of glorification is revelation of the Holy Trinity, unveiling 'I AM,' through 'I AM,' in 'I AM.' *Theosis* is not theoretical but doxological, glory ascribing glory to God. God is seer and seen in this spiritual seeing, not us, but it calls for our co-operation, our synergy, in the illumined heart. It is not knowledge about something but God's direct knowledge of God through God. None of our natural faculties can grasp this wisdom, but it spontaneously dissolves confusion and heals division.

The tradition imparts wisdom that purifies and illumines. It communicates union and communion in glory. Elders do not just discourse about God. They transmit the wisdom that reveals God in his Name.

29.

Theosis is called glorification because glory releases passions into glory so that their energy becomes limpid purity in primordial presence. Pride, anger, envy, sloth and the rest, all purify when the vanity in vainglory dissolves into glory and freedom. Passions are all manifestations of uncreated creative energy that has been contaminated by confusion or division. Emotions are released by wisdom and the Name, so that as radiance of pure awareness and primordial presence, 'I' and 'AM,' they are freed in the Holy Spirit to be as God intends. To rest in peace means to abide in the Name with wisdom, so that poisons are no longer poisonous and passions are no longer passions.

Christ 'goes away' so that he might send the Holy Spirit, whose coming as the Spirit of Truth frees every addictive passion from confusion, healing all fixations of division and separation. The Orthodox Christian Tradition prescribes the *praxis* of *theoria* to cure hatred of enemies with unselfish love, so that glory changes passions into glory by *theosis*. The Son returns to the Father, bearing us all with him. Enthroned on the right hand of the Father, he offers our humanity deified, transformed from glory to glory. There is no end to this doxological transcendence in God, from God to God.

If wisdom is to unveil the Name, we need deep faith in the Name to save. Division reigns as long as confusion persists. But when we put our whole-hearted trust in God's Name to save us, it does indeed save and the Kingdom of wisdom reigns. The effort and struggle to save ourselves is perverse when Christ is already freeing all sufferers and emptying all hells. To dream of being awake is not to awaken. The psyche can no more cure itself than dreaming can awaken from dreaming. Wisdom is true awakening that really does awaken from the dream, freeing the spirit from confusion. The Name saves by releasing all kinds of awareness into uncreated awareness, God's 'I,' and all modes of presence into uncreated presence, God's 'AM.' God is 'I AM,' revealing freedom from confusion in uncreated light. Wisdom unveils glory, delivering difference from division in uncreated glory.

30.

Liberating wisdom is uncreated light. The deifying Name is uncreated glory. Glorification sees illumination and deification as a single weave, an interweaving of light and glory that restores everything to its primordial purity. Purification is no longer a preparation for illumination but an expression of the uncreated light of deifying glory. The three stages of purification, illumination and glorification turn out to be the temporal unfolding of three inseparable and timeless dimensions of the uncreated light of divine glory. The temporal perspective is valid before the heart awakens to *theoria,* but once illumination sustains the *praxis* of *theoria,* the timeless vision of *theosis* begins to dawn. Illumination stands in between, at times partaking of timeless vision from above, at times descending to the temporal perspective from below.

Incompleteness is inevitably uneven, but wisdom bears witness to the timeless completeness of glory, by partaking in the renewing waters of uncreated light. Timeless completeness is infallible, as Denis and Palamas bear witness, but the rational and imaginative faculties are fallible. Language can face both ways, calling for the wisdom of discernment. No one lays claim to verbal infallibility, but the tradition partakes of the infallibility of the Holy Spirit to the extent that its fallibility is willing to humble itself and empty itself, to the glory of God alone.

Somehow the ark of wisdom manages to negotiate these turbulent waters without harm. It seeks refuge in the harbour of the Name, and trusts wisdom to the navigation, not itself. When thoughts, *logoismi,* arise, it is crucial to abide in the state of *theoria,* without wavering. Thoughts always fall short of the glory of God's Name, whereas spiritual vision sees what the Name unveils, for in the light of glory, the heart sees light in uncreated light. *Theoria* is luminous wisdom, a union of openness and freedom. Openness is revelation of 'I AM,' and freedom is limpid purity, the original clarity of the primordial state. Freedom from passions, *apatheia,* is not apathy but unselfish love released through the Name by wisdom. Selfish habits fall away gradually, though awakening is sudden and instantaneous. Wisdom unveils the glory of the Name by a hallowing transmission of the Kingdom of love's glory.

31.

Elders transmit great peace and blessing on earth just as angels do in heaven. Their spiritual state is free of self-interest because their hearts are open and free. Openness and freedom are the gift of God's Name, 'I AM.' The openness springs from the uncreated grace of God's 'I' and the freedom arises from the deifying presence of God's 'AM.' The key to the Kingdom of the Name is hallowing the Name aright, which is right glorification. It is the quintessence of Holy Orthodoxy, which is openness and freedom transmitted by prophets and saints, even when times are difficult and genuine sacred tradition is hard pressed.

The meaning of the Kingdom of glory transcends everything and is quite unlike anything else. The completeness of glory does not come and go. Wisdom discerns this glory without effort, having nothing to discard or adopt. Her radiance is ineffable openness and spontaneous freedom, which she discerns in the Name. Wisdom's injunction is to turn and see. Turning is *praxis* and seeing is *theoria*. The *praxis* of *theoria* undoes confusion and heals division. It reveals the glory of the Kingdom come, which does not waver even when we fall. Delusions arise but burn up in wisdom's gaze, leaving glory to give glory to God. Thoughts arise but wisdom does not waver. The enlightened scope of wisdom is ineffable, formless and imageless, as is the glory wisdom discerns.

Glory is ineffable and beyond description, imageless and beyond expression. But the eye of the heart wakes when wisdom dissolves confusion and unites what division puts asunder. There is no error in wisdom and no obscurity in the light of uncreated glory. Heretical extremes of confusion and division are purified when illumination opens and frees the heart. Narrow and shallow extremes are cured when glory transmits openness and freedom. The uncreated light of glory purifies the heart, so that glorification is normative for healthy communion. There is nothing created in the midst when turning turns and seeing sees. Nothing separates wisdom from God, whose essence is indivisible from his saving energies.

32.

There is no before or after in eternal life, which wisdom reveals when time is timeless in the eternal now. The divisions of time are no more. There is no here or there in glory, which wisdom unveils when heaven and earth declare the glory of God. Space is fundamentally unconditioned and indivisible in the ineffable light of glory. Conventional labels of time and space dissolve when confusion transmutes back into communion. All conditioned frames of reference are unseated by glory, though they remain relatively valid on their own plane. Fixations unfreeze and addictions release when glory dawns. For where the Spirit is, there is freedom. Once glory breaks free of restriction, wisdom rises into the fullness of the stature of the resurrected Christ.

The Fathers say that this ineffability transcends both affirmation and negation. Positive and negative extremes cannot intrude in the unobstructed sphere of integral wisdom. The enlightened intent of glory abides. Illumined awareness of God in the midst frees the heart from reacting reactively when confusion arises. Seers neither accept nor reject experiences that come and go. They abide in the Name with wisdom, laying aside all worldly care. They rest in carefree openness, free of the misconstruing of desire. For them, glory gives glory to God whatever happens. They are not hampered by changes of mood, any more than changes in the weather. Experiences come and go, but wisdom stands steadfast in glory, unfettered and uncontrived.

Wisdom is decisive, cutting through confusion, whereas glory is expansive, leaping over division. Wisdom is exact but not pedantic, ascribing all glory to God. She is simple but not simplistic in the primordial ground of being. Seers immersed in wisdom, whose glory is ever-present, know directly that there is no confusion or division between the created and the uncreated. They are not depending on rational argument, or hesitant, due to the complexity of phenomena. Free of confusion and delusion, they turn and see no division between anything and God. They do not stray from wisdom, knowing that to abide in Christ is their refuge and their strength. Glory, discerned by wisdom, leaves no trace, like uncreated energy, light of the Name.

33.

The power of the Word to make himself powerless without forfeiting the freedom inherent in this power, was for Saint Hilary a crucial insight into Christ's self-emptying love, his obedience even unto death. [2] This love unveils glory in the uttermost opposite of glory, undoing loss of glory that constitutes the fall from grace. The glory or *kabod* of God was, for the prophets, his resplendent weight and *gravitas,* his dignity and majesty. *Kabod-YHWH* was revealed on Sinai with the theophany of the Name, with the unveiling of holiness and power, with the enlightening 'countenance,' but there was something so ineffable here that the *mysterium tremendum* of God's glorious presence never strays from a cloud of unknowing. *Kabod-YHWH* is 'dazzling darkness' on Sinai and 'bright cloud' on Tabor, but Elijah was overwhelmed by the 'still small voice' of a gentle whisper, breathing the awesome Name, plunging him into ecstatic wonder.

In the New Covenant, the glory or *doxa* of God translates twenty-five Hebrew words including *kabod,* but never strays from the wondrous ineffability of doxological revelation. Glory is unveiled in Christ's obedience unto death, which glorifies the Father, and is consummated when the Father glorifies him. Glorification of the Father by the Son is reciprocated by glorification of the Son by the Father. Just as when we pray in his Name, our prayer is heard and fulfilled in him, so when we glorify God in him, God reciprocates with our glorification in him. The pathologies of vainglory are cured, not by us, but by him. 'Father, glorify thy Name.' [3] The hour of glorification of the Name is the whole meaning of Christ's life. Right glorification or Holy Orthodoxy is the ultimate meaning of our life in him. A voice from heaven says, 'I have glorified it and I will glorify it again.' Jesus says this voice comes for our sake, not for his. It opens to us his mysteries, the hidden wisdom of our glorification in his Name.

---

[2] See Phil 2: 6-11; Hilary's De Trinitate 9:41.

[3] John 12: 28 RSV.

34.

Holy Trinity unveils glory when God glorifies his Name and is glorified in his Name. The Spirit reveals the glory of the Name invested in the Son to the glory of the Father. If the Father is glorified in the Son, the Father glorifies the Son, with love's glory, unveiled in the Holy Spirit. Uncreated glory suddenly springs forth 'at once,' [4] with spontaneous immediacy in the timeless presence of freedom. There is no dithering or hesitation for glory. Uncreated creative glory acts 'at once.' Jesus does not speak from himself, but in the Father's Name, 'I AM.' He speaks in God's Name. He is the Word revealing God's Name. He sends the Spirit who bears witness to the eternal gospel of glory, for the world has fallen short of glory and cries out for healing.

Christ never seeks his own glory. Recognition never comes from self-regard. It arises in the Spirit from the Father. It is the gift of wisdom, which discerns glory in the beginning. All that the Father has is the Son's, in the Name, to the glory of the Father. *Doxa-Kabod* is love's glory unveiled in Holy Trinity. To see love's glory is to be where 'I AM' is revealed. [5] To see his glory is to be where he is. It is to discern the glory of the age to come right now, not in oneself or for oneself, but in the glory of the Name.

The Name unveils the glory of the Kingdom to come, by imparting this very glory as its radiant momentum. If Jesus is never in control of his own glorification, neither are we. He entrusts himself utterly to the Father, self-emptied of all glory, offering all glory to the Father. He is 'Lord of Glory' by virtue of this *kenosis,* this self-emptying, and his face is unveiled as glory in uncreated light. The Word transmits the Name, which unveils the Face of God in glory. Wisdom makes this glory known, knowing as she is known. The ineffable is unveiled as the ineffable by the ineffable. He is who he is. 'I AM' who 'I AM.'

---

[4] See John 13: 32.

[5] See John 17: 24.

35.

Wisdom is childlike trust in the simplicity and peace of glory. It is prayer in spirit and truth. It is ineffable gratitude and joy. It is insight into love's glory that transcends all sophistry. Christian wisdom never forgets that Scripture loves to pass over from prose to poetry for a reason, and that it ends with the Book of Revelation as wisdom song, *Hallelu Yah!* Transcending prose and poetry, wisdom is ineffable glorification. It is mystagogical doxology, wisdom unveiling the mysteries of glory. Glory is not reducible to anything else. Holiness, majesty, dignity and might are all interpenetrated with glory but differ from glory, as divine names differ, without division. Glorification is ineffably ineffable.

Doxa, in Greek, once meant opinion, a conception of something, but in the New Testament, it expresses God's self-revelation in many ineffable modes. It denotes doxological theophany in glory. Wisdom is manifold because glory is manifold, revealed in many kinds of theophany. The freedom of the glory frees wisdom too, liberating everything as it arises. Everything is liberated when glory descends in glory and wisdom discerns what perception overlooks.

To increase in wisdom is to grow in knowledge of glory. To deepen illumination means to partake more profoundly in glorification. There is no end to illumination, because uncreated glory is inexhaustible. Wisdom is the radiance of uncreated light unveiling glory from one degree of glory to another. This is glorification, increase in wisdom being the opening of love's glory to greater and greater glory. Increase in wisdom and growth in glory are both hidden with God in the inmost heart of Christ, where he eternally prays, 'Father, glorify thy Name,' and the Father eternally responds, 'I have glorified it, and I will glorify it again.' [6] Glorification lives the glory that shines forth from the mutual love of the Father and the Son, discerned by wisdom in the Spirit.

---

[6] John 12: 28 RSV.

36.

Christ is eternally praying, 'Father, keep them in thy Name, which thou hast given me, that they may be one, even as we are one.' [7] Christ has kept them in the Name, revealed by the Father to the Son. He has shepherded them in the wisdom of the glory of divine love. He has guarded them and preserved them from perdition in the saving Name. Now, in his great High Priest's prayer, he prays that all who are his shall be gathered in the Name. As Word, he has revealed the Name and hallowed them through the hallowed Name. He consecrates himself by hallowing the Name, so that they too may be consecrated in the Kingdom come.

The enlightened scope of this prayer of the Name explicitly includes all who down the ages hallow the Name, that we may all be one with the very same oneness that unites the Father and the Son. [8] The glory of the Name revealed by the Father in the Son is shared, that all may all be one as he is one with the Father in the Name. Glorification is this experience of glory in the Name, for God is 'I AM,' and 'I AM' is one. Oneness shines forth from the Name like light from the sun. Oneness is spontaneously present in the openness of glory, ineffably unveiling the glory of the Name.

Christ did not pray just once, long ago, that the Name would be glorified, but prays this prayer eternally in our midst, that we may be one, as he is one, partaking directly in the indivisibility of the Holy Trinity. The uncreated energy of glory is direct, and the oneness frees confusion to rise as communion and division to rise as differentiated union in the uncreated glory of the Name. Christ's prayer for glorification is a prayer that we shall be with him where he is, that we shall see him as he is, in glory, through his Name, 'I AM.' Glorification is the Father's eternal answer to this prayer, hidden in Christ from before the foundation of the world.

---

[7] John 17: 11 RSV.

[8] See John 17: 20-21.

37.

'Father, glorify thy Name.' [9]   In Gethsemane, Christ, asking 'Whom do you seek?' says, 'I AM.' They drew back and fell to the ground. [10]   The Name 'I AM' is glorified in his loving obedience unto death, his free submission to love's glory on the cross.   The cross of glory reveals what glorification really is, and hallows the Name so that the Kingdom really comes. The cup of salvation is full to the brim, and the grail is found again whenever the glory of the Name is unveiled to an awakened heart.   Recognition of God in the midst happens whenever the Name transmits the glory of God. Wisdom remembers God when God remembers all who turn and see.   Recognition is reflexive doxological reciprocation.   God is seer and seen as well as the seeing, which wisdom is in her discernment of the glory of the Name.   Language strains to transmit the mystery, which is hidden in Christ's prayer, that God will glory the Name.

Glory transcends cause and effect, just as the Name leaps over effort and strain.   The Name has lost nothing of its power to save and keep seers safe. Glory is not diluted over the centuries, but glorifies the glorified just as it always did.   The Name intends illumination and the ultimate point of this piercing is glorification, transcending conditioning.   Glorification of the Name is glorification by the Name.   'I AM' cuts through to glory, and glory leaps over shortfall from glory without effort.   The supreme secret of the Name is immersion in the genuineness of glory, which is timeless.

Glorifying *theosis* embraces everyone and everything with deification, not just the saint who prays.   But this is ineffable and remains inaccessible to curious scrutiny.   Wisdom beholds what perception overlooks, when she turns and sees what hard hearts cannot see.

---

[9]   John 12: 28 RSV.

[10]   See John 18: 4-8.

38.

Blessed be God, who in Christ transmits wisdom that discerns the glory of his Name, key to the mysteries of the Kingdom of God. Wisdom sees into the glory of the Holy of Holies, which is God's enlightened intent from before the foundation of the world, uniting all things in the Name. Our hidden destiny is to experience glorification, glory sealed by the Holy Spirit as guarantee of glory to come. The 'I AM' of glory imparts a spirit of revelatory wisdom, opening the eye of the heart to increasing knowledge of glory. The fullness of revelation lies in completeness of wisdom, calling to us to turn and see. The completeness is always already complete, even when we are painfully aware of our incompleteness. Prophecy transmits it and prayer assimilates it so that in its uncreated light, wisdom can restore the tradition and renew creation.

Wisdom bears witness to the completeness of God, who fills all in all. In wisdom, the Spirit raises us to eternal life even in this life. Glorification arises from the throne, which Christ shares in heaven with all who hallow the Name. The Name reveals where God is to be found, and wisdom is the uncreated grace of recognition, which calls for our whole-hearted trust. We were created for glorification, not for conventional ways and means that fall short of glory. Wisdom brings all who were far off nearer than near. Christ is the Great Peace that leaps over separation and cuts through confusion. In him, we all have access to wisdom in the Holy Spirit. Glorification is founded on the prophets, transmitted by the apostles, assimilated by the saints and handed on by elders in every generation.

So although our incompleteness is obvious, wisdom unveils the mysteries of glory, not in complete speech but in humble witness to the completeness of glory. This witness employs partial speech and radiant silence, pointing beyond both to the glory of the Name. Even the least of saints bears witness to this grace, knowing that it shines forth from the Name in uncreated light. It is not necessary to be somebody special to be a dwelling place for wisdom. Wisdom loves a pure and lowly heart, which suffers everything to the glory of God. Such suffering is always to the glory of God. Rooted and grounded in wisdom, God is glorified in his Name.

39.

Wisdom surpasses information and all knowledge based on information. Her insight into glory sustains the unity of the Spirit in the bond of peace. Her love is forbearing and kind, forgiving and generous. The glory of the Name of the One is one in all and all in one and all. Above all and through all, 'I AM' is in all as wisdom and for all as glory. Wisdom speaks the truth in love, renewing hearts by healing their scleroses. Avoiding destructive gossip, she transmits the grace of the glory of the Name. Curing vainglory, she unveils the glory of the Name. Her business is purification, illumination and glorification, but her home is glorification.

Calumny and slander are a kind of murder, because they murder how someone is seen and received, and so are incompatible with wisdom. Self-interested asceticism serves the selfish self, not wisdom, whereas wisdom purifies the heart. Wisdom redeems the time by hallowing the Name, discerning the glory of the Kingdom of God. God's will is done on earth as in heaven when illumination invites glorification to extinguish time in timeless glory.

Illumination sees light through light in light, and glory still to come, whereas glory sees light of glory as light of glory in the Kingdom come, discerning the glory of the age to come in the light of glory already present in the Name. Illumination is still in time, looking forward in hope. Glorification is timeless, partaking eternally in glory by ascribing glory now, so that glory is present now, as in the Kingdom of God. Illumination is the way things appear, as glory is approached. Glorification is the way it really is, just as it is. Glorification is timeless presence spontaneously present, fulfilling illumination, which sees 'in a glass darkly.' Wisdom sees 'face to face,' being God's seeing of God in God. [11]

---

[11] See 1 Cor 13: 12.

40.

Elders thank God for wisdom because she shepherds them, not because they presume to possess her. They pray for wisdom because without it there is no insight into the Name or knowledge of glory. A desert without wisdom is a desert without illumination or glorification, which is a wilderness without heart. There are those who sincerely reject wisdom, but they know not what they do.

There were controversies over wisdom and the Name almost a century ago, but time grants perspective and healing when Name and wisdom renew the tradition. Extremism tends to produce heresies, but there is no inherent heresy in either wisdom or the Name. The desert integrates all that is valid and true from controversy, in the silence that turns and sees. It sheds all that was exaggerated or extreme, extracting the kernel from the husk. Wisdom discerns the glory of the Name without curiosity or sophistry. She inspires an integral embrace that gives glory to God, without resort to extremism or extreme reactions to extremes. Glorification is the inheritance of the saints in light. It is the destiny inherent in the Name, which wisdom discerns in glory. All things are created in 'I AM,' whether invisible or visible. All things are created through 'I AM,' for 'I AM.'

'I AM' is before all and in him all things hold together. Christ reveals the Name with 'I AM' sayings, with and without predicates, such as 'I AM the way, the truth and the life,' and 'Before Abraham was, I AM.' [12] In this Name, all the completeness of the fullness of God comes to dwell. In this glory, the Great Peace has always dwelt, and saints bear witness to this, not merely as their opinion, but in wisdom. Old controversies are reconciled not in compromise but in God, who unveils his Name with wisdom, resolving what theological opinion was unable to resolve. It is in peace that the desert prays for peace, inspired by wisdom and the Name.

---

[12] See John 14:6 and 8:58.

41.

Wisdom is holy, blameless and irreproachable in Christ, for she stands steadfast amidst the shifting sands of controversy, stable and peaceful, despite negative gossip. Elders transmit wisdom in the Name, enabling the Word of God to be fully known. The mysteries of glory are experienced as glorification, Christ in us being the hope of this glory. Without wisdom, there can be no maturity in Christ. No hearts are knit together in love without wisdom, nor the treasure of the mysteries of glory made known.

The desert treasures wisdom because in Christ the completeness of the wisdom and fullness of God dwells. Buried with him by Baptism, saints rise with him by Chrismation and partake of eternal life in him in the Eucharist. Wisdom's mysteries of glory all have glorification in view. Without it, the sacraments lose all point. The mysteries of glory are the substance of the way, revelation of the Name its truth and its life. Christ is this substance and without wisdom he is annulled. Dead to all but him, wisdom is hid with him in God.

It follows that when someone is condemned for loving wisdom, it is Christ that is condemned. When someone is rejected for his Name's sake, it is Christ who is rejected. If someone has been raised with Christ, it is not really so surprising that they are rejected and condemned just as he was, and for the same reasons.

Glorification is hid with Christ in God. If Christ is our life, glorification will be our life too. Glory completes the suffering of Christ, so when we suffer because of the Name, it is all to his glory. When we suffer because wisdom is condemned, it is with his glory that we are glorified. To be in Christ is to abide in wisdom, renewed by wisdom in the hallowed Name.

Wisdom is lowly and kind, patient and forgiving, not contentious and extreme. Here in him, there is no 'them and us,' but Christ in the midst, unveiled in his Name, 'I AM.' Wisdom imparts wisdom songs to the glory of the Name.

42.

Uncreated light is worthless dung to those who reject wisdom and the Name. But glory values it like the pearl of great price, knowing it to be the fertile ground of wisdom and the Name. For in uncreated light, light sees light, and the eye of the heart awakens. Glory is first purification and then illumination, before it enters into the fullness of the stature of Christ as glorification. To dream that you have fallen asleep celebrating the Eucharist is like dreaming that you are awake. It is necessary to awaken, or uncreated light will remain a dream.

Narrow and shallow religion, although they differ on many things, sometimes agree that wisdom and the Name are heretical, and glory is delusion, unless it is future glory or the glory of the saints in heaven. The Palamite Councils might as well never have happened, or the Athonite Tome been written, in some conventional circles where Church Services are the Church's only prayer and the Jesus Prayer is shunned. Even monasticism is subject to these strictures, and ends up attending to externals, as if the tradition was a system of rules and regulations without trace of a wisdom transmission of the heart.

The living tradition of wisdom and the Name survives on the margins, although it lies at the heart of Orthodox Tradition. It transmits purification and illumination in the Name, with a view to glorification in wisdom. But once glory arises at centre, where all centres coincide, it unveils how things are, for it discerns the glory of the age to come, just as it is, eternally present even now.

Conventional religion sees glory as a dream, and saints in glory as comforting adornment in icons. But glory sees convention as a dream, and awakens the eye of the heart to shatter its delusions. Once wisdom and the Name are functional, prophets and apostles are heard once more, and angels gather round with saints, glad to be included again. Glorification is actually the way it really is, just as it is, not something very special that only dreams retain. *Theoria* is quite ordinary for *theosis*, being like the radiance that spontaneously shines from the rising of the sun, effortlessly dispelling dream with sleep, like nocturnal mist dissolved at dawn.

43.

Wisdom walks in glory, like a fragrant offering of incense to God. Wonder walks in light with wisdom, exposing what is not of God. The Name awakens wisdom, rising from the dead. Christ hides with God at centre, redeeming the time. Centred where all centres coincide, wonder embraces wisdom as she sings wisdom songs, turning psalms and hymns into Name hallowing chant. Wisdom is holy and without blemish in the Holy of Holies. Indifference to the Name has no place there. Fear and trembling are no more.

Wisdom is adorned with glory as she descends, making all things new. Death is no more, now that life is eternal in glory. As in the beginning, so at the end, wisdom wipes all tears away as she embraces the cries and pain. It is not that people in time do not die, nor that completeness abolishes incompleteness once and for all. Old things appear to go on in the dream of life, just as they always have, even as wisdom is making them new.

'I AM' is first and last, *alpha* and *omega,* wedded to wisdom in the Holy of Holies. Glory vests both Name and wisdom in the Kingdom of hallowing light. By this uncreated light, elders transmit what saints imbibe, and waters of eternal life flow forth. Bright like crystal, wisdom is a tree of life in the midst, bearing wondrous fruits of healing. Timeless glory permeates time, without ceasing to be timeless. The word of prophecy transmits the Name, in whose light the seer sees light. Truth is worthy of trust, so prayer hallows the Name and the Kingdom comes. The coming of 'I AM' through 'I AM' in 'I AM,' is right glorified when glorification receives it, not when coming is postponed and life is lived as if the resurrection never happened.

All curses lift in the Kingdom come, just as elders share the throne with its king. His face of grace is awake when wisdom's eye illumines their hearts. God is glorified, not angels, in this chant of angels and saints, as it rises like incense to the throne of grace. The Spirit seals prophecy and prayer until wisdom unveils the day of the Name. When that day comes, wisdom bears witness to the Name, the coming of 'I AM,' as souls in time pray, 'Come, Lord Jesus!' Christ hears their prayer, saying, 'I AM come in the hallowed Name.'

44.

Desert wisdom transmits the glory of the Name with hallowing doxology, so that in all circumstances, seeing nothing but God in the midst, the solitary prays, 'Glory be to thee, O Lord, glory be to thee.' Love's glory purifies the heart and illumines the soul, enjoining ascetic training in the *praxis* of *metanoia* and *theoria*. Exterior asceticism without *theoria* does not purify the heart. The injunction to turn and see has purification of the heart in view, that we may see. Illumination has glorification in view, that we may ascribe all glory to God: 'Glory be to thee.' The desert imparts the mysteries of wisdom, hidden with Christ in God. The Word reveals the Name for our glorification. The Spirit transmits wisdom for our deification. The wisdom of the Lord of glory is the wisdom of Christ crucified, which eyes do not perceive nor ears hear. Hearts cannot conceive love's glory, but when wisdom opens the eye of the heart, seers are seen as seeing sees, illumined by the Spirit.

If it is true that sometimes sophistry debases wisdom, it is by wisdom that this is discerned. Sophisticated cleverness is not confused with wisdom, nor conceptual subtlety substituted for genuine insight. The desert is not impressed with abstraction nor duped by dogmatism. Elders ascribe all glory to God, humbly renewing tradition in regenerated hearts. The Patristic heritage of wisdom and the Name is transmitted when elders impart the 'word' that undoes confusion so that through prayer it is assimilated without division. The key to tradition is direct revelation of glory through the Name, not verbal formulations, which are always indirect. Scripture and dogma point to the mysteries, but the mysteries of glory are not reducible to them.

There is a living tradition of prophecy and prayer, which communicates the uncreated grace of the Name, opening hearts to glory in the Kingdom of Light. Wisdom's living stream still waters the Holy of Holies, so that gardens enclosed in the desert can flower.

'Glory be to thee, O Lord, glory be to thee.'

45.

St Symeon the New Theologian agrees with St Denis and St Maximus that the Prayer of the Name sustains unceasing unveiling from glory to glory. Glory, though uncreated, is not fixated immobility, because the Spirit inspires unceasing prayer that rises from glory to glory without end. The saints bear witness that God is 'I AM,' and has revealed himself to us in glory. Their wisdom is not presumptuous speculation, but the expression of their experience of glorification. St Symeon handed on the same purifying illumination to the hesychasts, as the apostles had initiated in the saints. Wisdom is one, just as the glory of the Name is one. Glorification is not subject to changes of fashion or to clever originality. Uncreated light is infallible, but it does not follow that every formulation of doctrine or practice it inspires, is infallible.

The therapeutic wisdom of purification, illumination and glorification springs from the uncreated energy of glory, which purifies to illumine, and illumines to glorify the saints. The tradition is dynamic, imparting uncreated creative energy to all, energy that is experienced according to the spiritual state of each. The glory wisdom discerns in Christ is ineffable openness. It is expansive and uninterrupted. There is no heretical bias or extremism here, because the Spirit frees. The Name hallows everything, once it is hallowed.

When glory dawns, everything is glorified. That is why the saints are a blessing to their generation and leave blessing where they lived. Extremism confuses and divides, whereas wisdom sustains the beauty of difference in the truth of communion. Glory grounds everything in this ineffable openness, freeing wisdom from extremes of confusion and division.

The limpid purity of stillness releases energy from fixated obstructions, so it unites again with the uncreated energy of God.

Unrestricted freedom manifests in the enlightened scope of the Kingdom, just as unfettered love liberates all it embraces from heavy constraints.

Wisdom discerns the glory of the Name, transmitting timeless freedom.

46.

By ascribing all glory to the Father through the Son, the Spirit unveils the sphere of glory arising ineffably between the Father and the Son. This is the dwelling place of wisdom, the Kingdom of glory nestling between the Father and the Son. The Spirit proceeds eternally from the Father to abide in the Son, so is the first to unveil the homeland of mutual reciprocal abiding between the Father and the Son. Vainglory falls short of this because it confuses the uncreated and the created. Shortfall cannot ascribe glory to God, so Christ goes away. He sends the Spirit of Truth who leads us into wisdom, whose truth is whole. Wisdom sees from within God in the midst, transmitting doxological recognition.

The Spirit receives the Name from the Word and transmits it to us in wisdom. It is in the gift and reception of grace, not selfish possession, that the Spirit opens wisdom to the mystery of mutual glorification between the Father and the Son. The Spirit makes reciprocal glorification explicit, by unveiling total self-emptying at the heart of the Holy Trinity. Glorification of God turns into glorification by God, who destines us for glory in the indwelling of glory from before the foundation of the world. Glorification by God is his gift of blessing in the Spirit, to the praise of this glory. Wisdom opens the eye of the heart to revelation of the Name, for it is in the Name that wisdom dwells. Here, at centre, where all centres coincide, the inner man is one spirit with God, indivisibly and inseparably. This is unveiled by the Spirit of Truth not as a union of essence, but as a union born of uncreated grace.

Glory undoes all confusion between giver and gift so as to overcome all division between grace and graced. The 'praise of the glory of his grace' is wisdom's hidden song, hidden because it never exposes the mystery to objectifying scrutiny. Desert wisdom creates the genre of a 'Century' of 'Chapters' to transmit glorification, *doxazein*.

Glorification does not impart information but revelation of God in the midst. Elders praise the glory of grace by unveiling God in his Name, which transmits recognition of God, 'I AM' in the midst.

47.

Glorification, *doxazein*, ascribes all glory to God, right here where 'I AM' is uncreated unifying awareness arising as uncreated timeless presence. *HALLELU YAH* praises the glory of the Name, a glory that is inexhaustible even now as grace, whilst being unsurpassable then as vision face to face. Glorification offers 'praise, glory, wisdom, thanksgiving, honour, power and might to God, forever and ever.' [13]

Wisdom songs offer all wisdom, *pasa Sophia,* as glorification unto the ages of ages. For desert wisdom, glorification is no longer an external event in a far off future, but is its very life right now, its *theoria* and its *praxis*. The experience of uncreated grace imparts purifying illumination to all who turn and see. Such grace empowers glorification even to the last and least of brethren, to each and every sister, to each and every seer. Wisdom always has glorification in view as something ineffably given already even now.

The *Amen* that glorifies knows God from within. The Spirit reveals God as God, in God, not something created. But we cannot appropriate God, since God expropriates us of ourselves, when he dispossesses us of ourselves, revealing the glory of his Name. Our determination to be in control is undone right here, at centre, in the midst.

God became man precisely so that those who fall short of glory, because they have turned away from love, may yet be glorified. Faith trusts love's glory enough for the glory to break through.

All that was his becomes ours when we are no longer our own but his.

---

[13]   Rev 7:12. See Rev 11:17f, 12:10, 15:3f, 19:1-7 etc.

48.

Glorification lives for God by ascribing glory to God in his Name. Glory is dead to sin and alive to God, just as wisdom is alive to glory and dead to death. The *fiat* of deep faith does not conjure something new, but trusts the glory that is our timeless destiny from before time began. Faith is 'yes' to love's glory, which led Christ to his hour of glory, his death to save all. 'Yes' to this love comes from the 'yes' of this love, the 'yes' of Christ, which calls his Church into being. The *fiat* of the solitary is 'yes' to glory, the sphere of glory uniting the Father with the Son, to which the Spirit bears witness. The solitary is led into the desert, driven by the Spirit, but the Spirit unites him in Christ with all humanity, as he prays, 'ABBA, Father!' The Spirit confirms Christ in the midst, showing him that although alone, he is not alone, because 'I AM' is one, uniting many children of God, crying, 'ABBA, Father!'

Glorification is witness to the eternal generation of the Son before the foundation of the world. It is witness to Song of Songs mysteries at the heart of the Eucharist. What usurps God, in the fallen state, is offered as a living sacrifice, giving glory to God. Glorification of God turns into glorification by God in God, but this is God's doing not ours. Our 'yes' to this is to turn and see. We die to our conditioning as an expression of unconditioned wisdom. We stand out of ourselves ecstatically by opening ourselves to the sphere of love's glory. The Name reveals 'I AM' to be God's self-revelation in our midst. Wisdom lives for God by giving glory to God in his Name. The glory of the Name is saving. The glory of wisdom is illumining. The glory of God the Holy Trinity opens both to the freedom of glory, as glorification, which begins as proleptic anticipation in hope, and ends as ineffable openness to God. The Apostle says we have this openness, *parrhesia,* through faith and confidence in God. [14] The Patristic tradition calls this spiritual openness, *parrhesia,* which is the reverberation in us of the openness between the Father and the Son. The sphere of glory is this realm of ineffable openness.

---

[14] See Ephesians 3:12.

49.

Desert wisdom trusts the ineffable openness of glory as the glory of the Father transmitted to the Son, which the Son ascribes to the Father. The Spirit proceeds from the openness of the Father to abide in the openness of the Son, and to search out this ineffable openness in God, so that it can be transmitted to us. Wisdom shines forth as the light of the knowledge of the glory of God, unveiled as the ineffable openness of Christ to the Father, answering the openness of the Father to him. Glory is this openness discerned by wisdom. Wisdom is this openness discerning glory. The Spirit gives access even now to the glory that is to come, and to the ineffable openness that wisdom imparts. The Saints manifest this openness as confidence in God, knowing they are heard, knowing they receive the moment they ask.

The glory of the Name is revealed when vainglorious self-glorification is extinguished. Kenodox delusion is seen right through, so that right-glorifying Orthodox wisdom can flourish. Glory is the fruit of wisdom in the paradise garden of the heart. Wisdom is a tree of life and glorification is its fruit. The Eucharist gives thanks for the glory wisdom sees, and offers glorification as its true thanksgiving. Glorification is the fruit of this thanksgiving. Revelation of the Name is communication of the glory of God in the midst. Wisdom ascribes this glory to God, giving back the glory given. The gift of glory is revealed in the human heart, and the word of prophecy is assimilated as prayer of the heart. Glorification of God in God is the fruit of prophecy and prayer.

The Kingdom comes when the Name is hallowed, and the ineffable openness of glorification is its fruit. Without Christ in the midst, we can do nothing, just as without the Father, the Son can do nothing. The heart is the womb in which the Word plants the Name. Glory is the fruit of the hallowed womb, the harvest of glorification, which ascribes all glory to God. Wisdom is the living water that quenches thirst, and wisdom's spring wells up to eternal life. Streams of living water flow from heart to heart, transmitting wisdom. The fruit of wisdom is glory, transmitted from heart to heart, ascending from glory to glory.

50.

The glory of the Name overflows with an abundance that is inexhaustible. There is no end to the sacramental mysteries that flow forth from the Name. Baptism transmits turning so that Chrismation can transmit seeing, and the Eucharist blesses glorification, the ineffable openness of deifying union and communion. Grace overflows from the Name with an abundance that is ineffable. Wisdom is poured out with the Spirit, opening up insight after insight into the glory that is to come. When the veil is lifted, the heart sees. Love's glory is revealed in the wisdom that discerns it. The desert loves this wisdom and so retains its first love, its 'philosophy,' long after the word was debased in the schools.

A culture of gift flows forth from glorification. The gift and reception of glory inspire a simple giving, an unpretentious generosity that gives away, like the poor widow, all that she has. Her poverty is like Christ's, a wealth that is given away, a glory that is freed from selfishness by being generously shared. Desert monasticism lives from gift, even when baskets or rugs are woven in a spirit of generous joy. Grace does not calculate, but overflows with an abundance that inspires gift, a culture of gift that is profoundly countercultural.

Wisdom puts the Kingdom first, laying aside worldly care. Trust relies on God, giving thanks to God. More than abundant generosity in God inspires a culture of more than abundant generosity in us. Glorification of God arises as glory from God, returning to God the glory that God generously gives. Everything is ineffable gift, glory given and received.

The glory of the Name is sheer grace, awakening glorification of God in wisdom's integral embrace.

Wisdom is a miracle of grace, revealing mysteries of glory everywhere.

51.

Love's glory is to give back to God the glory of his love. His gift of love was free, so the giving of glory in glorification is always free. Love's glory is not oppressive closure, but an endless outpouring. It is grace given freely, freely received and lovingly glorified. Wisdom glorifies the Name that unveils glory. Glory has no stain any more than wisdom has. God is light and those who walk in light are by grace the light that seeing sees. They transmit light out of a God-given love that sees light and is light.

The pure in heart bear witness to the transparent translucence of glory. They do not ascribe glory to themselves. Glory dispossesses them of glory, which is ascribed to God. They do not confuse themselves with God, even though God is revealed in their midst. They know that glory cannot be calculated or appropriated like a possession. Love's glory is boundless, being both God's and ours without confusion or division. The formula of theophany, 'I am I AM, thy God,' [15] which underlies both covenants, reveals the 'Thou' in 'thy God,' a 'Thou' that is neither swallowed up by confusion, nor cut off by division. Love of God is our response to love's glory revealed in his Name, and love of neighbour is its spontaneous expression. Both love of God and love of neighbour spring from the uncreated energy of love's glory, which unveils the 'Thou' in the light of 'I AM.'

Love does not offend the brother for whom Christ died, although wisdom severs soul from spirit like a two-edged sword. The tension shows where the offence lies, not in the 'Thou' that is 'beloved,' but in the confusion which is offended by the Name. Wisdom lives in the light of the glory of the Name. Confusion arises but dissolves; emotions arise but are resolved. Glory blesses broken bodies and troubled souls, being generous with all who suffer. Completeness does not shun our incompleteness, but embraces it, holding us steady, in wisdom's embrace.

---

[15] Exodus 20:2, Leviticus 19:2 and throughout what scholars call the Holiness Code, as well as Isaiah 49:23, Ezekiel 6:7 and throughout the prophets.

52.

The Name is Great Peace, abolishing enmity, embracing all who are 'far off,' as God's beloved 'Thou,' in his Son. When the Name is revealed, all enmity between 'them' and 'us' is undone. Wisdom discerns the glory of the Name as uncreated creative unifying energy, dynamically unveiling the universal scope of 'I AM.' The Name crosses over to embrace the other as 'I AM.' The Name brings all who are far off nearer than near. All are brothers of the Son, who is the first of many brethren, in the Name. 'I AM' is our God, 'I AM' is one. [16] The *Shema* confesses the Name, which Christ transmits in glory by signs and 'I AM' sayings. The uncreated 'I' is ineffable openness embracing the uncreated 'AM,' timeless presence, the fruit of whose union is deifying oneness. Prophecy bears witness: 'I am I AM and there is no other. There is no God but I AM alone.' [17] Prayer in the Spirit takes this to heart and intercedes for all.

Love of God and love of neighbour are one in the Name, because whatever is done to the least of brothers is done to Christ, 'I AM' here in the midst. The glory of the Name preserves the unity of the Spirit in the bond of peace, because glory is the unifying destiny of all, and is given to all from before the foundation of the world. Since the other is 'I AM,' there is no division, but difference bearing witness to unity.

The gifts of wisdom and love differ, but do not divide, because wise love bears all things. Someone who thinks he is wise is far from wisdom, but someone who loves wisdom loves God, and God loves all who love wisdom and are known by him in his Name.

Wisdom discerns the glory of the Name.

The sphere of glory is the sphere of the Father's love.

---

[16] See Deut 6:4.

[17] See Isaiah 45:5.

53.

The Name openly reveals the hidden mystery of love's glory, not our love for God but God's love that deifies all. Christ's love reveals the Father's love, which the Spirit interprets as the glory of the revelatory Name. To have confidence in this Name and to love one another are two sides of the same mystery of glory. Faith in the Name supports recognition of God in one another, and love of one another in God. The glory of the Name unveiled by the Father to the Son and by the Son to us, in the Holy Spirit, grounds the communion of saints. The Name is glorified in the saints who are glorified by it. The communion of saints is rooted and grounded in the glory of the Name. Generated by the communion of the Father and the Son, in the Holy Spirit, glory hallows all who hallow the Name. Glorification, *doxazein*, is even now at work when wisdom opens the eye of the heart, and prayer of the heart ascribes glory to God.

Glorification of God in his Name opens us to the glory of love's communion between the Father and the Son. Glorification of the saints is hid in the hallowing of those who hallow the Name. The tradition contrasts this vision of glory 'as in a mirror' with vision of the Face of Christ, which is described as 'face to face.' When the heart turns to God revealed in his Name, the ineffable face of Christ in glory is unveiled, not as an object of curious scrutiny, but as wisdom's vision of glory, in the freedom of the Spirit.

The uncreated light of the eternal gospel of glory opens the eye of the heart to the ineffable openness of glory already accessible in the timeless presence of the Name. Christ in the midst is also the hope of glory because the glory to come is already present in the revelation of the Name. Glorification is not, however, self-concerned, but leaps over itself into the glory that is being revealed, cutting through every kind of self-interest. The glorified do not glory in their own private glorification but in wisdom's enlightened scope, which is the glorification of everyone and everything.

The revelation of glory in us, which the Spirit discerns, yearns with the sigh of the same Spirit, for the glory that is to come. Prayer of the heart is the ineffable sigh of the Spirit that lays hold of this glory to come.

54.

The Name is the *alpha* and *omega* of glorification. The glory in the beginning and at the end is one, but this oneness is timeless. The ages turn on this axis of uncreated glory in the midst. Wisdom turns on the axis of glory by initiating turning, *metanoia,* and transmitting *theoria,* illumination. Glorification lives the glory of the age to come in the midst of the present age, by discerning the uncreated grace at the heart of hope, and the uncreated light at the heart of the Name. Glorification is hid with Christ in God in such a way that Christ is wisdom's theophany. When Christ, who is our life, is this theophany of wisdom, we too shall be with him this theophany of glory.

The ages turn on an axis of glory that passes through the centre of all centres, where all centres coincide. The glory of the age to come is already come when wisdom discerns it as Christ in the midst. It is the glory the Father bestows upon the Son. It is the glory the Son ascribes to the Father. It is the glory the Spirit apprehends in the Son, the glory that reveals the Father, at the heart of their reciprocal abiding. The Spirit cries, 'Abba, beloved Father!' in our hearts, praying ineffably the prayer of glorification. The freedom of the glory is an ineffable openness, an inexplicable hope, a wordless prayer.

The Spirit intercedes with our spirit with ineffable sighs, bearing witness in our spirit that the glory of the Son is ours by grace. Love's glory is theophany, revelation of the glory in the midst of the Father and the Son, a love that seeks not its own. The realm of ineffable glory, in the heart of God the Holy Trinity, is the dwelling place of wisdom.

55.

Christian wisdom springs from Christ, whose vision of glory opens it to wisdom. Christ sees the glory of the Father in the Holy Spirit, and hands it over to us in the mysteries of glorification. This unveils our faces, so that we begin to reflect this glory as in a mirror.

Glorification is a lifetime of transformation into Christ, which begins with glory and ends with glory, in the Holy Spirit.

The wisdom is the vision, and the vision is Christ's, not ours. But the Spirit shares it with us so that it becomes ours.

Christ's wisdom is face to face, whereas our vision is reflection 'as in a mirror,' or as the Apostle says elsewhere, 'in a glass darkly.' Nevertheless, our unveiled face is a real reflection of glory.

The illumined 'eye' of the heart is 'turned,' and so sees the glory of 'I AM.' This seeing is wisdom, not our private vision, but the wisdom of Christ in the Holy Spirit.

The Spirit proceeds from the Father to abide in the Son, and without ceasing to abide in the Son, draw us all without exception into the sphere of this abiding.

Prayer of the heart assimilates the glory of this abiding.

Seers are transparent to this glory. The image of God is restored to likeness by glory.

Saints do not draw attention to themselves, nor do they boast of their own wisdom. But they do bear witness to wisdom that discerns the glory, knowing that where the Spirit is, there is freedom to discern.

Elders impart this wisdom in Christ, interpreting the mysteries of glory, transmitting love's glory in glorification.

56.

The tradition proclaims wisdom at the heart of the mysteries, primordial wisdom, which has glorification in view from before all ages. Wisdom is an eternal gospel, not the trendy wisdom of this present age, or of any age. It springs from the inmost depths of God that only the Spirit knows. Wisdom has glory in view, not in general, but personally. Wisdom has our glorification in view, each one of us, and all of us. But it is not forced on us. It is freely disclosed to us if we freely welcome this disclosure. The Spirit freely bestows the gift of wisdom without which the mysteries of glory would remain forever hidden. The Spirit grants wisdom so that we may receive the grace of glory.

The hidden wisdom of God has always been folly to anyone who is a stranger to the Holy Spirit. Recognition of God in his Name is an insight of wisdom, not an opinion. Wisdom is folly to hard hearts and blind eyes, deaf ears and closed minds. Glory is our destiny, but sclerosis of heart makes us oblivious to the fact. Wisdom is a gift to those who love glory, not their own glory, but the glory of God revealed by the cross of self-giving love. The divided mind confuses the uncreated and the created, and so it is inevitable that it sees wisdom as folly. Confusion blinds the heart so that it is incapable of discerning things in the light of wisdom. But the humble lover of wisdom does discern what wisdom reveals, and so is able to discern things in the light of wisdom.

Humble lovers of wisdom listen to the Spirit and so come to know unselfish love. The wisdom of love's glory is never conventional, never shallow and never narrow. Love of wisdom is the state of being always ready to be surprised by wisdom, surprised by glory, surprised by love. Seers know they see, because *theoria* is renewed by *metanoia* in every moment of their lives. But they make no claim to know what they shall be. All they know is that what they shall be is already revealed in Christ, and wisdom really does discern what the grace of Christ unveils. So desert wisdom does not claim to comprehend absolute wisdom, or impart a complete speech. It transmits the Name that reveals glory to wisdom.

57.

Desert wisdom transmits a measured prophecy and prayer that undoes confusion and heals division. Though measured, it imparts a wisdom that is incommensurable. Christ is evidence that the impossible is possible. God can become man; man can become God. In Christ, the impossible is actual, real, specific. Glorification is the impossible made actual. It is the deification of us all.

In Christ, the Name is hallowed and so the Kingdom comes. Glory has broken through and emptied hell. The world contradicts this. Death reigns as before. Glory is impossible. Glorification is impossible too. In Christ, the impossible is not only possible, but is actual when wisdom discerns glory in God's impossible love, and lives it as way, truth and life.

Wisdom is humbly radiant as wonder, amazed that the impossible is possible, and that the possible is actual. Love's glory is powerlessly present in the Name, powerlessly disempowering the fallen principalities and powers. Wisdom rejoices in the Name always, even in the very depths of hell. Can glorification ever be a safe option, or is it always an exposure to impossible extremes, extremes that can only be handled if extremism is avoided?

Wise love of wisdom does not usurp the completeness that is loved. It neither presumes nor despairs. Divine-human union is sheer paradox. It is impossible, but in Christ it is real, through the Spirit. Impasse is our life. Wisdom discerns glory but is not vainglorious. We know in part, in the light of the wisdom of completeness.

Tradition is healthy when it bears witness to completeness without usurping completeness.

58.

Wisdom imparts a mystical pedagogy of turning and an ascending anagogy of illumination, in order to fulfill a descending mystagogy of glorification. Turning awakens to God so that illumination sees. Glorification is experience of the reconstitution of all things in Christ, which illumination knows in part. Illumination sees 'through a glass darkly,' like a reflection in a mirror. Wisdom sees 'face to face,' in completeness, which is loved but not usurped. To know in part is to acknowledge glory now, in the light of love's glory to come.

Wisdom discerns the glory to come without profaning it. Her enigmas are radiant with glory, but no foothold is given for vainglory. Love's glory never ends. Prophecy, crucial to illumination, falls away. Prayer of the heart, the basis of spiritual knowledge, transcends itself when fulfilment comes. Only love's glory remains. Glorification is not reification of glory. Love knows best what glory is, as wisdom knows and bears witness.

The Spirit of Truth comes to help us in our weakness, opening us to remembrance of God in the light of love's glory. Purification and illumination are not, for glory, a means to an end, but are direct theophanies of glory, justifying the means, wisdom. As the *praxis* of *theoria*, turning sees. They purify and illumine together, being the uncreated creative energies of glory, breaking through from above, like sunlight on the hill.

From below, the temporal gospel looks forward to the Kingdom to come. From above, the same gospel is eternal, abiding in the Kingdom come. As purification and illumination deepen, they acquire a different hue. Glory turns and seeing sees, seeing seer and seen. Timeless wisdom discerns timeless glory in the Kingdom come. What looks like inconsistency or incoherence on the rational plane, makes obvious sense once glory opens and wisdom sees. Conflicting structures of eschatology fall into place once spiritual stages are clarified and spiritual states are distinguished without confusion or division. Knowing 'in part' has its place, but so has wisdom's vision 'face to face.' Knowing and being known fall into place once wisdom is loved and known again, as in the beginning.

59.

A widespread misconception of Semitic theism in the East is that all God-talk is reification of the ineffable. A common misconception of Eastern wisdom in the West is that its way of negation and the negation of the negation is nihilism. Each sees the other in the image of its own 'demons,' which can be a serious barrier to understanding, but presents no serious difficulty for wisdom. Christian wisdom is no stranger to apophatic traditions, and is not tempted to confuse them with nihilism. Difficulty arises, however, in circles that disdain wisdom, where the war of antagonistic 'demons' threatens to explode into political and social violence. Both sides talk at each other, but fail to engage, piling misconception upon misconception.

Wisdom loves the Name, which is neither of the East nor of the West. It unravels reification and overcomes nihilism as a normal part of its therapeutic regime. It cures both as an intrinsic ingredient of its integral functioning. That is why the 'demons' of reification and nihilism present no difficulty to wisdom. Deconstruction of 'demons' is her daily business. Christ is neither of the East, nor of the West, being 'I AM' in the midst. The wisdom of the Name transcends affirmation and negation, the affirmation of both and the negation of both, leaving no foothold. To dwell in the glory of the Name is to abide in the ineffable. To abide in the wisdom of Christ is to expand the heart into the boundless openness of unselfish love.

Love's openness is infinite. There is no conditioned way or means to reach such love. It springs from the Father's heart where it is one with the Son, and this is where the Spirit too abides. Beyond characterization, love's glory does not come and go. Love's openness is free of obstruction due to extremes of strain or stress. Glory unites heaven and earth in a most intimate embrace. Wisdom searches out this glory without bias and transmits the Name without self-interest.

Christ rises free of all frames of reference, sealed by the Spirit to free everything the moment it arises. He is in our midst, yet we persist on looking everywhere but where he is, 'I AM,' here in our midst.

60.

The illumined heart is a dwelling place for wisdom, gift of the Spirit, praying, '*Abba!* Beloved Father,' with our spirit, united through the Son to the Father. The Synoptic Gospels have purification in view and used to be read before Baptism, sacrament of *metanoia*. They offer parables of the Kingdom to turn the heart through the Name. The Gospel of John presupposes illumination, and has signs instead of parables, with 'I AM' sayings with and without predicates. It is read after Baptism and Chrismation to inspire illumination and the *praxis* of *theoria*. It is the spiritual Gospel of all who are participating in the Eucharist as glorification. The Gospel of Thomas imparts the mystical eschatology of *theosis,* within the ethos of early prophecy. It was treasured in at least one monastic library in Egypt, but was then lost for many centuries. Its perspective was not lost, however, for *theosis* remained the experience of all who practiced wisdom as glorification.

The Epistles of Saint Paul contain many references to *praxis, theoria* and *theosis,* although they do not use this terminology, referring to *theosis* as glorification. They are read all the year round, whereas the Gospel of John is read after Pascha and up to Pentecost, beginning with, 'In the beginning was the Word.' Both have glorification in view on the basis of purification and illumination. Wisdom is patient and kind, and never imposes herself, although on the Damascus road, Christ appeared with power in glory to the Apostle Paul. Externals are not at war with the heart, but act as a reminder of the remembrance of God. God is the subject of turning and seeing, just as God glorifies the saints, but never rides roughshod over freedom. Our co-operation, our synergy, is essential.

When wisdom is lost, purification is no longer *metanoia* but is reduced to abstention. Once the prayer of the heart awakens, purification is no longer a separate means to an end, but an expression of illumination. It is the *praxis* of *theoria.* So whilst from the standpoint of purification, *praxis* is the precondition of *theoria,* from the standpoint of illumination, the *praxis* of *theoria* is an integral co-inherence of turning and seeing.

61.

Christ is the Son, wisdom in person, transmitting mysteries of glory through the Name. Awakening to him in the midst, saints experience him in interconnected ways. Spiritual states are not rigid steps of a temporal sequence but Christ in different indivisible dimensions, revealed in the Spirit, in distinct but inseparable modes. The *praxis* of *theoria* cuts through the dualistic abstractions of active and contemplative life common in the Western Church. When purification of the heart is no longer central, *praxis* becomes external activity, and *theoria* becomes interior recollection, neither of which embrace the critical tension that keeps wisdom healthy and whole. There is a subtle spiritual snobbery that looks down its nose at 'lower' spiritual states, as if Christ was susceptible to the vacuous snootiness of vainglory. Christ is one and his glory is indivisible. Unselfish love does not preen itself on its superiority.

When the noetic faculty descends into the heart and remembers God, thoughts are released and their energy is purified by the remembrance of God. Instead of flitting from this to that, the heart is purified by hallowing the Name. Thought is normal for the rational faculty, handling the affairs of this world. The saints did not have to be morons in order to be saints. Some were very intelligent indeed. But they did experience prayer of the heart, and they did discover pure prayer. In some circles, purification has been watered down to a shallow moralistic puritanism. Wisdom is despised, and the prayer of the Name neglected. Patristic wisdom is not pious moralism. Nor is it religious rationalism. It does address the will and the intelligence, but it homes in on the heart. Wisdom unveils the Name to illumine the heart, sometimes called the *nous,* the noetic faculty, by certain Fathers.

The *nous* is the spiritual intelligence, the eye of the heart, not the rational faculty. Their confusion and divorce are symptoms of a widespread malaise. Prayer of the heart separates out the confusion so as to free them to co-operate. Illumination of the heart frees the rational faculty to function on its own level without usurping the heart. Enlightenment of the rational faculty has its place, but it is not confused with illumination of the heart, nor is a scholarly study of the Name confused with illumination through the Name.

62.

"Pray without ceasing." [18] Prayer without ceasing is not endless verbal prayers said without stopping. It refers to prayer of the heart, which is a state of illumination. It is the remembrance of God that is unceasing. It continues in sleep and purifies dreams. It is a state of freedom, a state of grace, born of the Holy Spirit. Glorification in this life is a state of illumination in the Holy Spirit, which discerns Christ in resurrection, ascension and glorification, and so rises above illumination. Glorification in God through God is also from God, descending from the Father to embrace us. It is always present 'above,' but is not a permanent state here 'below.' Neither illumination nor glorification can be appropriated, for both can be lost, when *theoria* wavers. Grace is not arbitrary, but we are, and we project our arbitrariness onto God.

Glorification is the prayer of the Name within the heart, turning it into a temple of the Spirit and a sanctuary of glory. It is not the same thing as verbal prayer with the rational mind, such as the Jesus Prayer, although it can take over from it, and also accompany it, once the eye of the heart awakens. The mind is aware of the action of both kinds of prayer, and gradually becomes familiar with both of them. In the state of glorification, prayer may fall away for a while, returning once illumination returns. Unselfish love does not seek its own self-interest, but loves because love loves. This is impossible when we unconsciously confuse ourselves with God in the midst. We are selfish because we are not God-centred. We are selfish because 'I AM' is usurped by 'me, me, me.' 'I am me,' we say, as if the tautology was self-evident, oblivious that 'I AM' is God's Name. Unselfish love and glory are indivisible. The Word of God severs soul from spirit like a two-edged sword. Glory is uncreated love as fire in purification, love as light in illumination and love as glory in glorification. Unselfish love is glorious, and is not conditioned by conditioning. It is the glory of the Father and the Son, disclosed by the Spirit, and is radically unconditioned.

---

[18] 1 Thess 5:17.

63.

The Name is Christ's gift of himself to us. It unveils light from light, God from God. But it is in the light of the Holy Spirit that the light of glory is revealed, not conventional opinion, however religious. Uncreated light is indivisible, but is not God in his essence. In this light, light from light is seen. The grace of the Spirit is light from light, opening the eye of the heart to light from light, 'I AM.' The Spirit descends to purify the heart and open it to the glorious mysteries of 'I AM.' The pure in heart are blessed because they see God revealed in his Name. The blessed are purified and illumined by the Name, once the Spirit opens the heart to wisdom. Without wisdom, we cannot know God, because reason can only know things in the created world.

Wisdom and glory are mysteries of the heart. Reason can help formulate dogma, but it cannot open the eye of the heart to the mysteries expressed in dogma. God is inconceivable, and so reason, useful in science and technology, has distinct limits when it comes to mysteries of glory. Patristic wisdom distinguishes between talk about God and speech that transmits wisdom and glory through the Name, and so communicates the eternal gospel of the Kingdom. Christ's knowledge of the Father is direct, not like reason, which argues from premises to a conclusion. He sends the Spirit to open us to the Name, which unveils love's glory between the Father and the Son.

The Spirit's knowledge of the Son is direct, not like a hazarded opinion. This directness has no direction out from God or towards God, as reason does. It is directionless and direct. Sound reason is useful for earthly things, and there is no problem with it. But when it comes to the mysteries of glory and the Name, wisdom is crucial, which is why the Apostle Paul imparts wisdom to the mature. [19] For the Name 'I AM' to be revelation of God, the eye of the heart needs to be opened. For the glory of the Kingdom to come, the Name needs to be hallowed. It is the Spirit who opens the eye of the heart. It is the Spirit who imparts wisdom that hallows the Name.

---

[19] See 1 Cor 2:7.

64.

Patristic wisdom has not always used the terminology of wisdom to communicate wisdom, but at a time when there is a widespread misconception that the Christian tradition lacks all wisdom, it is obliged to bring out its wisdom treasures for all to see. When Patristic wisdom points to the Biblical roots of Christian wisdom, it speaks the mind of Christ, which inspires the mind of Patristic wisdom. The dogma of the Holy Trinity is never confused with the ineffable mysteries that save through the Name. Scholars can grasp the dogma intellectually, with the help of sound conceptual analysis. But for the desert, this can never lead to the saving wisdom of the Triune Name.

Patristic wisdom never forgot that the heart must turn and see. Seeing, or *theoria,* is essential for revelation, and revelation is essential to wisdom. God transcends all concepts of glory or the Name, and so when the Name is unveiled in glory, all concepts fall away. Conceptual improvisation has its place in secular philosophy, but not in the desert. Patristic wisdom speaks of wisdom because it loves wisdom, not because it is impressed by sophistry. Patristic wisdom sees 'I AM' in glory, enthroned in the midst, filling the heart with uncreated light. Both covenants bear witness to the Name, in the light of the Holy Spirit. Patristic tradition loves the wisdom of the Name, which unifies both Testaments. The glory of the Name is uncreated. The luminous energy of the Name is uncreated. God is 'I AM' revealing himself in his Name.

Controversies over the Name and wisdom are inevitable in an environment that has only a tenuous hold on Patristic wisdom. Accusations of heresy are hurled to and fro, but fall short of the mysteries of wisdom and the Name. The fact that controversies occur, points indirectly to the energy of the Name and wisdom, and the fact that these mysteries are crucial in our troubled times. But controversy cannot be resolved by controversy alone, since mysteries of glory are not accessible to rational debate alone. It is Patristic wisdom that sees why the Bible says the Name is crucial for wisdom and wisdom for the Name. It imparts the Name in wisdom, showing that both controversies resolve themselves in the *praxis* of *theoria* .

65.

In theophanies of the Name, the glorified participate in the wisdom and glory of God. The Fathers do not say they partake of the essence of God, but in his uncreated energies, revealed by the Father, through the Son, in the Holy Spirit. When seers do speak of essence, they also speak of 'supra-essential essence,' to ensure that, on the basis of no confusion, no subtle division is read into God. Patristic terminology is not an attempt to grasp God conceptually, but to avoid extremes that spawn extremism, because extremism is incompatible with wisdom. Heresy is avoided because it spawns spiritual pathologies instead of curing them. It is pointed out to us, not out of prejudice, but out of concern for wholesome wisdom.

When the tradition loses touch with its therapeutic theopathy, it begins to degenerate into sophistry. The 'blind' begin to speak about the essence as if the essence was something knowable, and reification sets in so wisdom is lost. When Patristic wisdom speaks of essence and person, it is not objectifying the ineffable, but transmitting wisdom to awaken hearts. It also speaks of essence and energy, knowing that the unknowable really is unknowable. It does so out of love of wisdom and glory, to communicate the Name. It is bearing witness to glory with a wise unknowing, to free the Name from fixated preconceptions.

Desert wisdom knows there are not two glories, for God is one, and his Name, 'I AM,' is one. It is love's glory that 'proves' this, not syllogisms. It is light from light and God from God that reveals this, and it does so in uncreated light, gift of God the Holy Spirit. The glory of the Name is one. There are not two. Wisdom sees into the heart of this oneness, and knows it is ineffable. It does not harden ineffable oneness into a rational concept, even though it uses reason to distinguish wisdom from sophistry.

So Patristic wisdom speaks of one God in three persons, to transmit wisdom in uncreated light. It never forgets that God is inconceivable and ineffable, in his uncreated energies as well as in his essence. When the Word reveals the Name, words are used, but concepts fall away when wisdom sees the glory of 'I AM' in uncreated light.

66.

The Patristic distinction between essence and energy is not a hardened dualistic division, as we can see when the Fathers speak of essence as 'super-essential mystery,' and energy as 'essential energy.' There is origination, generation and procession, not because speculation says so, but because this is how revelation is revealed and unfolds. 'I AM' from 'I AM,' is seen in 'I AM,' not as three separate things, but as three persons revealing one glory, one wisdom and one Name. It is ineffable mystery even as it is the heart of Patristic wisdom, handed down in the desert, by angels and by saints. Satanic confusion and demonic division confuse the uncreated and the created, causing division between the uncreated and the created. The discernment of spirits is called for because confusion parodies communion and division pretends to be healthy difference.

Wisdom is called mystical theology when discernment of spirits comes to the aid of purification and illumination of the heart. The Spirit of wisdom is everywhere present and fills all things, but discernment is needed if the machinations of confusion and the deviations of division are to be seen right through. The insight of wisdom sees through confusion and division. That is why the Patristic tradition, treasured in the desert, loves wisdom. Wisdom is not optional but indispensible for all who love her.

The tradition does not claim to own wisdom, as if Christ belongs to an exclusive clique of traditionalists alone. It humbly bears witness to wisdom in love, giving all glory to God. The tradition imparts light to the world, fanning the spark of the Name into flame. 'I AM' is the 'light of the world,' and desires recognition in every heart. 'I AM' is glory in heaven, longing to be hallowed on earth. The Name is common to all three persons, but its manner or mode of being the Name is specific to each person. There are not three 'I AMs,' because 'I AM' is one. But the way in which the Name is origination, generation or procession differs. It is revelation that unveils this difference, and it is wisdom that discerns this difference, distinguishing difference from division by hallowing without confusion the oneness of the Name.

67.

The Word who reveals the Name, and the Spirit who discerns what is revealed, are from the Father. The Father unveils the Name through the Son, in the Holy Spirit. In the language of dogmatics, the Father is unoriginate, the origin of the Son is by generation, and of the Spirit by procession. The desert does not stop short at theological definitions, but bears witness that Christ indwells the glory of the Father as the Father indwells him. Christ's 'I AM' sayings, with and without predicates, reveal God in his Name. Christ abides in the glory of the Father, discerned by the Spirit, through the Name. On Sinai, on Tabor, on the mount of the heart, Christ unveils the Name in uncreated glory in his midst, right here in our midst. The Name is hallowed in glory by wisdom everywhere that the Lord's Prayer is actually prayed, rather than merely repeated by rote.

The uncreated Word at the heart of the Lord's Prayer and also of the Jesus Prayer, is the revelation of the Name. Wisdom discerns the glory of the Name by right hallowing it, saying, 'Hallowed be thy Name, thy Kingdom come.' 'Thine is the Kingdom, the power and the glory.' 'Glory be to thee, O Lord, glory be to thee.' What is important to elders in the desert is transmission of wisdom through the Name. It is illumination sustained in purity of heart. It is glorification sustained by hallowing.

When the mind turns and awakens to Christ in the midst, it sees uncreated not created light of glory. There is no resemblance between the uncreated and the created, and the uncreated is inconceivable. The remembrance of God is possible only because the uncreated grace of the Holy Spirit opens the 'eye' of the heart. The 'single eye' sees light of glory in uncreated light, and is not reducible to the exercise of metaphysical discrimination. For Patristic Wisdom, the union of the uncreated and the created is uncreated, and so ineffable. To see uncreated light, it is necessary to be in uncreated light, through uncreated light, which is ineffable. This is illumination, and from the standpoint of illumination, illumination is the basis of glorification. From the standpoint of glorification, illumination is the radiance of glorification, since glorification is the basis of everything.

68.

To hallow the Name of the Holy Trinity is to harrow the hells of confusion and division in the power of the glory of 'I AM.' The uncreated creative energy of the Father redeems as well as creates all that there is, through the energy of the Word, in the energy of the Holy Spirit. This is the expression of wisdom's vision of the glory of the Name. Wisdom recreates all that there is in the power of the Name, and in the mystery of Holy Saturday, descends into hell to empty the prisons of pride. The glory of resurrection, ascension and also glorification itself, is hid with Christ in God, waiting to be revealed by the Holy Spirit.

It is not in our power to undo pride or cure vainglory, but it is in the power of Christ in his Name. So we hallow the Name as he taught us, praying the Name in the heart. The Name harrows the hells of confusion and division when it is hallowed, which is how the Kingdom comes. To hallow the Name on earth, as in heaven, is to fulfil the will of the Father in the heart of the Son, as discerned by the Holy Spirit. It is not in our power to see this, but it is in the power of the wisdom of the Spirit, if we let the Spirit unite with our spirit in holy vision and co-operation. This awakens the eye of the heart to the inner principles of everything, which Christ frees to rise with him in resurrection. In Christ, the inner energy of everything ascends with him to heaven. In him, the *logoi* of the *Logos* himself are glorified in the glorified Name.

When Christ says he has been working, and that his working is the Father at work, he speaks of this holy work of hallowing the Name, including harrowing hells. Confusion dissolves when wisdom sees right through. Division heals when glory descends from heaven. It is not sophisticated speculation that sees this but wisdom. It is not vainglory that does this, but the glory of the Name. The blessed are glorified gradually, but the grace is uncreated, simultaneous and sudden. Wisdom spells out for us what is being given in uncreated grace, not in created words, but in uncreated words of the Word himself. Revelation is spelt out with the help of created words, and passed on from elder to disciple from generation to generation.

69.

The ages, *aionas,* of the angels, archangels, cherubim, seraphim and heavenly powers, are neither eternal, as God is, nor temporal, as we are. They are dimensions of time in heaven unlike our measurable time on earth, but they are addressed by the Name when wisdom weds heaven and earth. The powers include fallen powers, traditionally called demons, whose powers are undone by Christ in the ethereal realms. The fallen powers fall short of the glory of God and so are powers of darkness. But they do partake of the creative energies of God, or they would not be at all. God's love and glory embrace heaven and earth, including hells. But outer darkness experiences love and glory differently from the glorified. It experiences love's glory as hell not heaven. Wisdom is not ignorant of the devices of darkness, the darkness of confusion and the fires of division. Confusion parodies union so that division can parody difference, reducing union to confusion.

When the demon appears as an angel of light, it comes from outside and its machinations are external. It tries to get us to confuse the created with the uncreated so as to usurp the uncreated with the created. It divides the created from the uncreated, proliferating divisions everywhere. But it can never actually usurp God in the midst. The Name reveals the uncreated at centre and the created off centre, where it can enter into communion with the uncreated. It reveals this in uncreated light. Demonic parodies have form, shape, and external characteristics, because they intend confusion between the created and the uncreated. Such lights come and go, unlike uncreated light, which is everywhere present and fills all things.

Wisdom discerns these spirits, whether they are of God or not. Death subjects us to spiritual death by subjecting us to fear of death. Glory overcomes death by death and so undoes the power of death. Christ sees through satanic confusion with wisdom, and overcomes demonic division in the glory of the Name. Fallen powers are rendered powerless by wisdom and the Name. The wiles of devils are empty vanity when discernment of spirits sees through them. Purification undoes confusion so that illumination can heal division. When glory hallows the Name aright, confusion and division are no more.

70.

Christ is the image of God and we are created in the image of God, which means we are created in him. Confusion would have us usurp Christ by claiming we are the image of God, cutting us off from the Son, who is the image of the Father. When God the Word becomes man, the Son remains the image of the Father, so by mutual exchange of characteristics, the human Jesus is also the image of the Father. The Name in Christ restores communion by extinguishing confusion. Glory in Christ restores the image and dissolves division.

We who are created in the image of God are also created to be in the likeness of God, and glorification is realization of this likeness. The Word and the Spirit have glorification in view from the beginning, intending wisdom and the Name. Christ is the image and likeness of God, in whom we are recreated in his image and likeness, through wisdom and the Name. In Christ, illumination restores the image and glorification the likeness, fulfilled in the remembrance of God.

When the memory of God is lost because of confusion, we are cut off from remembrance of God. Illumination restores the memory of God to us so that in glorification, not only do we remember God, but God remembers us. Patristic wisdom imparts grace in the Name, which grants eternal life. The soul is not understood to be naturally immortal, but partakes of eternal life by grace. Seers see God by the grace of God, in the uncreated light of glory. Glorification embraces body and soul together, deifying both. Man is not God by nature, nor does man by nature see God as his divine nature. Confusions like this are commonplace, but wisdom sees through them if we are prepared to see with the eye of the heart. The heart sees what reason and the senses cannot see, once it is illumined. If it remains blind, the heart remains hard. Reason and the sensing mind cannot then see what the spirit in the heart sees.

The Name draws our *nous* down into the heart, so that turning, we may see, illumined by the Holy Spirit, in the bond of peace. Wisdom restores us in Christ to illumination in the image of God and glorification in the likeness of God.

71.

In many translations of Patristic wisdom texts, the word *nous* is translated as 'mind,' but *nous* and *dianoia*, mind, are distinguished by the Fathers, who never taught that the mind or rational faculty descends into the heart in prayer of the heart. It is the *nous* that descends into the heart, not the mind, and noetic prayer, not 'mental' prayer, is the prayer of the heart. Originally, the Fathers spoke of the heart, *kardia*, and the spirit, *pneuma*, using the Semitic terminology of the Bible. They gradually made use of the distinction between *nous*, or the noetic faculty, and *logos*, or the rational faculty, eventually distinguishing the praying faculty, *nous*, from the rational faculty, sometimes called *logos*, reason, and sometimes *dianoia*, reasoning.

Patristic terminology is not consistent, but what is important is that noetic awareness in the heart is not confused with rational thoughts, *logoismi*. Prayer of the heart is remembrance of God in the heart. *Nous* is the word the Fathers used to express our spiritual capacity to awaken to God in the heart. When prayer of the heart awakens, it is the Spirit who prays, through the *nous*, in the heart. In the fallen state, the *nous* wanders about confusing itself with thoughts, emotions and sensations, whereas it needs to descend into the heart if the eye of the heart is to awaken to God in the midst.

In divine vision, we transcend our senses and our rational capacities, but they remain available for our everyday affairs, so that we can function normally. Reason translates the ineffable experience of vision into human language, so that it can be communicated. When the *nous* unites with the heart in vision of God, desire and anger are purified of selfishness and restored to their original unselfishness as the desiring and incensive energies of the soul. Saints desire the good of others and show wrath at the injustice that oppresses others. They are not the victims of insensitive indifference, but free of the pathological passions of selfish anger and self-interested desire.

Illumination is at first sought through the outer purification of the *nous*, but once illumination is given, it is then the inner purification of the *nous* through the *praxis* of *theoria*. Love is purified and illumined by seeing, so that unselfish love can flower in glorification.

72.

There is glorification of God in words and symbols, in the Liturgy and services of the Church, but there is also spiritual glorification of God, when the Holy Spirit prays wordlessly with our spirit in the illumined heart. The Apostle Paul refers to this when he speaks of praying in the Spirit and praying with the understanding. [20] Verbal prayer and spiritual prayer can take place simultaneously, but they are not confused, because the Spirit descends at Pentecost to grant spiritual prayer and glorification in the Holy Spirit, not more verbal prayers.

Mystical theology is not clever speculation but pure prayer in spirit and in truth. Theology can talk about God without pure prayer, but it cannot be mystical theology transmitting the mysteries of glory with wisdom through the Name. Mystical theology is the wisdom of the cross, which Saint Isaac says has two aspects, a *praxis,* such as patience in tribulation, and a *theoria,* as in pure prayer, where the Spirit prays with our Spirit, crying, '*Abba,* Father!'

The spiritual power of the cross is the wisdom of uncreated self-emptying love, which is the empowering energy of glorification. It is hidden with Christ in God, waiting to be revealed, loved and known. The Spirit discerns it in the mysteries of glory that fallen powers cannot pry into or make their own. The 'I AM' of glory reconciles all the opposites of creation within his reconciliation of the creation with the uncreated. The uncreated cross is wisdom discerning the glory of the Name in every dimension and on every level.

The mysteries of glory transmit this uncreated energy of glory so that everything can partake of glorification. But without wisdom, the externals are 'letter' not 'spirit,' and there is no life, no way and no truth. Love's glory, revealed by the Father to the Son, is given in the Spirit to all who hallow God's Name. This transmits spiritual glorification of God, through spiritual glorification by God, glorification in spirit and in truth.

---

[20] See 1 Cor 14:15.

73.

Illumination is glory experienced in uncreated light, through revelation of the Name. The glory the Father gives the Son, in the Name, is given to the apostles, so that it can be passed on to the saints. They see the glory of the Name in glorification, because being in Christ means being in him in his glorification, as well as his resurrection and ascension. Christ has declared the Name to his disciples, to illumine them, and he says he will declare the Name to them, in their future glorification. He will unveil love's coming glory to them for their glorification, so that the love of the Father for the Son will be theirs too. Coming glory is the glory of the coming Kingdom. It is union with Christ in his ascension. It is the gift of the Paraclete at Pentecost.

Christ goes away in order to come as resurrection, ascension and glorification, unveiling his Kingdom of resurrection, ascension and glorification in the descent of the Paraclete at Pentecost. He comes not as he was, but in love's mysteries of glory. He comes as Baptism, Chrismation and Eucharist, experienced as purification, illumination and glorification. The unfolding of the deifying economy of glory is hidden in the Name, and discerned by the Spirit for our purification, illumination and glorification. Wisdom is this discernment and glory is its hidden content.

Pentecost reveals the communion of the glorified in the revelation of the Name. The glory of the Kingdom is uncreated, which means the Church is not of this world. It is the radiance of the glory of God's Name. Christ is the indivisibility of 'I AM' in heaven, hallowed on earth as in heaven. The glory of 'I AM' is uncreated, and is only seen when the Spirit of Truth opens the 'eye' of the heart. The Paraclete is sent in the Name, the same Name above all names that the Father reveals to the Son. Pentecost opens the Name as glorification, on the basis of purification and illumination. The Paraclete transmits all mysteries, transmuting all 'words' of the Word into the remembrance of God. Above all, the Paraclete imparts glorification, which is ineffable, and it does so by means of the ineffable. 'I AM' is ineffably one in God and many in us without confusion or division. The Name is one with the mystery of mysteries, broken but not divided, eaten but not consumed.

74.

The wisdom of the Paraclete discerns what the wisdom of Christ reveals in the Name, which has its source in the Father's timeless gift of his Name 'I AM' to the Son. Wisdom imparts mysteries of the ineffable oneness of the Trinity as well as of hypostatic difference between the persons. Both the oneness and the differences are glorious as well as beautiful, but there are no words that can do them complete justice. Wisdom beholds their glory as perfect completeness in unbiased openness and ineffable stillness. Wonder experiences this glory as spontaneous presence in indivisible oneness. The wisdom of the Paraclete is key to these mysteries of glory, which lie at the heart of the Church in glory. Without it, we are reduced to the externals of institutions and administration. Without it, the extremism of ecclesiastical and political extremes takes over. Without it, the heresies of confusion swallow up communion, and the heresies of division insinuate themselves as separation, so that wholeness falls apart. It is not a question of 'them' and 'us,' the baddies out there against the goodies here with us. Schism is itself a symptom of the pathology that the wisdom of the Paraclete alone can cure.

The wisdom of the Paraclete is the mystery of peace, the peace prayed for in the Litany, the peace that proleptically precedes the prayer. Peace is presupposed, so peace is given. Forgiveness is the basis of forgiveness, as light is the basis of light and glory of glory. Pentecost presupposes the resurrection and ascension, and so glorification embraces the mysteries of Pascha and Pentecost, revealing the interconnectedness of everything for wisdom. The wisdom of the Paraclete is omnipresent and omniscient, communicating communion without confusion or division. The mystery of the Eucharist transmits Christ's glorified humanity to us, so each and every one is by grace Christ as a whole in the glory of his wholeness. Pentecost transmits wholeness, revealing wholeness according to the whole, which is what 'catholic' means. The Paraclete, the Spirit of Truth, gradually reveals mysteries of glory, which we could not have received before. They are always already present in Christ, but the Paraclete searches them out for us one by one, when we are ready to receive them.

75.

The Spirit of Truth imparts all truth, the truth of the whole. Wisdom discerns wholeness in the mysteries of glory, but this wholeness is impaired by our limited capacity to bear it. However deep our glorification becomes, divine completeness is always impaired by the incompleteness of our capacity to bear it. So elders bear witness to Christ's wholeness in its completeness, even as they are aware that it is impaired by our incompleteness. They uphold the 'critical tension,' as Archimandrite Sophrony used to put it.

It is not that there is another truth beyond Pentecost that will gradually supersede it. It is that Pentecost guides us into all truth, and as a whole, but we cannot bear it all, so the Spirit comes to help us in our incompleteness, bearing witness to completeness with wisdom's humble awareness of our incompleteness.

The Church does not claim to posses completeness but bears witness to completeness so that we may live in the light of its glory, giving all glory to God. Wisdom turns and sees nothing created in the midst. 'I AM' is not something created, but God's self-revelation in our midst. The light of the glory of 'I AM' is 'all truth,' which the Paraclete discerns and communicates to us, in the measure that we are able to bear it. Pentecost proclaims the Name so that we can begin to imbibe 'all truth,' without usurping God, who alone right glorifies the glory of the Name.

Pentecost communicates the mystery of the entire wholeness of the completeness of glory to everyone in Christ, without usurping God. This is truly wondrous. With every tongue of uncreated fire, the wholeness of the completeness comes to dwell in us. This is the experience of glorification. It is really awesome.

Broken but not divided, the Lamb is eaten but not consumed. This is the mystery of union. The uncreated fire of the Name consumes confusion but creation is not consumed. This is the mystery of communion. Glorification is union and communion discerned by wisdom in the Name.

76.

Pentecostal fire imparts all truth from within as well as from without, deifying the saints, but deification deifies all, not just separate individuals. 'All truth' embraces all. The limit to completeness is our capacity to receive it, which is why glorification imparts completeness in accordance with our freedom and not against it. Our 'yes' is our 'Amen,' saying, 'Glory be to thee, O Lord, glory be to thee.'

'All truth' means glorification, which the Spirit reveals as purifying fire in tongues of flame, and uncreated light in flames of love. 'All truth' is love's glory deifying all things in the saints. Glorification at Pentecost is normal, not the special privilege of very few. It is normative and so imparts things as they are. It is grace and so is not the result of effort and strain. It is given to all, but not forced on all, since it respects our freedom and our capacity to receive it.

It remains a fact, however, that conventional religion distances itself from glorification, preferring the narrows and shallows of external rules and institutional regulations. 'All truth' becomes 'our truth' or 'my truth' when self-interest calls the tune. Wholeness is narrowed down to an ideology, a weapon with which to exclude 'them' from 'us.' Completeness is made shallow enough for all to use as a method of exclusion. This is inevitable, for it is the price love pays for love's respect for freedom. It is the price wisdom pays for love's respect for our incapacity to receive the Spirit of Truth.

To be formed in Christ, however, is to be transformed in Spirit and Truth, hallowed by hallowing the glory of the Name. The narrows and shallows are invited to trust the depths of glory unveiled in the Name. They are free to say no, but love's glory invites them to come and see, to turn and see. Wisdom is patient and kind. She never imposes out of a will to power.

Oneness in freedom cannot be imposed. Glory is not forced on us. To be with him where he is, means to be 'I AM' from 'I AM.' Pentecost recreates creation anew in every moment. The Paraclete imparts glorification to all who give glory to God.

77.

Illumination is already a foretaste of the experience of glorification, as is purification. By illumination, the Spirit pledges glorification. In the mysteries of glory, all parts are the whole, revealing the truth of the whole. The whole Christ is present in every part of the Lamb, and all who partake of the Lamb, participate in the whole Christ. When *theoria* is right glorification of the Name, *praxis* is orthodox not kenodox. Orthodoxy is doxology that exposes the vanity at the heart of vainglory, the confusion at the heart of kenodoxy.

Unity among us arises from the oneness of the glory of the Name. It is not an external phenomenon but an ineffable radiance from the light of glory discerned in wisdom. Glorification is the enlightened intent of Pentecost, which the Paraclete discerns and passes on from elders to saints from generation to generation.

Religion exists to console the soul emotionally and give it hope of salvation after death. Patristic tradition is not religion but wisdom that severs soul from spirit like a two-edged sword. It transmits spirit and truth to the heart, not conventional formation but doxological transformation. Wisdom imparts eternal life through death in Christ, resurrection life through resurrection in Christ, glorification life through glorification with Christ. It is not religion but the end of religion, although there has been no lack of determination in conventional circles to dumb it down to religion again.

Wisdom values prophecy that transmits the Name and prayer that assimilates the Name in the heart. It values teaching inspired by wisdom and miracles that are signs of glory. It values healing that cures the passions, and interpretations that help healing happen. It values varieties of tongues because no two people are the same. Tongues of fire are various because wisdom is manifold, well able to speak to every heart, however different the context and background. [21] Patristic wisdom is integral and manifold in the light of the glory of the Name.

---

[21] See 1 Cor 12:28.

78.

Wisdom is recognized by the fruit of her mysteries, love without self-interest that does not seek its own. [22] The desert loves wisdom because she transmits the glory of the Name and keeps alive the mysteries of glory revealed to the prophets and apostles. In an age that sees monasticism as a parasitical cancer, it is rare to find anyone who is familiar with its therapeutic theopathy, still less those who have experience of its cures at first hand. In fact, it has always known of the cancers of the spirit that harden the heart, and the scleroses of the soul that blind it to God.

Fear of death is rooted in selfish self-love, and selfish love is determined by the fear of death. The wisdom of the cross overcomes fear of death by dying to selfish self-love. There is no fear in unselfish love, because unselfish love casts out fear. [23] The wisdom of the Paraclete leads fear out of fear, into love free of fear. The Spirit of Truth leads fear into 'all truth,' the truth of love's glory in the hallowed Name.

The Paraclete prays in the illumined heart, freeing it from fear, freeing it for unselfish love, that seeks not its own. This love is the Biblical mind, which is the mind of Christ that inspires the Patristic mind. It is not sophistry but wisdom, heir to the wisdom of Christ, generating sons by grace with the Son, daughters of light in wisdom. Love's glory is the glory of unselfish love experienced in glorification. All else falls away. Love alone remains. Love loves because love loves. Love knows as it is known. Love's glory never ends.

---

[22] See 1 Cor 13:5.

[23] See 1 John 4:18.

79.

The Name transmits peace not fear. 'I AM' says, 'Fear not! Be not afraid!' 'My peace I give unto you.' Transmission of peace is wisdom's gift in the Name. It opens the eye of the heart. It frees the *nous* to unite with the heart in profound *theoria,* because in profound *metanoia,* the *nous* turns and sees. Saint Symeon the New Theologian renewed integral Orthodox Tradition with the wisdom of uncreated light. The Hesychasts handed on this transmission of light. Illumination is wisdom's dwelling place. It sees the uncreated energies of glory on earth as in heaven. It awakens to these energies as 'words' of the Word, giving glory to God in his Name.

Illumination raises us from fear and roots us in love, unselfish love that does not seek its own. The sterile servility of fear and the selfish asceticism of punishment, merit and reward, fall away when love's glory begins to purify the heart. The cup of martyrdom is a baptism of love, called glorification, and it goes beyond resurrection, and even beyond illumination rooted in resurrection. Fragrance of glory is like incense, rising as form into the formless prayer of love.

It is not pietistic sentiment but uncreated light that opens the 'eye' of the heart. Saint Symeon bears witness to this in 'Hymns of Love.' Glorification is participation in uncreated glory, because in uncreated light, light sees light. God in God sees God, not clever scrutiny prying into the divine to glorify itself. Glorification is union with God in the Holy Spirit, deification by grace in the Name. It is sanctification by wisdom through the vision of God. It is overlooked when the *praxis* of *theoria* is neglected and wisdom is disdained.

Glorification is Pentecost lived and loved, known as the wisdom of the Paraclete alone knows, hid with Christ in God. It is ineffable even in its radiance, invisible even in vision. Both the *theoria* we call illumination and the *theosis* we call glorification are ineffable. Verbal prayers fall away in the stillness of recognition, when turning sees and vision is struck dumb. But prayer returns when speech is called for, and the Name is verbally hallowed again. It is not that glory comes and goes, but we do, in this life, as we attend to this or that. Glory is how it is, as it is, as the Name reveals.

80.

Language is symbolic when it transmits ineffable mysteries by means of words and images. Theology is suspended as mystical theology begins to transmit the mysteries, because they cannot be grasped conceptually. The term 'theologian' is used of Saint John, Saint Gregcry and Saint Symeon, but means they saw deeply into the glory of Christ in his Name. Mystical theology lives from *theoria* and from the *praxis* of *theoria,* which sees nothing created in the midst. Nothing created usurps 'I AM' here. The Name reveals where God is to be found. Hallowed aright, the Name unveils the Kingdom of glory in the midst. Right glorification is the indispensible basis of the experience of glorification, not sophisticated speculation or metaphysical discrimination. If metaphysics usurps wisdom, things go awry. An overweening mind is no substitute for an illumined heart, but a good mind can reflect the mysteries of the heart and express them, as the Fathers did.

Mystical theology employs symbols to transmit states of union and communion with God, which cannot be conceived or comprehended. Glorification transcends conceptual discrimination, so elders employ prophetic symbols to inspire pure prayer of the heart. They certainly do think conceptually but do not let thoughts usurp vision, or something created usurp God in the midst. They love others, but do not confuse this with unselfish love that does not seek its own. Self-love lies at the root of all other passions, so the Name begins by uprooting the confusion that deludes our energies and capacities. Having undone confusion between the created and the uncreated in the midst, the Name then heals the divisions predetermined by confusion. This cures vainglory by freeing glory from vanity. Vainglory then transmutes into right glorification, the indispensible basis of glorification and its mysteries.

Mystical theology prays purely as pure prayer, as Evagrius saw, prayer that purifies and illumines the heart so that glorification rises above vainglory. The pure heart is poor in spirit because it sees through the vanities of riches of all kinds. The pure heart lets glory through, because it is no longer hard. A single eye sees the truth of the whole wholly, and is whole. Glory sees glory and is glorified.

81.

Vision of glory imparts union and communion, as the saints bear witness. Glorification transmits communion of saints, which believers trust, but faith in vision does not usurp vision. Confidence in *theoria* is called for, but blind beleif is no substitute for *theoria*. Elders communicate knowledge in the Name that transcends secular knowledge, but they know that secular knowledge has its place. As long as it does not usurp divine knowledge, but humbly serves it, all is well.

Glory grounds vision and so wisdom, but without wisdom, glory goes unnoticed and is ignored. Wisdom is not an abstraction, nor is a concept of wisdom ever to be confused with actual wisdom. Glorification is glory discerned by wisdom, glory that sustains wisdom. Wisdom knows as she is known, which is glorification, but the saints do not confuse wisdom with themselves. They bear witness to wisdom, in the light of wisdom, giving all glory to God. Even in ecstatic moments of vision, glory belongs to God, and the glorified ascribe all glory to God. Patristic wisdom is not in competition with Biblical wisdom but is sustained and confirmed by it. The reason that Patristic wisdom came to an end in the West is that scholastic philosophy thought it was superior, and that the Fathers had been superseded. In the East, Patristic wisdom is not dead, although it is under siege from conventional religion.

Glorification and mission are one, for the Spirit is sent for the same reason as the apostles were sent, to impart purifying light of glory in the Name. Mission has wisdom and glory in view, to bless the glorified in the Name. The idea that mission has nothing to do with the desert is disproved over and over again. The history of Orthodox mission and monasticism refutes such misconceptions, and is witness to the Paraclete who inspires both.

Glorification and mission are the light and the radiance of Pentecost, which the Paraclete transmits anew in wisdom, to renew the Patristic tradition. Patristic tradition, which lives from wisdom, has no end, for wisdom, and the glory it discerns, have no end.

82.

Obedience without glory is vulnerable to all kinds of deviation, whereas obedience to the glorified is obedience to God, ascribing all glory to God. It is not subjection to psychological abuse. In some circles, there is no discernment of spirits, so they are confused. The Spirit intercedes for us in such circumstances, knowing better how we should pray and act. Pentecost is not over, so there is always hope, hope that is grounded in the Spirit's pledge, glory to come revealed even now, glory now guaranteeing glory to come.

When theology degenerates into ideology, fundamentalism is inevitable. When spiritual paternity and maternity degenerate into psychological abuse, wisdom has been lost. The cure lies in glory and the Name, which wisdom imparts with the help of living prophecy and prayer of the heart. Pentecost can restore and renew all degenerations, because wisdom makes all things new.

The mysteries of the Kingdom are one in the glory of the Name. They transmit the uncreated light of glory through the Name. Baptism transmits *metanoia* in the inmost heart, opening wisdom's single eye to God. Chrismation transmits *theoria* in the illumined heart, opening it to the uncreated light of glory. The Eucharist transmits *theosis* in glorification, opening the heart to all mysteries of glory, in the ineffable presence and invisible oneness of God.

The oneness of Baptism and Chrismation is experienced in the oneness of *metanoia* and *theoria,* which is the oneness of *praxis* and *theoria.* Baptism and Chrismation are one in the oneness transmitted by the Eucharist, the union and communion experienced in glorification. The mysteries of glory all transmit wondrous oneness, one spirit with the oneness of the Paraclete, the oneness revealed at Pentecost. Pentecost happens anew in every moment when the Name is hallowed and the Kingdom comes. The Patristic age is not over because Pentecost is not over. There has been no closure, and so there is no rupture with the oneness unveiled in the mysteries of glory in the Name.

83.

Baptism in the early Church involved threefold immersion in the waters of initiation, accompanied by threefold invocation of the Thrice Holy Name. It transmits the mysteries of turning and the remission of sins. Chrismation seals the gift of the Holy Spirit with the words, 'The seal of the gift of the Holy Spirit.' The Paraclete seals initiation in the Name with the gift of the Holy Spirit.

Chrism transforms the heart into a temple of the Holy Spirit, where the Spirit's prayer in the heart gives all glory to God. God is glorified in spirit and truth, that is, in God's glorification of God in the heart. The Holy Spirit illumines the heart, and prays in spirit and truth within it. It is this that makes the heart a temple of the Holy Spirit. It is this that constitutes the royalty of its sacred priesthood.

The Liturgy of the Church hallows the Name to awaken liturgy of the heart, in which the Spirit searches out the mysteries of Communion in the Body and Blood of Christ and communicates them. We offer 'rational worship' in the Liturgy of the Church, whereas God offers 'spiritual worship' in the liturgy of the heart. 'Spiritual worship' is the prayer of the Paraclete in the heart, and the Paraclete's prayer is unceasing.

The mysteries of the Eucharist communicate communion in accordance with the spiritual state of the communicant, as purification, illumination and glorification. The same tongue of fire purifies, illumines or glorifies. When the mysteries are dumbed down, they cease to heal as mysteries and become religious services. Their therapeutic efficacy is ignored because there is no prayer of the Spirit in the heart. The glory of the Name is overlooked because there is no wisdom.

The Eucharistic Liturgy remains what it always was. It hallows the Name and communicates the Body and Blood of Christ to us, broken but not divided, shared but not consumed. The mysteries of communion remain primordially pure, like wisdom, which discerns them. We come and go, but the glory is as it is, just as it is.

84.

Running through and beneath the rivers of ethereal fire is God's own uncreated fire, creating and recreating all things new. This fire is God's uncreated creative energy in two presences, two divine names, wisdom and glory, the wisdom of God's 'I' and the glory of God's 'AM.' The Holy Name 'I AM' is a union of God's wisdom and glory, which the fall confuses and divides. The 'I' is confused when the created usurps the uncreated on the throne of the heart, and the 'AM' is divided when vainglory deprives glory of its beloved, God. Wisdom, when confused, and glory, when divided, fall from God and so fall apart, as self-love and idolatrous love, egocentric delusion and delusive reification.

When wisdom and glory descend from heaven, it is to cure all 'powers' of confusion and to heal all 'powers' of division in the Name. Wisdom weds glory in God's wondrous Kingdom of power and glory, creating all things new as descending glorification. Wisdom discerns that what purification looked forward to, has already come in illumination, and what illumination looked forward to, has already come in glorification.

Wisdom's sevenfold light makes us children of light in the threefold perfection of wisdom, and children of glory in the fourfold wholeness of wisdom. The sevenfold mystery is twelvefold when the Kingdom of glory is revealed, and the fourfold wholeness of deified creation is multiplied by the threefold perfection of the Holy Trinity. The difference between seven and twelve is the difference between addition of perfection and wholeness, and multiplication, which symbolizes wisdom's glory as ineffable expanding completeness. The numbers do not matter. The wisdom of the Paraclete, translucent in the heart, is crucial. The glory wisdom beholds, radiant as glorification, matters. It is why we are here.

But wisdom knows it is the Name that unveils these mysteries, opening the eye of the heart. She does not attract attention to herself. She bears witness to Christ and the Name the Father bequeaths to us through him.

85.

When wisdom descends, it is as a bride, revealing Song of Songs mysteries at the heart of the throne. Saint Denys speaks of a divine *eros* here, where a sacred *temenos* encloses mysteries of descent as a bridal chamber and Holy of Holies. It has been called a rose-garden, in which wisdom is enthroned, a symbol of paradise in which wisdom offers her feast of love. A crystal fountain lies sealed in the midst of a bower of bliss, in this spiritual paradise, because when the bride descends, the fall is undone and the sensible and the spiritual are one.

Saint Maximus says that male and female conjoin in the earthly paradise at the point where it conjoins with the spiritual paradise, which is where heaven weds earth, and both wed intelligible gardens where God weds creation in the heaven of heavens. Maximus' five mediations are the descending bride ascending in conjugal embrace with Christ. They are mysteries of his bride the Church, lived as a mystery of a Song of Songs. The beloved is to be found hidden in her secret garden with its high walls and sealed fountain. It was a lost garden when wisdom was exiled, but is found again when she unveils glory in the heart. Paradise is not a place in space or a moment in time, but is a timeless garden of sacred alchemy, which is a cloister garden of forgotten mysteries that only wisdom remembers. The Song of Songs says the bride herself is the garden, and Saint Gregory of Nyssa inspires us to see what the glory of the descending bride is really like, veiled as a Song of Songs.

Wisdom descends as the bride of Christ in the mysteries of glorification. The garden is symbolic, as is the Song of Songs, but spiritual marriage is love's glory when wisdom has the deification of all things in view. The cosmic liturgy of the awakened heart derives from Christly Eros, divine, human and cosmic in scope. The scope of wisdom is the enlightened intent of the Paraclete, unveiling the mysteries of glory in the Name. The Word reveals the Name which the Father imparts to the Son, but without the wisdom of the Paraclete, its treasures would remain hidden. Christly Eros is the revelation of the Holy Trinity, not sterile dogma, but burning, boundless love.

86.

For wisdom in the desert, dogma is life, remembrance of God in tongues of fire. Wisdom turns and sees in the hidden silence of the night. For the schools, dogma is conceptual form, requiring rigorous definition in the fires of debate. There is talk about talk but no one remembers to see. For the desert, wisdom is primordially pure in awakened hearts, if we abide in her ineffable expanse. She never strays from the Father's revelation of the Name to the Son, in the timeless glory of the Paraclete. Glorification arises in the limpid purity of the heart, when the Spirit prays the prayer of the Name. The prayer of the Paraclete is unceasing, like an ocean of boundless love. Waves come and go, but the prayer is unceasing. Such prayer transcends verbal prayers as the divine transcends the human, but deified humanity is given glimpses of its glory as a guarantee of its truth.

Renunciation without turning is blind, leaving us lost in the dark. Real *metanoia* turns and sees, so is no longer blind. When the blind lead the blind, the world is a ditch, but no one notices. All have fallen from glory, but no one knows what glory is, so no one sees what they have lost. Rumours make us wonder, but few are ready to awaken to the wonder of wisdom. Confusion arises in the omnipresence of the Name that can dissolve it, just as division arises in the omniscience of wisdom that can cure it. Neither confusion, nor division, have real existence in God, because both distort what exists in God by usurping him.

Communion cures confusion, and union heals division, discerned by wisdom in the glory of the Name. The ineffable openness of wisdom turns and sees the presence of oneness in the Name 'I AM.' Wonder receives what wisdom sees so that prophecy can communicate it and prayer assimilate it in the illumined heart. Ineffable wonder invites glory to unveil glory without end. This is how glorification unfolds, but who can say what this is, or why, since it is ineffable? Unknowable by us yet known to God, the Paraclete shares it with us in a still small voice, like a gentle whisper in the heart. When we come to the end of ourselves, wisdom discerns what the Name reveals, imparting the glory of the age to come.

87.

The desert speaks of a second baptism, which like the first is a baptism of uncreated light. It is a baptism in the light of the glory of the Name, just like the first, but the second baptism is monastic initiation. Monastic tonsure is called second baptism because it transmits prayer of the heart and the *praxis* of *theoria*. Prayer of the heart is the unceasing prayer of the Holy Spirit in the heart, not verbal prayers said without stopping in church or cell. The worldliness of the imperial church was the result of a profound loss of confidence in the *praxis* of *theoria,* a sacred trust, which the desert continues to transmit to this day as prayer of the heart. The second baptism recapitulates the first for a culture that has lost *theoria* and is no longer centred on *theosis*.

Patristic wisdom inspires prophecy and prayer, being grounded in prophecy and sustained by prayer. If it were a thing of the past, the New Age would be right: Christianity would be shallow moralism and sentimental pietism, not wisdom. If Christ is without wisdom, then those who love wisdom must look further to the East. But Patristic tradition, renewed by Hesychasm, transmits Christ as wisdom in glory of uncreated light. In the experience of glorification, it is Christ in the midst that wisdom sees, and Christ sends the Paracletic light by which he is seen. Suddenly, and unexpectedly, the Paraclete descends with glory as a pledge of glory, and initiates the growth in glory that illumines the heart.

As Christ received glory from the Father, and transmitted it to the Apostles, Saint Symeon the New Theologian bears witness that the glory he is given, he also passes on, and Saint Gregory Palamas, experiencing this glory on the Holy Mountain, defends its transmission in the Hagioritic Tome. The wisdom of the Word unveils the glory of the Name, confirmed by the wisdom of the Spirit in glorification by the Name. Transmission is direct, from God in God to the glory of God, not from men to the glory of men. On the other hand, in the Spirit, elders share indirectly in the directness of God, giving all glory to God. The wisdom received by elders without self-interest, is passed on without reserve, renewing Patristic wisdom in age after age.

88.

The desert holds to an older wisdom, for its love of wisdom derives from a primordial surrender, obedience to the Father's will, the Spirit crying, 'Thy will be done,' imparting union and communion. The Son prays, 'Abba, Father, for you all things are possible; take this cup from me! Yet not what I will, but what you will.' [24] The Spirit conjoins with our spirit when, in the midst of our pain, we give glory to God, so that the suffering is no longer ours, but an epiphany of communion, union with Christ in our midst.

'Thy will be done,' undoes the vicious circle of self-glorification with the doxological circle of right glorification, the deifying circle of *perichoresis*. It says 'Amen' to union and communion in the Name. The Spirit inspires this perichoretic wisdom of deifying surrender to the source, obedience to the origin, the Father from whom all things are arising through the Son. Such wisdom is not the work of rational speculation, but the fruit of experience. It is not invented but received. It is not studied but lived.

Patristic wisdom speaks of spiritual filiation in terms of communion, not merely adoption as an external legal fiction. The traditional distinction between filiation by nature and filiation by grace is radically apophatic, since filiation by nature is ineffable. We cannot conceive or define it. Filiation by adoption is a cultural metaphor, but what it seeks to express is real. Deification is not docetic, just as the incarnation is not docetic. Communion is not a fiction because God really became human.

The wisdom of the Paraclete communicates our union and communion with the Son, searching out the hidden depths of our participation in the Son's indwelling of the Father, and the Father's indwelling of the Son. As sons and daughters in the Son, we indwell the Father in the Spirit, who communicates communion. What we shall be in glorification will be the epiphany of this communion.

---

[24] See Mark 14:36; also Matthew 25:39; Luke 22:42, John 12:27.

89.

'I AM,' being both uncreated timeless awareness and uncreated primordial presence, causes to be all that there is. Nothing falls outside the limpid purity of this luminous glory. The Name is saving because it releases even as it causes to be all that there is, freeing glory to ascribe glory in glory to God.

The Name is above all names and all ways and means as well. In the spirit and truth of the awakened heart, uncreated awareness and uncreated presence are one, upstream from all bifurcation of seer and seen. This unifies all that there is, in the primordial ground, the Father's heart of light, who generates the Son as light of the world. Proceeding from the Father to abide in the Son, the Spirit sees this seeing as the seer, and this seer as the seen, revealing the Trinity of persons at the heart of light.

Ineffable in essence, glorious in energy, the sphere of the Name is free of fixations as glory ascribes glory in glory to God. Heaven and earth are translucent with glory as they wed in oneness and interpenetrate in openness within the realms of the Name. Wisdom rejoices to breathe this glory in with every breath, aspiring to inspire every heart with light.

The Name causes to be, as 'I AM WHO I AM,' so there is nothing arising that does not bear witness to the light of the glory of the Name, 'I AM.' The Name releases and frees, as 'I AM from I AM,' being the Son's fulfilling of the Father's will, 'Thy will be done.' Throughout all worlds, everything is glory, giving glory through the Son, just as everything is glorified with uncreated glory, in the Son, through the Spirit. The sphere of glory is without bounds, so sound, like light, is giving glory too. The form of the Name as primordial sound is *Hallelu Yah*! 'I AM' shines as it is praised, illumines as it glorifies, deifying every heart, hallowing heaven and earth, in its hallowing light.

90.

There is a most intimate connection between hallowing the Name and what the Bible and the Fathers call crowning, depicted in the iconographical tradition as the halo of glory. Christ is crowned with glory and honour, so union in Christ inherently includes crowning. [25] The crown, *stephanos,* is a crown of life, of incorruptible glory, whose symbols include the crown of gold and the radiant halo. Both the Old and the New Testament often refer to the crown of glory in connection with the experience of glorification, but the crown of wisdom is also an important theme. The crown of wisdom is a crown of joy, a crown of righteousness in Christ, who crowns all who are known of him.

The crown of thorns reveals that this is not glory as the world knows it, for the crowns of the elders are cast before the throne of the crucified, whose glory is discerned as the wisdom of the cross. Patristic wisdom is the wisdom of the cross, not a worldly wisdom of externals. It discerns the glory at the heart of the Name, not the shallow celebrity of a famous name. This is the glory that transfixes the heart, like an axis of uncreated light, unveiling the radiance of the Name. "I and the Father are one." [26] " He who has seen me has seen the Father." [27] "The Father is in me and I am in the Father." [28] The glory of this oneness is shared in glory with all in whom the Name is hallowed. It crowns angels and saints, elders and all who receive their transmission of the Name. It includes all who truly partake of him in the communion of the Eucharist. It includes all who experience glorification in the mysteries of his crowning. The Name crowns wisdom with glory.

---

[25]   See Hebrews 2:7-9; Rev 2:10 and 4:4 and 4:10.

[26]   John 10:30 RSV.

[27]   John 14:9 RSV.

[28]   John 10:38 RSV.

91.

Wisdom cuts through all forms of egocentric identification, subjective, objective and inter-subjective, releasing bondage into freedom. The Name leaps right over all forms of affirmation and negation, unveiling the ineffable radiance of the ineffable. The leap frees 'I AM' from all conditioning conditions, so that all perceptions are penetrated by insight into unconditioned wisdom. Instead of depending on this to renounce that, the Name imparts equanimity directly, unveiling the peace that passes all understanding. It awakens to peace as it is, not to a false peace that is conditioned by its opposition to its opposite. Wisdom actively penetrates right through confusion so that the Name restores communion. The Name effectively dissolves all division due to confusion, so that wisdom heals separation through union. Nothing conditioned can save us from our conditioning, so we put our whole-hearted trust in the unconditioned wisdom of Christ's saving Name to save us.

Wisdom always transcends every conception of it, however correct from an Orthodox point of view. Patristic tradition does not cultivate monistic or dualistic extremes, but releases all identification based on extremes into un-fabricated glory, ascribing glory to God. The Name 'I AM' is not this or that. Freedom from passions is without aversion or attachment to this or that. Wisdom knows 'I AM' is uncreated, not something created, so confusion dissolves and divisions collapse. Wisdom rests in peace, abiding in the Name. 'Amen' says 'So be it!' to the peace that passes all understanding, beyond identification with conditioned identities. It does not confuse conditioned with unconditioned peace, nor assume conditioning can condition the unconditioned. 'Amen' says 'So be it!' to the self-emptying love that does not identify with fixated extremes, subjective, objective or inter-subjective. A compulsive yes or no, to this or that, imprisons the heart in extremes, making unselfish love impossible. 'Amen' says 'So be it!' to the wisdom that turns the *nous* and reverses the mind's oblivious tendency to go out into perceptions, thoughts and emotions. Wisdom hallows the Name in glory instead.

92.

The 'now' of 'vision in a glass darkly' is contrasted, by the Apostle, with 'then', when vision shall see 'face to face.' The Macarian and the Dionysian witness is that in *theoria* and *theosis,* there is already an anticipation of the 'then.' Saint Symeon the New Theologian, too, participates in this sacred polyphony that bears witness to this theophany of glory 'then.' The 'then' is already 'now' in this epiphany of the Name in the awakened heart. The 'then' is even 'now,' when wisdom dawns. The hallowed Name is 'now' in the Kingdom come.

Capacity for wisdom 'now' points to wisdom's capacity as such. All relative capacity depends on capacity itself, but what does wisdom's capacity itself depend on? What is her capacity beyond all opposition and even coincidence of opposites? Can anything be said of wisdom's capacity to awaken to capacity as the 'now' of glory and the Name? Is our incapacity not a humble capacity for wisdom's capacity for completeness? Does it not bear witness to pure capacity for this completeness?

Wisdom questions us to help clarify the heart, mirroring God's ineffable capacity. Such questions help the heart to hallow the Name as infinite capacity, without falling into fixation or obscuration. They serve a timeless love of wisdom.

Prophecy employs poetic symbolism so as to reveal the dynamic capacity of the Name. Contrary images point to the ineffable rather than define the indefinable. Different divine names reveal God without reification of God, correcting each other in turn.

Prayer uses language up to the point when vision takes over and transcends imagery, and the Spirit intercedes for us with sighs and groans too deep for words.

Wisdom searches hearts beyond word and image, discerning spirits in the dynamic capacity of the Holy Spirit.

93.

Prayer is invocation and remembrance of God in his Name, hallowing heaven and earth with great peace. God loves peace and we desire peace, so in the Litanies of the Liturgy we begin with peace when we pray for peace. Prayer with vision is prayer in wisdom, prayer in Spirit that hallows Truth. God hears all who praise him, and glorifies all who glorify him. *Hallelu Yah* is praise of God in which God shines forth. It is too holy to translate, so we pray it still, just as it was always prayed, and God reciprocates, just as he always did. The seer is in the world but not of it when seeing sees as she is seen, 'face to face,' no longer as 'in a glass darkly.' Love of wisdom raises us out of ourselves and of the world, freeing us from what Diadochus calls 'gross and cloddish density.' The wisdom is subtle but it frees. Wisdom herself initiates desire for wisdom, which she blesses by giving herself, inspiring deepening love of wisdom without end.

Prophecy initiates the heart into prayer of the Name, so that mind and heart can heal. It teaches remembrance of God in his Name, welding us to the glory of his love. Wisdom humbles the soul, helping her to discern between what is real and what is counterfeit, what is of God and what is parody.

Prayer kindles a living flame of love for God that frees us from fantasy and doubt, drawing the body into the soul's ineffable love that is one spirit with the light of the Holy Spirit. Such prayer cleaves with ineffable simplicity to love's glorification of God, and the heart is then pregnant, through the energy of the Holy Spirit, with ineffable love and joy.

Wisdom is rooted in spiritual vision, *theoria,* not perception of luminous apparitions. The glory is not seen in visible form, by sight, but with the eye of the heart, invisibly. Faith does see, but by *theoria,* not by sight. Christ fills body, soul and spirit with his deifying presence, but is not visible as an object to un-awakened sight. The mysteries are veiled to sight even as they are revealed to wisdom, a paradox that wisdom handles but the world cannot. The world's criticism is inevitable, but Christ takes no notice, a legacy of courage that encourages wisdom to flourish.

94.

God the Holy Trinity is God in and for himself, becoming personally other than himself, knowing himself as other, and as other, knowing himself, without ceasing to be himself. God is true God in mysterious recognition of himself as other, negating himself without losing himself without end. Trinity is intrinsic negation that negates negation, and with each negation, God never ceases to be God. God holds steady as God, embracing boundless self-negation, never ceasing to be God, even as he empties himself of himself endlessly, in the power of love and glory.

Wisdom purifies, illumines, and glorifies as way, truth and life, when 'I AM' is revealed in the Holy Trinity, God's Name as his other in our midst. In the Son, the Father is other, but is so indivisibly. In the Name, God is other, without ceasing to be God. Wisdom negates negation as boundless self-negation, without ceasing to be the wisdom of God. It is the wisdom of the Holy Spirit discerning the glory of the Son. It is the wisdom that sees that 'I and the Father are one.'

Saint Maximus summed up the mysteries of wisdom's indivisibility when desert solitaries fled to fortress monasteries, to escape the violence of marauding tribes. Wisdom is radiant, simple and complete, for there is no division between wisdom and God.

In the Monastery of the Stoudion, behind the massive walls of Constantinople, Nikitas handed on what he received from Symeon, which was the tradition of Maximus, which is the Patristic wisdom of Evagrius, Macarius, and Denys. He imparts a pedagogy to the monasteries that turns the *nous* back to God in the midst, an anagogy that raises the heart to illumination, and a mystagogy that inducts body, soul and spirit into deep deifying union, the angelic estate also called glorification.

Wisdom is radiant prophecy when prayer is simple and complete.

Wisdom generates prophecy of prayer to glorify God in his Name.

95.

Wisdom illumines the heart by inspiring it to turn, *metanoia,* and see, *theoria.* The practice of turning purifies the heart so that seeing can illumine it. Remembrance of God means that when passionate thoughts arise, they find God here in the midst and so nothing to get hold of.

Remembrance of God releases and liberates the pure heart, which sees nothing but God in the midst. Remembrance of God is gratitude and joy that frees the energy of passions to transform, allowing them to transmute into glory to God. The state of glorification is simply the state of remembrance and recognition of God, in which glory no longer falls short of God in the midst. It is the state of right glorification that gives Orthodoxy its name.

There are many ways and many means, but wisdom turns them all into remembrance of God, when she raises 'knowing in part' into the fullness of her wholeness. Ascetical effort is sometimes viewed as an attempt to win grace as a reward, or as merit that qualifies one to receive grace. This mistake is perhaps inevitable when self-obsession still holds the heart in its imperious grip. We become sick when we fall short of glory in the midst, confusing the created with the uncreated. Vainglory sets in and messes everything up, including asceticism.

Prince Myshkin in the 'Idiot' speaks of being 'saved by beauty,' and Dostoievsky's vision is prophecy that sees we are all responsible for everyone and everything here at centre, where God is 'I AM' in the midst. In an age when science and technology call the tune, the poets are sometimes prophets and the artist is sometimes the seer, whose vision does what prophecy once did, bringing wisdom back into the world. Wisdom discerns glory in oblique ways, so that prayer of the Name can flourish at the heart of secularization in the modern world.

Wisdom's remedies spell out how the Kingdom comes by hallowing the Name. Her dispensation of purification, illumination and deification restores the heart, by glorification, to the Holy of Holies.

96.

Self-love disfigures glory until wisdom exposes the vacuity of vanity, releasing vainglory to be glory to God in the midst. The cross of selfless love, and the resurrection of love's glory, together express wisdom's enlightened intent and extend her scope into a boundless, glorious openness. The argument between salvation through faith alone or through meritorious works falls away once love's glory breaks through. Love trusts love and the works of love. Love is not love that shuts out in any way, or condemns to outer darkness the enemy it hates. Saint Silouan said that the criterion of true Orthodoxy is love of enemies. Right glorification is selfless, boundless love.

Resurrection and glorification live out of Christ-like love of enemies. Love neither judges nor is judged, for the reification of God as judge is a mythic image that liberates into its own future when love's glory dawns. The saints have always known that what is judged already is never judged again, so they judge not lest they are judged. Love sorts out sheep from goats, and gives goats the dispensation of wisdom they require to pass from fire, to light, to glory. Love's judgment does not judge, which turns out to be love's searing judgment by glory. Love's glory knows.

Wisdom sees God always, knowing that our seeing will be for us infernal flame or God's living flame of love. She offers us her remedies of fire and light and glory, so that we can learn from her how to experience glory as heaven rather than hell. Those in glorification experience glory as glorification, those in illumination, glory as illumination, and those in purification, glory as purification. The Fathers say that from outside glory and against glory, glory is an intolerable flame, burning regret, consuming remorse.

Wisdom is the vision of God in glory, from glory to glory. It is union in consuming fire and uncreated light even now, so that then it will be blessing, in love's glory, in the life to come.

97.

Satanic confusion, or egoism, is unconscious until wisdom unveils the Name. God's self-revelation is saying, 'I am I AM, that is my Name, and I will not give my glory to another!' [29] 'I, even I, am I AM.' [30] 'For, I am I AM, thy God.' [31]

The formula of theophany, in the light of the 'I AM' sayings in John's Gospel, unveils why the Church bore witness, from the earliest times, that Jesus is 'I AM' or Lord. What Jesus did was to reveal the Name, not in its external reified form, 'Lord,' but in its wisdom revelation as 'I AM.' He did so to undo confusion, but those who were suffering from unconscious confusion, thought he was himself guilty of confusion. They accused him of blasphemy and cried, 'Crucify him.'

Maximus explores *aporia,* also called *ambigua,* many of which he finds in the writings of Gregory the Theologian, Bishop of Nazianzen. As in his 'Questions and Responses,' his 'Ambigua' and 'Ad Thalassium,' *aporia* are difficult points in Scripture or in Gregory that present an obstacle to the mind, providing opportunities for the heart to awaken to illumination.

Prophecy handles scandalous impasse to awaken wisdom. Prayer lives scandalous impasse as breakthrough to glory. Wisdom leaps over impasse into the glory of the age to come. Glory adorns the sphere of the Name so that whatever arises gives glory to God. Nothing actually strays from the heavens of glory even on earth, because in God nothing falls from the grace of the Name. The fall from glory is not ultimately real in God although it seems real within the sphere of confusion it engenders.

---

[29] See Isaiah 42: 8.

[30] See Isaiah 43: 11.

[31] See Isaiah 43: 3; Exodus 20: 2; Leviticus 19: 2 and throughout the Holiness Code.

98.

Wisdom descends from heaven to reveal to us the uncreated creative energy of glory that is creating us, and uniting us with the angel of our being who intercedes for us with unceasing prayer. Above all, wisdom seeks to unveil Christ in our midst, revealing God's Name in the Holy Spirit. In the Spirit, through Christ, wisdom returns us to God anew in every instant. We die into God anew in every instant. God also raises us from the dead anew in every moment, freed from the fallen 'powers' of confusion and division.

In the seventh heaven of the throne, fire and light are seen as the uncreated glory of ineffable love. In the sixth, love's glory is refracted through the prism of four archangels, Michael, Gabriel, Raphael and Oriel, also called Nuriel and Fanuel. In the fifth heaven, love's glory is seen as ineffable beauty. In the fourth, love's victory is seen as ineffable power. In the third, love's glory is fierce rigour, countering all that is against love. The second heaven is the foundation of heavens, and the first, which is the Kingdom of God, recapitulates the highest heaven of wisdom and the Name. Prophecy proclaims the Kingdom of love and prayer as it passes through many heavens, many modes of glory.

Enoch and Elijah were masters of ascent as descent, and descent as ascent. They were prophets of prayer for whom ascent and descent were both Chariot vision. Wisdom raises on high the King of all when Cherubic vision is throne vision in the seven hells as well as the seven heavens. There is no end to glorification in the hallowed Name, which disempowers hells to expand the heavens. Fallen 'powers' are disarmed. Satanic confusion is consumed by fire. Diabolical division is dissolved in light.

The disciples of Enoch and Elijah were masters of chariot vision, which loves to hide with Christ in God, rather than vaunt itself or get puffed up. Throne vision is love's hidden work of hallowing glorification.

Throne vision is also 'Trisagion' vision, descending with, 'Holy, holy, holy,' into every last dark corner of all souls.

99.

Dissonance between prophecy and opinion may sometimes arise when elders are asked for a word, empty themselves of their own opinion and say only what God gives them to say. There can be times when they are given a word that contradicts their own opinion. Of course, they impart the word from God, not their opinion. If, later, the elder recalls his opinion, and is in doubt about the word that was given, there is a difficulty. The disciple is presented with a living *aporion*. Is he to continue to receive the original word, given as a 'word' from God, or is he to take account, out of love and respect for his elder, of the elder's contrary opinion, which confirms his contrary but unstated opinion in the past?

The elder would be the first to say that we are living from God, not men, the Word, not opinion. On the other hand, those closest to the elder are also closest to his opinions, and for love of him, they are keen to listen to him. An *ambigua* or difficulty arises at the interface between prophecy from God and the human opinion of a God-inspired elder.

The disciple in this case is thrown back on God-given resolution of a difficulty, which is not open to resolution on the plane on which it arises. The resolution of a difficulty of this nature is only possible in the fire and light of awakening. The elder that transmits tradition at this level is working in the spirit of profound wisdom, transcending opinion.

A tradition that receives prophecy with gratitude and love, can be a tradition of profound wisdom, unafraid of difficulties.

Wisdom loves the Name 'I AM,' which reveals God in every moment to renew all things. Prophecy reveals Emmanuel, 'God with us,' in his Name. Prayer prays, 'Come, Lord Jesus!' in wisdom's grace.

The glory of God shall be poured out on all, that in his Name, all shall be saved.

100.

There is an ineffable union between wisdom and the Name. Its transmission is ineffable, and lies hidden at the heart of sacred tradition. Wisdom offers herself to all and is received according to the capacity of each. The tradition of the Name is mystical prophecy, which receives rites and dogmas and transmits them as mysteries of love's glory. Wisdom mysteries have in view union and communion with God.

Wisdom is one as well as manifold, the same in all, unique in each. The Church is one in the Name, but is never the same, because conditions are constantly changing. Wisdom bears witness to a double economy, one in heaven and one on earth. Her economy of glory is ever one, but her mysterious unfolding is forever changing.

Wisdom is one and the Name is one, one tradition at the heart of all. It is the ineffable *Epiclesis* that transforms form, transmitting formless union and communion, revealing grace to be uncreated not created. Doubly apophatic, because it negates the negation, it undoes reification whenever it arises. Infinite ineffability bears witness to ineffable completeness, grounding our incompleteness in ineffable groundless completeness.

Wisdom is ineffable openness communicating completeness, calling us forth from the known to embrace the unknown. Wisdom is the mystagogue of the ineffable, spelling out secret tradition as union in the awakened heart. Hidden with Christ in God, she whispers, 'Turn and see.'

The Holy Spirit is witness to wisdom in illumined hearts. We are fallible and flawed in countless ways, but the Spirit makes up for this ineffably, imparting completeness through wisdom to broken hearts. Every day is Pentecost for wisdom, imparting tongues of fire. There is no end to completeness in the hallowed Name.

Wisdom transmits indivisibility as both prophecy of the Name and prayer in glory. Prophecy transmits indivisibility in the Name. Prayer lives indivisibility as glory.

WISDOM, GLORY

AND THE NAME

SECOND CENTURY

1.

Christ indwells the ineffable sphere of the Father, primordial source of his oneness of being as the Son, and original ground of the Holy Spirit, who proceeds from the Father to indwell him.

As primordial source of the Word and Spirit, the Father is the ultimate source of the Name uttered by the Word, and of wisdom, gift of the Spirit. The union of the Name and wisdom is timeless communion in the ultimate ground of glory.

Christ imparts union as communion in glory to all in the ineffable sphere of the Father. He shares the radiance of his throne of glory with hosts of angels and saints as *YHWH SABAOTH*. He extends the sphere of glory from heaven to earth when he weds an earthly heaven to a heavenly earth in the Name. He extends the perfection of wisdom into our incompleteness as wisdom's perfect completeness, unveiled in glory through the Name.

The sphere of glory is the ocean of purification and the womb of illumination in the hallowed Name. It is the ineffable sphere of the Father revealed by the Son. It is the life-giving sphere of the Spirit infusing recognition of God in his Name.

Christ is the wisdom he teaches, because in him teacher and teaching are one, indivisible in hearts taught by his Name. He is primordial wisdom communicating union in oneness of being, saying, 'I am I AM thy God; there is no other.' Prophecy says, 'Listen and attend! Holy is the Name 'I AM.'' Prayer of the heart listens and attends, rightly hallowing the Name.

The three spheres of the Name interpenetrate without obstruction, being the glory of the Father from whom the Name originates, the glory of the Son through whom the Name is revealed, and the glory of the Spirit in whom the Name is hallowed. The three spheres are hypostatically distinct and indivisibly one in essence and nature, and in oneness of energy and activity as Name of glory and wisdom of Christ.

2.

The Name resounds and the sound is the meaning, the *Logos,* causing to be all that there is. 'I AM' is in the beginning is always now, and shall always ever be. When the Logos speaks, he says, 'I am He who is, who was and who is to come.' 'I am I AM, causing to be all that there is.' The Name whispers its secret: 'I' is ineffable omniscience. 'AM' is incomprehensible omnipresence. Glory is uncreated energy and wisdom is the divine discernment of glory, hallowing God's Name.

Wisdom is the virgin womb that gives wondrous birth to the Name, by being the glory that right glorifies, like a Cherubic Throne. Glory is not something special added to the given. It is the given-ness of the given, called uncreated grace. It is the saving radiance of 'I AM,' called uncreated light.

'I AM,' God's Name, defines God to be indefinable, ineffable and incomprehensible. Glory is ineffable purity as 'I' and ineffable presence as 'AM.' Wisdom discerns pure presence pervading all in all, without confusion or division. God is un-reified purity as 'I' and un-objectified presence as 'AM.' Purity is not an object of possible experience, nor presence something that can be defined conceptually.

Understanding comes from wisdom, not sophisticated argument or subtle analysis. Misunderstanding is dispelled by direct recognition of God in his Name, not from dualistic thought about God apart from his Name. Understanding neither confuses nor divides, letting oneness be oneness and the indivisible be indivisible. Understanding lets the ineffable be ineffable, as in the beginning, so in the end.

The Name 'I AM' is pure presence of glory which wisdom sees, rainbow radiance of uncreated light ascribing glory to God. Wisdom cuts through confusion whilst glory crosses over all division, abiding in the Kingdom of the Holy of Holies. Wisdom stands steadfast in glorification of the hallowed Name, resting in peace beyond strain or stress.

3.

Wisdom is faith rising into the fullness of its glory. Wisdom transcends blind faith, that sees in a glass darkly, when she sees face to face, seeing as she is seen. Faith is to sight what wisdom is to faith. Wisdom sees face to face when faith rises into the glory that her symbols signify. The sons of resurrection watch and pray, standing steadfast in wisdom with the watchfulness of angels.

The *stasis* of solitaries unifies the Name, reintegrating the divine 'I' and 'AM,' inspiring the integral simplicity of seers. It refers to the one-pointed single-mindedness of angelic watchers, shared by spiritual elders. Solitude, simplicity and oneness are not originally external regulations but spiritual states. Early Syrian monasticism inspired the Macarian and the Dionysian writings, transmitting *Ihidaya* to the desert for centuries to come.

'Dazzling darkness' is divine presence overwhelming the heart with awe struck wonder. When God is 'I AM,' we are God's other, arising off centre with God in the midst. Luminous wisdom is an awareness of God's presence that transcends all determination. The symbol of 'dazzling darkness,' where darkness signifies excess, not lack of light, expresses ineffable difference utterly transcending every relative difference. Form veils glory but faith unveils form so as to reveal the glory it symbolized. Faith knows by unknowing that what knowledge cannot know is revealed to wisdom.

Prophetic mystagogy initiates the heart into the mysteries of the Name. Desert tradition transmits this as the mystery of *Ihidayah,* singleness of heart, which wisdom awakens in the sons and daughters of the Covenant of the Name. It is the oneness of the Only-Begotten, *monogenes,* unveiled in single-eyed vision, timeless awareness of uncreated presence, divided by the fall. The eye of the heart opens suddenly at the breaking of bread, revealing 'who he is,' before Abraham was. Prophecy bears witness to the tree of life in the garden of paradise. Prayer unites heaven and earth round an axis of light in the Holy of Holies.

4.

Wisdom reveals the Name 'I AM,' knowing that 'I 'and the 'Father' are one. Confusion re-veils the Name, glorifies 'me' instead of 'I AM,' and separates 'me' from the Father. All ways and means that are conditioned by confusion are predetermined by separation. Wisdom is exiled and the Name veiled. The 'I AM' sayings of Christ are ascribed to him in such a way that exclusive reification condemns deification as irredeemably demonic. Instead of revealing the Name, revelation is distanced so that it cannot impinge on hearts or awaken *theoria*. The Name is never actually hallowed even though the 'Lord's Prayer' is said by rote every day. Wisdom waits for hearts to turn and see, refusing to impose.

It is not that the Name is not always holy, only that without wisdom there is no hallowing. God, for God, is always God. It is just that there is no recognition and so no remembrance of God. God is 'I AM,' but nobody sees that this unveils God in the midst. Seeing is wisdom not visualization, insight not just sight. Those who cling to ways and means think wisdom and glory are for the age to come, not tongues of flame descending now. For them Pentecost is back then or still to come, not glory awakening wisdom in the illumined heart.

Wisdom has no need of ways or means, because for wisdom all ways and means are already complete in the glory that unveils their incomparable completeness. The strains and stresses of conditioned effort all fall short of the completeness they desire, whilst the Name freely imparts completeness, discerned by wisdom as the eternal glory of unconditioned grace. There are no ways or means towards the sphere of the eternal gospel, because all ways and means are already its glorious expression.

Wisdom returns to unveil again the re-veiled Name, knowing that 'I' and the 'Father' are one. 'I' and the 'Father' have always been one, so ways and means to unify them all miss the mark. The eternal gospel invites recognition to leap right over separation, freeing wisdom to sever confusion. The temporal gospel is most truly itself when it transcends itself as the completeness it envisions.

5.

The name Jesus, *'Yah shuah,'* means the Name 'I AM' saves. He was given this name, humanly, because divinely, the Father gave his Name 'I AM' to him, that he should save God's people from confusion. Jesus is 'I AM,' to the glory of God the Father. [32] This primordial witness is the quintessence of all revelation in the Christian tradition and heart of spiritual awakening in the saints. Recognition of 'I AM' saves, delivers and liberates. The Word never strays from revealing this. The Spirit's seal never ceases to witness to this. Whatever happens, this is decisive. Seeking this only serves to separate 'I' from 'AM,' knower from known, whereas true knowing knows as it is known. 'I' is not subject here and 'AM' object there, for God is one, one 'I AM' revealing God to God in God. There is no division here now that confusion has dissolved.

Whatever is arising, 'I AM' is 'I AM' here at centre, where all centres coincide. Christ is 'I AM' in the midst and shall always be this ground of being, well-being and ever-being. The wisdom of Saint Maximus is witness to Christ, the sure foundation of Christian wisdom in this and every age.

Some make enormous effort to practice meditation, fixating on meditation and ignoring the Name, forgetting that the Name and wisdom have been present from the beginning. 'I AM who I AM' is ever present from the foundation of the world, if we would only turn and see. A 'way' can become an obstacle in the way, a 'means' can be an avoidance of what it means to seek.

Glory does not stray from glory or wisdom from wisdom here in the revelatory Name. Glory is not elation followed by deflation any more than wisdom is something special followed by something ordinary. 'I AM' is ever present and aware of the presence we call God, revealing God in our midst in his Name.

---

[32] See Math 1:21; Phil 2:11 RSV.

6.

Wisdom stands steadfast in the inseparability of the uncreated and the created, in the indivisibility of the intelligible and the sensible. There is no need to be in doubt just because doubts arise. Doubts are able to dissolve into the great doubt that dissolves all the barren certainties that get in the way. Doubts resolve themselves in the inseparability of the indivisible, Christ in our midst.

Remembrance of God is not a remembering of memories nor is recollection a fixation on recollections. Remembrance hallows the Name upstream from memories, free of fixation and artificial recollection. Remembrance of God is unceasing prayer imparting unwavering peace to the heart in the purity of recollection. It is not artificial effort but the natural expression of wisdom when she turns and sees.

Confusion is the root of every separation and division, so the tradition diagnoses pathology and prescribes wisdom to cure confusion. Afflictions transform when distraction dissolves, and confusion transmutes into wisdom. Watchfulness abides as sober vigilance, the *nipsis* of the desert fathers, not self-interested efforts or self-obsessed activities.

The real asceticism is wisdom, the state of seeing, and the *praxis* of *theoria,* which purifies and illumines the heart. Glorification is the crowning of wisdom, our co-operation being the 'Amen' of pure attention, *prosochi,* expression of the heart's original limpidity.

When the *nous* descends into the heart, pure prayer is unceasing as the Spirit's prayer in us. Unceasing prayer is wisdom's natural state; it is we who get confused and distracted. Distraction and meditation clarify confusion as wisdom practices attention, *prosochi,* freeing awareness of fixation and self-interested obsession.

Clarity is unwavering in the primordial state, even in sleep. The *nous* is translucent, empty and clear. Hearts are pure with wisdom's clarity, enabling glory to be truly loved and known.

7.

The glory of the Name is purification in boundless and infinite freedom. Hallowing the Name is illumination in blessing and peace. Wisdom discerns the glory of the Name to be the key to glorification. Transmission of the Name opens the heaven of the heart. Glory is unimpeded when wisdom is direct. Wonder is wholly direct in its ineffability. Recognition hallows the Name at all times so that the Kingdom comes in all places at once.

Jesus bears witness that the filial 'I AM' can do nothing without the paternal 'I AM,' whose original oneness is prior. Inseparability is the dwelling place of paternal wisdom. Indivisibility is the key to filial wisdom, for which hallowing the Name is decisive, because the Name saves and frees. Spiritual wisdom sees 'I AM' causes to be in such a way that what comes to be frees into glory in every moment, which unceasing prayer assimilates. It is this that elders call glorification.

Deep faith does more than just believe in beliefs. It trusts the Name's power to save and trusts this holy trust to free things as they arise, just as they are, without interference from outside.

Wisdom shares her treasures with all, paternal wisdom as the source of revelation, filial wisdom as the revelation of the Name, spiritual wisdom interpreting revelation, so that it can be assimilated holistically. Christ in the midst is the glorification that enters into expanding glorification without end. He is the Alpha and the Omega of wisdom.

Union with Christ in resurrection turns the *nous* and awakens the heart to the mysteries of purification. Union with Christ in ascension enlightens the *nous* and restores the eye of the heart to vision of the mysteries of illumination. Union with Christ in his enthronement on high deifies the whole creation in the hallowed Name and unifies the heart in the mysteries of glorification.

These are the unfolding mysteries of glory hidden with Christ in God's Name, and wisdom is the Spirit's seal, opened as revelation, when pure prayer indwells the heart and rightly hallows the Name.

8.

The Eternal Gospel (Rev 14:6) communicates the glory of the Kingdom, which is the spirit that fulfils the letter of the temporal gospel. There are many heavens of glory in the Kingdom that Christ transmits, and many hells are liberated as confusion is restored to communion and division is transmuted into union. It is wisdom's true turning into the indivisibility of 'I AM' that lifts the veil of the literal and unveils the Spirit of Truth. It is 'I AM' the Spirit that really frees freedom to be free. If to see him as he is, it is necessary to be like him, then *theoria* in him as image of God cries out for *theosis* in him, likeness to him as deification in him. Christ descends into hells to harrow them with glory, the glory of his burning boundless love. His glory is translucent, his love transparent, in the Name that turns confusion back into communion. His burning love consumes confusion like an all-consuming fire. It empties vanity of vanity so that vainglory is free to ascribe glory to God again. This empties hells of infernal division in the fires of burning boundless love.

Wisdom does not force hells into subjection by bruit necessity but woos them to turn and see hell's fires as love, and love as glory, in the mysteries of resurrection and ascent. Love's true glory is wisdom's way with all that disdains wisdom and clings to separation. The Kingdom of glory is the Kingdom of the Name, for 'I AM' is God and God is all in all.

The Apostle says Christ gives us all things together with him, which means we are no longer a mere creature among many creatures, but comprise the whole creation, intelligible and sensible, invisible and visible, eternal and temporal, in Christ who is all in all. When Christ delivers the Kingdom to the Father, he hands back communion free of confusion, union free of division, God being all in all. All are one as God is one, oneness that holds together the dignity of difference and the beauty of oneness without confusion. There is no separation in the glory of this love, no confusion that can separate, no division that can destroy the union and communion at the heart of this love. Wisdom knows this, and is this union in being known, hid with Christ in God.

9.

'Powers' of separation and confusion try to overpower us but in Christ are overcome. 'Powers' cannot overpower wisdom, or confuse glory at the heart of the Name above all names. That is why we take refuge in the Name, which is a tower of strength for all who abide with wisdom.

The glory in the beginning and at the end, before and after the time of the fallen 'powers,' is wisdom's realm of uncreated light. From glory, through glory and to glory is wisdom's sphere of uncreated glory. From wisdom, through wisdom and to wisdom are glory's realms of uncreated grace. Wisdom is above all, through all and in all, discerning the glory of the age to come, glory above all, through all and in all. Wisdom is all in all, discerning glory all in all, in the uncreated spheres of the Name.

The Spirit of Truth blows where he wills, revealing depths in the Name that we have yet to fathom, taught by the Spirit of Truth. 'I AM' is way and truth and life in new and unexpected ways, as we answer the call to transcend the narrows and shallows of fear. To come up higher is to partake of love's feast, not to look down on fear with disdain.

Christ hands back his Kingdom to the Father free of confusion and division. 'Powers' of confusion and separation are overcome in him, so his Kingdom shows no trace of them. Where confusion reigned, communion rings. Where separation ruled, union sings. The 'powers' cannot overpower the Name, nor their reign insinuate itself between wisdom and glory in the Kingdom of God. THAT this is so is wisdom's witness, not WHAT it entails. HOW or WHY it is as it is, is ineffable. Theories of atonement all fall short of the glory they seek to explain. Theological speculation always falls short of the mysteries it desires to express.

The desert abides in peace in the wisdom it transmits. It does not attempt to explain the gaps, which yawn at us like chasms whose depths are unfathomed.

10.

Wisdom discerns the Eternal Gospel of glory hidden with Christ in God, glory that overcomes all powers of confusion and separation in invisible, intelligible worlds through the Name. The temporal gospel is the same gospel as the Eternal Gospel, but it is temporal because it contrasts this present age with the age to come. It is the gospel as it appears in time, with an age to come that has not yet come. The glory of the Eternal Gospel is the same glory but revealed in the timeless presence of the age to come, which wisdom searches out and sees in timeless vision by right hallowing the Name so the Kingdom comes. Wisdom discerns this glory even now in the hallowed Name, in the second coming of Christ in the Eucharist, in the Advent of 'I AM.'

It is not that the temporal gospel is permanently superseded, because it reflects how the gospel looks prior to illumination, when it is not yet ready for glorification. The temporal gospel lasts until illumination dawns, but compared with the Eternal Gospel of glorification, it sees 'in a glass darkly' and not 'face to face.' This frees wisdom to discern the glory of the age to come as it comes in the hallowed Name, revealed in the timeless moment, the eternal now of God's Kingdom of the Name.

Wisdom sees confusion dissolve into communion and separation transmute into union at the heart of the glory of the hallowing Name. This puts right the wrongs of the fall, which hides with Christ in God, waiting to be discerned from before the foundation of the world. It is the revelation of the love that seeks not its own, unveiled by the Spirit of Truth when the seals are undone. There are no limits to the pure capacity of this love, no bounds to the openness of this grace. The 'powers' of confusion and separation are disarmed. They lose their power to delude and deceive. They are released as confusion is restored to communion and separation is transformed into union in the Name.

The light of the glory of the Eternal Gospel has no limit as it shines its uncreated light into our hearts as illumination, and permeates all worlds as glorification, in the radiant power of the Name.

11.

There is no confusion or separation in love's glory that seeks not its own. It is the glory of the Eternal Gospel revealed in the Apocalypse, Revelation 14:6, the glory which wisdom sees and welcomes in the mysteries of glorification. Seeing 'face to face' does not refer to external perception but to the unveiled face of 'I AM.' Seeing in a mirror, obscurely, falls away when wisdom unveils the Holy of Holies. The gospel is temporal when we still cling to time, unable to rise in Christ or ascend with him into eternal glory.

The Eternal Gospel is the temporal gospel seen 'face to face,' revealed in the unveiled face of glory through the Name. Seeing 'through a glass darkly' is not yet glorification, also called deification, *theosis*. The mysteries conceal glory under the veil of an icon or image, and if the icon seeks to preserve itself for its own sake, it obscures the revelation of the glory it prefigures. The spiritually blind fall short of glory by confusing the icon with the glory, as if the icon as such were the mystery. The literal 'letter' of form is always vulnerable to shortfall. Symbols truly participate in what they symbolize but if the heart is hard, it treats the symbol as an end in itself and so falls short of the glory, which is its truth. Symbols lie when they are ends in themselves, and what is literally true becomes spiritually false. They do not let glory through.

The temporal gospel is not false but falls short of glory unless it turns and gives way to the light of illumination. Its truth as an icon of the Eternal Gospel, is unveiled in the light of glorification. Its truth unveils all symbolic forms, and is already partaking in the resurrection light of illumination. But resurrection, ascension and glorification unveil glory in increasing glory, opening transfiguration with glory beyond light.

Illumination handles icons that are images of the glory they depict, until their indirectness gives way to the directionless directness of glory. This is the mystery of glorification, no longer seeing 'in a glass darkly,' but in the 'unveiled face of glory.' The seal is the Spirit's pledge, promising that illumination already partakes in the light of glory. The unsealing of those seals is glorification in the Holy of Holies.

12.

Illumination sees 'through a glass darkly,' living from the first resurrection in Christ, which is baptism, whereas glorification sees 'face to face,' living from the second resurrection, which is ascension and glorification in Christ. Here below, in the shadows of time, the Eternal Gospel takes on a temporal appearance as a temporal gospel. It is not false, nor is it 'dead letter,' but it is not yet all that it shall be in the age to come. The first veil was torn from top to bottom at illumination, but the second veil, concealing the Holy of Holies, is not rent until the experience of glorification. The Eternal Gospel imparts glorification, which unveils the Holy of Holies. The ages end here in the timeless presence of the Holy of Holies.

It is the spiritual states of illumination or glorification that make the difference. The Fathers are describing the way things are seen as we ascend from light to glory. The Gospel is one in the *hypostasis* of Christ, but we see it as light or glory in the light of our capacity. The veils are rent to the extent that glory reigns, and the key to this is revelation of the Name.

Icons veil the glory they reveal, and reveal the glory by being rent, so to speak, from top to bottom. Translucence renders the veils more and more transparent, letting glory through. Icons veil the mysteries of glory but it is wisdom's task to discern the glory that they veil. Wisdom imparts turning that seeing may see. The turning turns the *nous* right round, revealing 'I AM' our God in the midst. *Theoria* removes veils one by one, opening the eye of the heart. It unites the *nous* with God in the heart, inspiring illumination then glorification. The veil is rent from the top, which is the beginning, to the bottom, which is the end of all worlds. The Name is the beginning and the end, the *arche* and the *telos* of the revelation of glory in the Holy of Holies. Wisdom discerns these mysteries which sensation and thought overlook, judging all things but judged by none. The Mount of Transfiguration is symbol of the ascent that unveils glory step by step, transcending the human points of view that have not yet awakened to 'I AM.' Wisdom sees God with God's own single eye, rending veils of glory.

13.

Christ's death overcomes the deaths of confusion and separation, unveiling the Holy of Holies. The outer and the inner veils are both rent when wisdom discerns the glory of both resurrections. The completeness of wisdom is perfected when the inner veil is removed and the Cherubic Hymn unveils the mysteries of glorification. Illumination rends the outer veil so that purification can prepare to unveil the Holy of Holies.

The Apocalypse, at Revelation 14:6, calls the severing of the second veil an Eternal Gospel. Love's death to death overcomes death in glory, unveiling resurrection within resurrection. The unveiled face of glory is the unveiled face of 'I AM,' transforming image into likeness. Illumination remains bright as light, but like the morning star, which does not cease to shine, appears to be overwhelmed by glory's rising light. The star appears to decrease but in fact illumination remains illumination even in glorification. The Kingdom of light is subsumed within the glory of the Holy of Holies, even though the vessel is frail and the vesture is poor. We are clothed despite this in light then glory.

Wisdom searches out the hidden depths of God in the Holy Spirit, never exhausting the mysteries, or letting us lay claim to them as our own. The depth of glory in glorification is discerned, not by us on our own, using only our own strength, but by wisdom, which is ineffable. Sophistry tries to pry into mysteries, but wisdom is unsearchable and passes all understanding.

Human capacity can never lay claim to wisdom. She withdraws the moment we try to grasp and possess her, rising free of all our self-interest. She knows our narcissism and our neuroses, and gently loves us out of the confusion and separation which give rise to them. Wisdom is God with us, our Emmanuel, curing our ills.

Christ in God overcomes all 'powers' of confusion and separation, which leave no trace in the presence of glory. Illumination is witness to the first unveiling, glorification to the second. The Eternal Gospel completes what the temporal envisions, overcoming the 'powers' that stood in the way.

14.

Wisdom's descent as glorification weds ascent as illumination, to integrate all Christianity's shadows, which it has not been possible to integrate before. Christ is the integration of ascension and glorification, and it is in him that religion's shadows are diagnosed and healed. When fear rules, love is not permitted to integrate and heal, and wisdom is deprived of a dwelling place among us. When glorification weds ascension, love cures fear, together with all division and separation that characterize unbalanced ascent.

The divine-human marriage of glorification and ascension in Christ is present from the beginning in wisdom and the Name. It inspires the holy work of the remembrance of God in the prayer of the Name. Hallowing the Name hallows heaven and earth in union and communion, which wed the uncreated and the created in the Spirit's interceding sigh. Tongues of fire descend to awaken hearts to Pentecostal flame, here in the midst where glorification weds ascension as unselfish, boundless love.

It is this love that cures fear and heals religion's blind spots so that it transcends and includes as wisdom in the ineffable mysteries of glorification. Wisdom as ascent is creation rising towards God, meeting wisdom as uncreated grace descending from God towards creation. Wisdom unveils the face of creation to the unveiled face of God.

It has been argued that Orthodox theology has no need of wisdom, because it can function perfectly well without it. That may have happened in the past, but at a time when humanity cries out for wisdom to survive, to insist that Orthodox Christianity has no need of wisdom is to fail to see who Christ is. It is to fall short of both illumination and glorification, leaving religion to drown in its shadows.

Ascent and descent meet on the holy ladder of the Name, where earth ascends and heaven descends by hallowing. Ascension and glorification interpenetrate in Christ, so in us they unite in the mysteries of union and communion.

117

15.

The desert is not interested in sophiological speculation, but in Christ, whose wisdom embraces illumination and glorification. Difference between the uncreated and the created is not division, because in the indivisibility of Christ, divisive opposition is done away. In him, creation is fully graced, hallowed by the Name. 'I AM' is revealed in the dwelling place of wisdom, where ascent and descent meet on the ladder of the Name.

'I AM' is present in this place of awe and wonder, the sanctuary of wisdom where angels and elders meet to behold the eternal presence of the glory in the age to come. But 'I AM' we did not know, because we had driven out wisdom. We say ' I am this or that,' but vainglory had deprived us of insight. We ascribed the glory to ourselves, unconscious of our confusion of ourselves with God. We had forgotten that 'I AM' was God's Name. We had forgotten to listen to our guardian angels of the Name, whose prayer for us is unceasing discernment of 'I AM.' Wisdom lives everything in the uncreated light of resurrection, including the mysteries of ascension and glorification. Christ offers to raise all who are illumined by resurrection into ascension and glorification, but not against their will. If we are determined to reject wisdom, ascension and glorification remain permanently opaque and obscure.

We are free to inhabit the narrows and shallows and to pretend that nothing transcends them. The narrows live from the terrors of fear, and the shallows live from the need to feel safe, confusing safety with salvation. Neither listens to the desire of the heart to awaken, reducing religion to consolation, leaving confusion uncured. The generous capacity of desert wisdom remains intact even in troubled times, because Christ is not only risen, but ascended and glorified too. If wisdom is excluded, ascension and glorification are neglected, and the fullness of the stature of Christ curtailed. Curtailed religion can console but not transform, sustain convention but not deify. Wisdom waits until hearts open to ascent, and then ascend beyond ascent to include descending glorification in the Name.

16.

Controversies over the Name or wisdom are not resolved by partisan revivals of past movements, but in the living transmission of the fullness of Orthodox Tradition, hallowing the Name with wisdom. The energy of controversy is redeemed without extremism, so that the Name is rightly hallowed, and wisdom discerned by the Spirit, in an integral embrace. At a time when wisdom and the Name are often neglected and even forgotten, it is no surprise to find controversy in circles where the *praxis* of *theoria* is alien, and outside the monastic cell, prayer of the Name in the heart is regarded with suspicion. The consequence is confusion that subverts communion and separation that subverts union, undermining the indivisibility of wisdom and the inseparability of the Name.

In the past, monks were sometimes embroiled in controversy, and caught up in opinionated extremes. But the centre of gravity within Orthodox Hesychasm is peace, free of the extremism of exclusive extremes. Tradition transmits the Name in wisdom, without confusion or division, avoiding the temptations of subversive extremes. This resolves old controversies in the natural flow of transmission, clarifying old obscurities in living wisdom springs. The Eucharist anticipates the Kingdom, so it is no surprise to find Eucharistic wisdom doing the same when the Name is revealed in the liturgy of the heart. Since Christ is remembered in his Kingdom at the Liturgy, wisdom does not neglect his ascension and glorification when the uncreated light of resurrection is imparted to the heart. It is God who remembers us in ascension and glorification, if we can find it in us to be his 'Amen.'

The whole of the *Anaphora* takes place after the second coming of Christ, according to the symbolism of the Liturgy. It is no surprise, then, to discover wisdom lives in the light of the second coming, living as though the age to come had already come. Since Christ is risen, ascended and glorified, wisdom opens these mysteries to us as always already present in our midst. Every day is for wisdom an eighth day, the timeless presence that comes when chronological time is no more. The remote future is already present in the Name, as is the beginning, in Christ who is wisdom present in our midst.

17.

Fear avoids the void of 'I AM,' seeing nothing created at centre as a void to be avoided at all costs. Love's glory embraces the void of 'I AM,' seeing God is nothing created at centre, to be loved free of fear's obsession with counting the cost. The culture of fear produces religion that flees God, treating the void as a black hole to be avoided at all cost. Love's glory offers remedies to religion that cure its pathologies of fear by unveiling the nothing so feared by religion, revealing God.

There is a postmodern spirituality that hates religion, called New Age spirituality by some, which is haunted by two ghosts, nihilism and narcissism. Wisdom accepts that spirituality is shallow when it rejects all religion as narrow, always well aware that not all religion is narrow, just as not all spirituality is shallow. Wisdom was hidden in the midst of religion for millennia, and offers her depths to spirituality, inviting it out from the shallows. Wisdom diagnoses nihilism as pathological wisdom, and narcissism as pathological psychologism, offering generous remedies to both.

Wisdom offers therapies to heal religion of its narrowness, and cure spirituality of its shallowness, aware that division has its way of negation, which it does not confuse with God's. A pathological spirituality spawns a way of negation that subverts communion with confusions in the image of its fears, whereas the uncreated 'no-thing' undoes confusion to restore communion, in the image of unselfish love.

Nihilism and narcissism spring from the same diseased root, which wisdom cures by applying remedies of glory and the Name. Nihilism is fear's jaundiced view of the void, which love embraces as God. Narcissism is fear's subversion of the Name, confusing 'I AM' with 'me,' writ large by the 'me, me' generation of baby boomers, as their 'New Age.' Wisdom transmits the Name to sever 'me' from 'I AM,' curing the subversions of narcissism at their root, together with separation, from which sick religion suffered for millennia.

Wisdom's theopathy is wondrous, truly awesome in its power to disempower 'powers' and cure pathologies.

18.

Love's holy work, in the silence of the night, is prayer of the heart, hallowing the Name. Wisdom in the inner desert calls for the greater love that lays down its life for fear, its friend, because unless love befriends fear, what hope is there that fear will ever transcend fear? Unless the Spirit intercedes for fear, what basis is there for fear to learn to trust love and so to rise into the fullness of resurrection? In the middle of the night, in the silence of the desert cell, the unceasing prayer of the Spirit in the heart is heard again, not as someone's prayer, but as God's prayer in them, hallowing the Name in the midst of fear's darkest hells. This is where the sweat bleeds, in this garden of Gethsemane, love's cure of fear on a Mount of Olives, undoing the subversions that drive fear to terror beside the Cedron stream. Oneness with Christ in death and resurrection must include this prayer in the garden, this synergy of wills, 'not my will but thy will be done.' Hallowing the Name can only let the Kingdom come if God's will is done, love's will that fear be lovingly freed of fear, wooing fear to free fear from terror.

Christ in time back then is timeless now, in this prayer of the heart that woos fear beyond fear. Love loves because love loves, here, addressing the root centres of fear, fear for our survival, fear for our safety, and fear of losing control. When the centre of gravity is fear, love is out of the question. So what does love do? Die for the friend. Love loves right through to the end. Love befriends fear for love's sake, bringing love right down into fear's root hells. Unless love reaches here, terror will reign, and where terror reigns, fear rules, without end. Name hallowing remains nominal without the garden, without Gethsemane's harrowing of fear by love in the stillness of the night. The reign of terror is very old, going back long before the twin towers fell. The rule of fear is older still, going back to the original fall from love. Or is it that fear's falls only become visible in the light of love's glory in the age to come? Was there ever an original paradise from which love fell into fear, or is paradise love's future projected back into fear's mythic past? Love hallows the narrows of fear, harrowing the shallows of terror with costly love, in the silence of the desert.

19.

The ruling 'powers' of confusion and separation are the particular concern of wisdom in the desert. This wisdom is imparted to the mature for the glorification of the saints, although it remains a secret and hidden wisdom until the 'eye' of the heart is opened by the grace of the Holy Spirit. Perception ruled by the 'powers' of confusion and separation remains blind. Thoughts dominated by the 'powers' of delusion and division are deaf to wisdom. The 'powers' crucify 'I AM' and subvert the glory of the Name.

Desert wisdom has always been spiritual warfare with these 'powers,' because its task is to address these 'powers' in heavenly places to make wisdom known to them. [33] This is the holy work of right glorification, which undoes the subversions of confusion to restore communion, and cures the pathologies of separation to restore union. A grace is given that engages with these 'powers' on behalf of all. It is the grace of wisdom, which discerns Christ as wisdom and the Holy Trinity as the key to wisdom, so that the 'powers' of confusion and separation are disempowered.

Wisdom's work is a work of unselfish love in the power of the glory of Christ crucified. It is the love at the heart of the Cross, the love that is rooted and grounded in the destiny of glorification that love had in mind from before the foundation of the world. It is this love that hopes for the restoration of all things in God, the Orthodox mystery of *apokatastasis panton,* taught by Saint Gregory of Nyssa and Saint Maximus, Saint Isaac the Syrian and Saint Silouan the Athonite. Love cannot bear the damnation of the damned, so it prays for the salvation of all. The condemnations of the Fifth Ecumenical Council refer to certain misunderstandings of this mystery of love, not to the mystery itself. Love taught Saint Silouan to pray for the salvation of all, and to know there is no limit to the power of love to disempower the 'powers' of confusion and separation.

---

[33] See Ephesians 3:10, 1Cor 2: 6-7.

20.

The resurrected body of Christ in glory passes through locked doors of fear and disempowers the 'powers' of confusion and separation. Recognition is crucial, for without it the 'I AM' of glory is not seen, and the Name is not hallowed. Our bodies are not fixed entities so they can partake in glorification from root to crown, grounded in the mysteries of resurrection, which embrace both body and soul. The ultimate state of all lies in beholding the glory of God's burning, boundless love, which is blessing for the blessed but torment for fear that rejects love. Love purifies, illumines and glorifies body and soul, transforming fear into love.

Love respects freedom, including fear's freedom to prefer fear to love, though love cannot bear that fear condemns itself to terror and torment for ever. So love is crucified with Christ again and again, even though Christ's crucifixion is once and for all. Terrorism is fear unable to transcend fear, unwilling to rise to love, suffering torment and hell even in this life. Love cannot bear to ignore such suffering and so prays for all, that all shall be saved.

Desert wisdom engages with terrorism by a costly love, love that engages with religion's shadow by wooing fear to transcend fear and rise into the heart of love. Instead of standing aloof, love loves, for that is what love does, even when confronted with freedom that chooses terror and rejects love. Love suffers, in Christ, bearing with fear, yet disempowers the 'powers' that give rise to fear. Glorification is the experience of the glory of Christ crucified, at the hidden interface between love and fear.

Little wonder that few let themselves be chosen by this crazy love, or let desert wisdom anywhere near, for fear of losing control. Fear cannot comprehend the love that draws someone into the desert to do business with fear. Fear cannot understand love or risk releasing fear. Nor can fear take seriously the hope that Christ in glory will restore all things. Fear recoils from glorification, disdains illumination and avoids purification, for a reason. Love is the death of fear. Fear rises as love.

21.

Wisdom in the Liturgy looks back to the second coming of Christ in glory as well as to his death, resurrection and ascension into heaven. Beyond time, in the timeless presence of Christ glorified, glorification yields up wisdom mysteries to all, once they are transcending the trammels of fear. In his *Mystagogia,* Saint Maximus discerns a wisdom of *anamnesis* at the heart of the Eucharist, which remembers Christ's second coming in glory as always already present in the Church's Liturgy and also in the prayer of the Name in the heart. For when the Name is hallowed, the Kingdom comes.

Christ's coming again in glory is the mystery of judgment of the living and the dead. Judgment is love's mystery, which lies in unselfish love, love that judges not. Judging no one, love's judgment of the living and the dead is true. Suspended between these searing paradoxes of love, the desert experiences judgment in the fires of glorification. Fear rejects love and so experiences glory as torment in fear's fires. Love raises fear from fear to experience glory as glorification. At the living centre of these paradoxes, the resurrection of Christ puts fear to death, and with it the fear of death.

The desert holds the extremes together without letting them regress into extremism. Refusing to define the ineffable, wisdom is witness to the literal exteriors breaking open to let glory through. Sophistry clings to its rationalism and its anthropomorphism, unable to resist prying into the mysteries. Juridical and penal metaphors run riot over the mysteries of love, spawning horrors that haunt the shadows of Christian tradition like ghosts. Wisdom, aware of the shadows, turns back to Christ in the midst, in whose light shadows are no longer shadows but a texture of light and shade which lets glory through.

Wisdom dances the timeless mysteries, transcending cause and effect. 'Powers' that subject us to confusion and separation are disempowered by the hallowed Name. Wisdom remembers the second coming of Christ, discerning the glory of the Kingdom come.

22.

Wisdom imparts participation in glory not information about glorification. God empties his glory into signs and symbols that impart his glory to us for our glorification. For Saint Maximus, symbols interconnect, so that symbolism in one context finds symbolic counterparts in others, so that all symbolism is multi-contextual, resonating in all dimensions at once. Wisdom's vision of the interconnectedness of everything communicates the Great Peace to all, saying, 'Fear not, for the 'powers' of confusion and separation are overcome.' The kiss of peace excludes no one in this peace of the Name: 'I AM, peace be with you, be not afraid!'

Time imagines eternity in moving images of the timeless, for as sages taught, time is the moving image of eternity. The symbol of the censing of the Church expresses a hallowing of everything by love, love's censing from the One to the many and the many to the One, revealing the One in the many and the many in the One. Love creates symbols like incense to create us anew in glory, creating a loving history of enigmas to awaken wisdom for our glorification.

The desert is not imparting information but deification in answer to incarnation, glorification in answer to purification and illumination. The wilderness is a garden in which the beauty of love is cultivated. Just as God is beautiful and loves beauty, as glory deifying all, so the saints are beautiful and love beauty through their glorification of God. The grace of the angelic estate incorporates them into the realms of heavenly hosts, who cultivate beauty by hallowing the Name. Wisdom imparts angelic beauty of glory through the renewal of prophecy and the inspiration of prayer.

Love's depths of beauty in God, call forth depths of beauty from us, in answer to love's self-emptying of fear, emptying fear into love. Wisdom empties fear of fear and love into love, curing fear of fear and love through love.

23.

Icons are love's symbols to cure fear, not snaps of exteriors to console fear. Icons, like mysteries, unite what confusion divides, so as to wed what separation tears asunder. Icons can be apophatic theophanies, freeing us from the addictions of fear. The 'play' of images frees fear from fear, so that the poetry of prophecy can mediate love through love.

The 'language' of icons is not the conventional logic of linear perspective, but the doxological 'logic' of the mediatory *Logos,* for which seer and seen are one. It is the iconic language of prayer, which is translucent, suffering glory to shine forth through the Name. It is the revelation of the unveiled face of glory.

Icons invite first personal recognition rather than pass on third personal information, like a photograph. They reveal the face, in the self-emptying of the unveiled face, not the confronting face that invites confrontation. 'Face to face' vision, *theoria,* is not confrontational but contemplative. It refers to the revelation of 'I AM,' not to an objectification of third person perception, which neither sees nor understands.

Icons communicate the communion of saints, a communion of love, not confrontation driven by fear. They impart life beyond death, divine life that is no longer dominated by the fear of death. They overcome death by dying to fear, bearing witness to eternal life. They bear witness to 'I AM.'

Icons of the Mother of God deploy temple symbolism, as do the Akathist Hymn and the Christmas liturgical texts. She is the Holy of Holies and the ark in the midst, the crown that glorifies and the joy of the glorified. She is the veil that protects the Holy from profane gaze, preserving the mysteries of love.

Glory indwells icons that impart glory in return. Icons still our fears to unveil the face of holy love. Wisdom inspires icons to free fear from fear, imparting love through love, saying, 'I AM, be not afraid! Love as I have loved you; love as I love.'

24.

Sincere fear lives in terror of getting deluded, unaware that delusion in the form of confusion is the unconscious root of fear. Delusion haunts fear like a ghost, but all attempts to avoid delusion without addressing unconscious confusion are doomed. Fear's despair is in fact a true insight into the nature of fear, which is without hope as long as fear clings to fear, trying to avoid delusion without curing delusion.

Wisdom crowns love that descends to the ultimate root of fear, where hells of confusion and separation generate fear. It hallows love that is unafraid to face the unconscious root of fear. Instead of struggling to avoid delusions whilst leaving delusion intact, driven by terror of delusion, fear lays down its life for the sake of the Name and rises as illumination into fearless love and glorification. Instead of trying to save itself without grace, as fear afraid to lose control, love descends to undo confusion, so as to cure separation and terror. But if love is to descend to confusion's lowest hell, it needs wisdom, if it is not to be seduced back into terror and fear.

Wisdom encircles love to preserve it from the delusions of fear. It cuts through confusion and dissolves division so as to cure separation. Love is crowned with glory in the divine presence, free of confusion and freed from separation. Love is consecrated by the halo of the Name, which enthrones God in the midst, releasing fear's delusions to rise as love from deepest hells. Wisdom opens the mystery of the Name as love, right in the midst of fear's worst fears, disempowering the 'powers' of terror. Wisdom opens the mysteries of glory as love, so that fear dissolves into love and rises as love to give glory to God. Thus, the 'powers' of confusion and separation that rule fear are overcome by burning love and crowned with wisdom's tongues of fire.

Crowning is hid with Christ in God in a world that has lost touch with gnomic mysteries. Even elders rarely hint at what Scripture and tradition refer to again and again. It is as if the mysteries of glorification were under siege, although the Name still has power to disempower 'powers' of confusion and separation.

25.

Wisdom opens glory in the Name to cure fear, trusting love to heal terror.   Glory is ineffable openness and the Name is timeless oneness, transmitting love's presence that cures fear. Wisdom turns and sees, calling fear to trust sound seeing and rise as love. When trust trusts wisdom to see as she sees, love can abide and release fear into wisdom, freeing fear to rise into the spheres of glory.

Wisdom is free of the fixations of fear when as love she abides as the release of terror. The Name undoes confusion between the uncreated and the created here in the midst, releasing fear to rise as love into the mysteries of glorification. Wisdom hallows the Name as way, truth and life, anchoring the *praxis* of *theoria* in recognition of 'I AM.' The perfection of wisdom transmits great peace in the completeness of the glory of the Name.

Orthodox Tradition, including Scripture, is intricate and complex but the conflicted textures are not crucial. What is crucial is wisdom's transmission of the Name, which undoes confusion to ground communion in sound union, revealing the indivisible mysteries of Christ. By unveiling the oneness of Christ in the Holy Trinity, and his union of natures, everything is released into the glory of the Name. Knowing 'I AM,' God is known, all in God, God in all.

Primordial glory is uncreated, so contrived effort, being created, is beside the point. Wisdom discerning glory is not grounded in created causality, so all ascetical conditioning, being created, misses the point. Synergy with uncreated grace should never be confused with self-improvement, or uncreated glory with created vanity. Glory in the beginning is uncreated, in the end is uncreated and grace is uncreated in between. The glory of the Name is beyond thought and never becomes objectified like an object of thought.   It is impossible to liken glory to anything created, but wisdom discerns uncreated presence in the midst. How it is seen differs in accordance with our state, not what it is, uncreated grace.

The injunction to turn and see grounds wisdom in the glory of the Name, delivering terror from separation by raising fear to love.

26.

Wisdom discerns glory through the Name, knowing that glorification of God is the indispensible key to 'right-glorification,' which is what integral Orthodoxy is all about. It is grounded in purifying union and illumining communion, the Kingdom of God the Holy Trinity.

A wisdom round cell in a hornbeam glade can symbolize axial peace, the central fire a world axis, *axis mundi,* here at the apex of the heart, representing Christ in God at centre, wisdom's centre of all centres, in whom all centres coincide. Christ here at centre is the great peace of illuminating grace and the great peace of deifying blessing, and in him there is no argument, though there is difference, between grace and blessing.

God speaks and his servant hears, saying, 'Thy will be done.' Peace passing all understanding is not as the world gives, but as the still small voice within is whispering, saying, 'I am I AM thy God and there is no other.' 'Turn and see 'I AM' in glory in the midst.' The Spirit is freedom's release into peace and such peace never forsakes anyone. But when we forsake grace, grace appears to us to forsake us as we fall short of glory. Peace remains grace and blessing in the Name, recalling us to its Kingdom of light.

Jesus knew that of himself he could do nothing. He does not confuse 'I AM' with his humanity apart from God. The 'I AM' that is way, truth and life, is God the Word in glory, one with the Father. God's Kingdom of glory is within us. His uncreated creative life is giving eternal life to us. His wisdom is uncreated creative light, in whose light we see light. Wisdom restores glory to glory in the heavenly realms of the awakened heart, hallowing earth as in heaven through the Name.

Wisdom awakens the 'eye of the heart' to the uncreated glory of the Holy Name. It is unveiled in the Father's original light, through the transmission of the filial Word, in the radiant clarity of the Holy Spirit.

27.

Prophecy renews itself with the help of the poetry of temple wisdom, whilst prayer renews itself through empowerment in the Name. Inspiring both renewals is the Pentecost of purification, realizing *metanoia,* the Ascension to illumination, realizing *theoria,* and Glorification, realizing *theosis.* The three stages of wisdom are empowered by the mysteries of Baptism, Chrismation and the Eucharist, all of which have ancient roots in temple wisdom. The poetry and ritual of wisdom matters because it expresses the ineffable in the language of the ineffable, which veils as well as unveils the mysteries. It functions as an iconic and symbolic realm in which the ineffable mysteries of the heart can find safe expression.

The Temple itself was often sacked, and twice destroyed, but its wisdom lives on in prophecy and prayer. The desert returns to temple wisdom because Christ is that High Priestly wisdom, renewing temple wisdom in age after age. Prophecy transmits the Name, and prayer is its assimilation through wisdom, renewing desert *ihidayah* in each generation. It is the transmission of wisdom and the Name that nourishes *ihidayah,* not external movements or rebuilding programmes. The renewal of monastic institutions and buildings may or may not be an expression of quintessential *ihidayah.* Christ is handed on in the heart of the tradition, by wisdom and the Name, unveiling the Holy of Holies.

Both Joseph of Volokalamsk, with the 'possessors,' who advocated large monastic properties, and Nil Sorsky, with the 'non-possessors,' who advocated hesychasteria, hermitages and sketes, sought to retain the tradition of *metanoia* and *theoria.* Saint Silouan and Archimandrite Sophrony bear witness to a living stream that flows freely beneath the Holy of Holies, renewing *ihidaya* even in our own day. Love's glory of wisdom, being free of self-interest, is passed on without reserve, renewing tradition in generation after generation.

The language of veiling and unveiling is temple poetry, as is the symbolism of light and glory. Prophecy employs it to communicate communion in wisdom and to inspire prayer in the temple of the heart, hallowed by the glory of the Name.

28.

It is the Spirit not the letter of the *logos* that gathers into one all who are known by Name. It is purification not puritanism that severs confusion. It is illumination not intellectual speculation that cures separation. It is glorification not formulation that frees. The *nous* steps back and turns, in the inmost heart, so wisdom sees. Seeing penetrates right through, once turning opens a way. Patristic wisdom did not end with Photius or Palamas, but lives on in elders whenever prophecy renews prayer that all shall be saved. Wisdom's scope embraces all in Christ when love seeks not its own. Wonder's sphere is peace in the Spirit, passing all understanding.

Christ in glory is discerned by wisdom in the Spirit to be ineffable openness, infinitely able to heal the narrows of fear. As wisdom, Christ is indivisible oneness with unlimited capacity to draw us safely out from the shallows of indifference into the depths of uncreated presence. The narrows and shallows of curtailed religion need the resurrection, ascension and glorification of Christ to draw them up and out. Without Christ in his ineffable wisdom, religion condemns itself, shut down in fear and rejecting love. It condemns itself to the hells of fear and sins against the Spirit by demonizing the grace God sends to save it. Christ is patient and kind, waiting for Christians to let Baptism restore them, and Chrismation illumine them.

Free in God of all compulsion and restriction, glory frees us through God from all compulsion and restriction. Unconditioned in uncreated openness, glory does not waver as conditions come and go. We waver, but we do not confuse ourselves with the glory of God's Name, but let it anoint and illumine us. The unrestricted completeness of wisdom comes to help us in our incompleteness, so that what is definitive for us is wisdom's completeness not our incompleteness. What is decisive for us is Christ in glory, not the restricted compulsions of terror.

29.

The glory of the Name is our original destiny coming to meet us from the age to come, to complete us. It inspires wisdom to discern seven heavens and seven hells, so as wisdom ascends into seven heavens through illumination, glory descends into seven corresponding hells through glorification, undoing the prisons of pride and vanity one by one. Wisdom ascends as illumination, and descends as glorification, undoing the narrows and shallows of the fall.

Wisdom purifies by turning and burning off the impurities of pride. Wisdom illumines by dissolving divisions and crystallizing the confusions of vanity. Wisdom glorifies by freeing restrictions and releasing the compulsions of fixated fear. Wisdom glorifies by integrating all undone hells into opening heavens, which is love's hope that all shall be saved, writ large as love's consummation in God the Holy Trinity.

When accused, love is patient with fear and does not retaliate. Love is forbearing and kind when fear condemns love to hell for not condemning the damned. Wisdom inspires love to watch and wait until fear is ready to rise with Christ to love.

Love is not jealous of fear, nor does love boast like a puffed up bubble. Love is not arrogant or rude to fear, nor does it insist on imposing love on fear. Love does not resent fear or get irritable when fear condemns love to the hells that fear inevitably spawns. Love does not rejoice when fear gets it all wrong again and again.

Instead, love rejoices when fear begins to rise with Christ into unselfish love. Love in Christ bears all things, even persecution by fear. Love believes that Christ can raise fear. Love hopes Christ's ascension includes fear. Love endures Christ's glorification as it descends down into the infernal roots of fear to heal them.

This is the glory of the Cross of Christ, which is the glory of unselfish love, discerned by wisdom as our destiny, present as our origin and our end, our alpha and our omega.

30.

Purification is the outer veil of turning, and illumination is the inner veil of seeing. Both 'pass away' when the unveiled secret of the Holy Name is revealed in the Holy of Holies. 'I AM' is the completion of the perfection of completeness when purification perfects, illumination completes and glorification consummates our incompleteness, perfecting completeness without end.

'I AM' is the paternal source and filial meaning of perfecting, completing and completeness as they proceed from the paternal source to be fulfilled in the filial meaning. The paternal Source of both the filial Word and the proceeding Spirit, rejoice as one in the Name and wisdom. As the creative uncreated energies and the unifying activity of God, wisdom and the Name differentiate in order to unite all that there is.

'I AM' is the unknowable essence, and its uncreated creative creativity, giving rise to all that there is. Past, present and future are timeless in the presence of the oneness of 'I AM.' Knower and known are one for purification. Seer and seen are one for illumination. The glory of 'I AM' is present everywhere, permeating ethereal space with tongues of flame, translucent air, purifying fire, cleansing water and crystallizing earth.

The Name is the apex of all ways and means. It is the peak of all ascent and the effulgence of all glory. Wisdom sees through delusion into the heart of the Holy of Holies, revealing glorification to be the perfection of purification and the completion of illumination. Christ kindles the wisdom that perfects and completes fire, light and glory in the temple of the heart.

Filial wisdom arises from paternal wisdom from which spiritual wisdom proceeds. The Name reveals 'I AM' in the midst. Wisdom gives glory to God alone. Completeness is already accomplished in God by God through God, so all effort and strain miss the point. Neither elder nor disciple can lay claim to anything here. The point is not them, but Christ in their midst. All else falls short of the glory. Their no-thing-ness here at centre is no basis for nihilism because it generously embraces all that there is.

31.

'I AM' saves just as it is. God in the midst is not a conditioned effect nor is uncreated presence caused by anything created. Remembrance of God is recognition, not undistracted concentration that binds hearts in knots. Nothing distracts Christ in the midst and it is Christ who saves not us. The greatness of the Name consists in Christ's ability to lighten all burdens and release all binds. Christ is 'I AM' before Abraham was, but we fail to recognize him. It is not that he fails us but that we fall short of the glory of his Name. 'Amen' says 'So be it!' or 'Just so!' to the Name, 'yes' to its spontaneous and effortless saving grace.

'Amen' to the Name unfolds as 'yes' to primordial perfection as pure being, seeing as well being, and oneness as eternal being, in the light of the glory of Holy Trinity. 'I AM' causes to be like a vine and its branches, or a body and its members. Symbols of the Name transmit uncreated purity, light and glory to the heart. There is nothing special here, nothing to gawp at, just wisdom and wonder seeing nothing created in the midst. Wisdom sees nothing to be seen where the Name reveals God, freeing the heart from addictions to bliss.

Recognition of 'I AM' sees the oneness of 'I AM,' the union of the Father and the Son, transcending yet embracing form. The Paraclete descends with tongues of fire, fire of ether, fire of air, fire of water, fire of earth and fire of fire. Pentecost is timeless in the 'now' of this unravelling flame. The infernal roots of the fall are purified and illumined as wisdom descends with Christ into hell, and glory unravels glory to glory in God.

Purity is release, light is spontaneous, glory is presence at the heart of remembrance. 'Powers' are disempowered of the power to delude. It is not that the mind is deliberately fabricating this, rather that the remembrance of God is this. It is not visualization of the harrowing of hell, but Name hallowing, which unveils wisdom to the 'powers,' as the Apostle hinted long ago. [34]

---

[34] See Ephesians 3:10.

32.

In the ineffable openness of timeless presence and primordial oneness, always now, there is the cessation and recreation of everything in every moment. At this critical juncture, the Name is hallowed so the Kingdom comes. God's will is done on earth as it is always done in heaven. When the uncreated glory of Christ arises, then too, in this same glory, the glory of our epiphany appears with him. When the ineffable openness of the Name is revealed, then too the timeless presence and primordial oneness of glory are unveiled with him. Christophany and epiphany are timelessly present and primordially one in the ineffable openness of wisdom.

Dying anew in every moment means we are born again in every moment, when prophecy gives us the initiatory Prayer of the Name: 'Hallowed be thy Name on earth, as it is in heaven.' Dying now before we die, the Word gives us his own pure prayer: 'Thy Kingdom come on earth, as it is in heaven.' Our epiphany answers his Christophany when we are given his synergy prayer: 'Thy will be done on earth, as it is in heaven.'

Death is the dissolution of earth into water, water into fire, fire into air, and air into awareness of glory. The inner radiance of glory is revealed in 'I AM who I AM,' revelation of the Name, saying: 'Thou art my beloved Son, in whom I am well pleased.' The filial and the paternal mystery of the THOU are revealed with the epiphany of 'I AM,' Christ's theophany. Prophecy says: 'Recognize God in this Name. Awaken to God in this Name. Dwell with God, through this Name.' Prayer does so by hallowing the Name.

The radiance of glory of the Name is the uncreated light of the Way, which is unselfish love. The oneness of Father and Son is ours in this epiphany, that we may be one as God is one. Terror arises when fear despairs, but recognition of 'I AM' cuts through. Christ descends to the hells of terror and fear on Holy Saturday, which is timeless grace now his primordial presence is present in our midst. Terror arises but the Name saves. Fear arises but the Name saves. 'Hallowed be thy Name.'

33.

Prayer dissolves fear in uncreated light, in those who call upon the Name that saves. When terror arises from fear that despairs, it is dissolved into a body of light. The Name saves in the timeless presence of ineffable openness and primordial oneness. Prayer takes refuge in glory in the midst of terror, giving glory to God. This liberates fear into a body of expansive glory. But if fear turns consistently away from uncreated light, insisting it is not worthy, the freedom of fear to refuse love is respected, though love bleeds. The fires of earth, water, fire, air and glory descend to purify and illumine fear, but if fear refuses their merciful light, fear's freedom is love's Cross. Fear chooses hell, which God offers as heaven, but terror experiences as hell, because it despairs.

Fear is free to refuse to trust love and cling to fear's familiar hell of terror and despair, experiencing love's mercy as wrath. Prophecy descends to impart prayer of the Name to turn despair to hope, renewing trust in love so that fear can dissolve into light. Hells are heavens that fear cannot trust, love that terror sees as wrath in its despair. Hell's wrongs are righted in the Name, unless fear persists in clinging to them, despite all dispensations of grace.

Terror is fear sharpened by despair, which love heals by raising it in Christ into the mysteries of ascension through illumination and the mysteries of enthronement through glorification. Hells confuse in order to separate us from the heavens of the Name. Heavens reclaim their 'powers' from hells in the power of the Name, ascribing all glory to God. 'Powers' are disempowered as enemies of God, empowering us to pray: 'Thy will be done. Thy Kingdom come in the hallowed Name.' Fear rises by trusting love, healing despair, and releasing terror into glory.

At the moment of death in every moment, the Name is hallowed to invert the subversions of fear, terror's confusions and despair's divisions. Dying before we die in every moment, we live resurrection, ascension and glorification as Christ's inversion of satanic subversion. The glory of the Name is ascribed by wisdom to God, inverting subversion.

34.

The Name liberates anew in every moment in the timeless presence of ineffable openness and primordial oneness. Subversions invert as 'powers' are disempowered. Hells are emptied as heavens expand and glory rises from glory to glory in the spheres of the Kingdom. The veils rend as the glory fills all in all in the Holy of Holies. Recognition of 'I AM' is the key to the remembrance of God in the midst. Hearts are pierced to the core by uncreated light as ascent passes over into glory in Christ, who is glorification of God by God in the midst. Recognition of 'I AM' restores the remembrance of God anew in every moment, dying to death and rising to life in timeless freedom.

The way is straight and there are many points of possible deviation, all of which straighten back when the straight path of the Name inverts the subversions. We die daily as we die to death's sting anew in every moment by hallowing the Name. Negative obscuration arises, but dissolves like mist in the sunlight of the saving Name. Remembrance of God holds wisdom steady in the midst. Temptations come and go but wisdom stands steadfast, as we say in the Liturgy, again and again. Liberation through recognition is wisdom's way, wisdom's ladder of truth, wisdom's life-giving cure of terror and fear.

Remembrance of God never forgets that God's wrath is his love, that love's uncreated energy of wrath when love is thwarted is never anything other than love. So love does not fear wrath at the judgment, because love is in peaceful accord with love, well able to release negativity as it arises, restoring love to love. Love burns as it purifies so as to illumine. Love illumines as it glorifies so as to deify. The judgment is timeless presence in the ineffable openness and primordial oneness of the Name. We live it moment by moment in glorification.

Obstacles are opportunities for love to deepen as it penetrates the depths of fear to release the negativity of terror. Love does not fear terror but turns towards it to win its trust, opening hells to heavens in the Name.

35.

There is no compulsion in love because love reveres freedom from compulsion to woo terror from violence. Love liberates fear when recognition releases terror through the remembrance of God. Love's hallowing is unceasing as it cures fear by love and terror by wisdom in the ascending, descending glory of the Holy of Holies. Glorification of God by God recreates the being, wellbeing and eternal being of timeless presence in the inter-being of ineffable openness and primordial oneness. Prayer of the Name is 'learned by heart' when Christ is seen in the midst: 'I AM, fear not!'

Pentecost welcomes the Paraclete's tongues of fire, fire of glory in fires of air, fires of air in fires of fire, fires of fire in fires of water, fires of water in fires of earth. Glorification embraces descent as well as ascent, where saints meet angels on the ladder of the Name, and each rung is a pure realm of wisdom and glory whose axis is the Name. Wisdom abides as ineffable openness in the timeless presence of glory. Love is selflessly unselfish in its compassion for fear. Wisdom is selflessly unselfish in its harrowing of terror.

Wisdom offers her completeness to our stories by helping us see incompleteness in the uncreated light of completeness. Fear's dysfunctional stories are retold until ineffable openness frees us to retell them in increasingly functional ways. Scripture is woven of stories that retell stories as prophecy inspiring pure prayer. Prayer is openness to wisdom's completeness coming to recreate us in our incompleteness.

The cycles of meaning never end, just as the expansive glory of the *Logos* has no limit. Christ sends the Spirit of Truth to reveal new dimensions that we had overlooked before. He is forever 'going away' so the Spirit can come, opening us in freedom. The tradition is coherent when wisdom diagnoses pathologies of incoherence and turns incompleteness into an integral moment of her unfolding completeness. The extremes are overcome and integrated as the stories unfold. It is the shepherd *Logos* that enfolds what is unfolding into the fold of textured completeness.

36.

Saint Mark the Ascetic says the remembrance of God is suffering of heart endured in a spirit of devotion. Forgetfulness of God is self-indulgence and insensitivity. [35] Remembrance of God cures passions, addiction to pathological fixations, in the uncreated flame of dispassionate freedom, *apatheia,* and healing stillness, *hesychia.* The watchful, listening openness of attentive remembrance is grounded in recognition of God in the midst. The Name saves by turning the *nous* and opening the 'eye' of the heart, deifying body, soul and spirit in uncreated light. Transfiguration is timeless presence, boundless in scope, releasing passions into ineffable openness in the uncreated oneness and beauty of the glory of God. The Tome of the Holy Mountain defends all who partake in the glory of the age to come against accusations of heresy and delusion. It confirms glorification as fulfilment of Scripture in prophecy and prayer, by transmitting Patristic wisdom as Hesychasm from generation to generation.

Remembrance of God is nourished by attention, *prosoche,* which Hesychios says sustains unceasing prayer in the stillness of the heart. The Name and wisdom mutually support each other as *praxis* and *theoria.* Passions dissolve as turning sees and seeing turns seeking outside in. A turned *nous* can guard the heart's invocation of the Name because it sustains union with God in the Great Peace. An ineffable but unwavering freedom permeates the remembrance of God, seeing light through light, knowing as God knows the mysteries of glory. Communion is ecstatic but unceasing to the degree that wisdom is quite ordinary, and we live uncreated energy creatively in everyday life. It is as 'I AM' that God is remembered, remembers and is remembering anew in every moment. This is no objectified triadology, trapped in sentimentalized extremes, but translucent wisdom aware of who recollects and who is recollected in transfigured recollection of God.

---

[35] Philokalia Vol 1 p 137.

37.

The illumined heart is a throne of God, a moving chariot throne that ascends to heaven and descends to earth discerning glory in the Name. It is the place of grace where the Spirit prays with our spirit sighing: 'Abba, Father!' Interceding for the salvation of all, the heaven of the heart is restored when the Spirit turns tombs of the dead into wombs of the Spirit in the light of the glory of resurrection. The heart suffers this turning, pierced by wisdom's blade.

The heart endures this seeing, transfixed in the midst by costly love. Awareness descends to where the pain is, without hesitation. The heart's stigmata pierces, burns and bleeds, drawing awareness to where God's tongue of flame severs soul from spirit in the midst. Confusion is consumed, leaving communion with the hallowing Name. Suffering is ecstatic with bright joy when the Name awakens recognition of God.

Self-indulgence is insensitive to God in the midst. Insensitivity is blind to 'I AM' being God's Name. Self-obsession is caught up in confusion, incapable of overcoming separation from God. The heart suffers the revelation of the Name and endures glory discerned by wisdom. It undergoes glorification as joyous mourning, martyred by wisdom's blessed severance in the midst. Patient surrender to the given kindles remembrance of God, as Saint Mark the Ascetic points out. Resistance indulges self-obsession and oblivious distraction. Stony insensibility hardens the heart, infecting it with sclerosis of spirit.

Remembrance of God, Saint Diadochus reminds us, burns off the impurities of the passions like a refiner's fire. It includes remembrance of death, judgment, heaven and hell, because wisdom puts death to death, imparts judgment that ends judgment, heaven that empties hell and restores hell to heaven. Humble sorrow for sin asks forgiveness from all, out of love for all, giving thanks to God. Such humility is spontaneous and free, not self-interested and self-obsessed. Such wisdom lives uncreated light as grace of tears, as Saint Isaac teaches. Wisdom tears are not of this world.

38.

The Elder Barsanuphius regarded himself as a 'slave on a mission.' [36] He sees himself as a man under obedience, a man with a mission or commission. For him, the elder is under obedience to the inspiration of the Holy Spirit, responsible before God for the transmission of the Sacred Tradition. Wisdom's commission is transmission. The mission is communication of the Name, transmission of the word of prophecy, which saves and heals. Such prophecy is apostolic because it is sent. It is apostolic because it is under obedience to the mission of wisdom.

The desert tradition of Gaza retained a sense of obedience to the mission of the prophets and apostles, to the roots of Scripture in inspiration, to the confessors and martyrs who laboured unto death. In the desert, the sayings of the Fathers are living prophecy which does not die out, though it may be under siege from cultures that are oblivious to the culture of the heart. It is a culture of discernment and humour, of kindness and wisdom. It is a culture of openness concealed by the hermitage, hidden from the scrutiny of prying curiosity. It transmits this ineffable openness to laymen and bishops, monks and hermits, without discrimination. It imparts prophecy, inspiring prayer, in a spirit of wisdom and wonder. The elder is a prophet and an apostle who hides these functions from objectification so as to save them for the sacred function of transmission.

Desert wisdom is concerned with spiritual discernment rather than external discipline, with personal inspiration rather than institutional subjection. Archimandrite Sophrony was under obedience to inspiration, and laboured to serve the mysteries of 'I AM.' His insight was made accessible to many. His inspiration pierced the heart like a two-edged sword. It is the invisibility of the Name, revealing God in the midst. It is the inspiration that transmits wisdom, renewing tradition as healing.

---

[36] Letters of Barsanuphius and John Letter 139 SVS p 7.

39.

Saint Maximus the Confessor imparts Christ as the wisdom of unconfused indivisibility, and of inseparable union in all dimensions. For Maximus, Christ's wisdom is divine and human, as well as cosmic in scope. It defines by letting the ineffable remain ineffable. It defines by putting wisdom centre stage, not theological definition, though it does so with theological rigour. Maximus speaks of 'stumbling and staggering,' rather than systematic speculation, true to the desert's awareness of the difference between wisdom and sophistry. He comments on Ephesians 1 and Colossians 1:15-23, recapitulating all lesser reconciliations in Christ. He transmits Patristic wisdom as heir to Scriptural wisdom in both covenants.

It is impossible to overstate the importance of both Denys and Maximus for Orthodox Tradition as it rises into the discernments of integral wisdom. It is a wisdom that acknowledges the incompleteness of this present time without losing touch with the completeness of the glory of the age to come. It is a wisdom that discerns differences without letting them degenerate into divisions, and discerns unity that does not disintegrate into confusion. Wisdom, not sophistication, is the point of intellectual rigour. Christ, not abstraction, is unveiled here in the midst.

For Maximus, ascetic *praxis* dances hand in hand with *theoria mystikos,* for wisdom integrates them without confusing or dividing them. Everything is seen within the prism of deification, including the incompleteness that apparently opposes completeness. Wounds are wombs, which birth Christ in wondrous ways. Christ turns temptations into transformations, fallen 'powers' into empowerments of wisdom. Divested of subservience to fallen 'powers,' glorification in Christ gives glory to God, empowering disempowerment of fallen 'powers'. We put our trust in wisdom to turn and see, giving glory back to God in the midst. We follow through to mysteries of glory that are ineffable, knowing we do not know, but that God knows, sharing his knowledge with us through wisdom.

40.

Saint Isaac says that Gehenna is not retribution for evil but the guiding hand of compassionate loving kindness leading us to the glory of the age to come. The cunning of love's wisdom uses hell to restore heaven, death to teach resurrection, torment to cure terror, fire to heal fear. Death is a blessed restoration of paradise through resurrection. Divine wrath is not vengeance but vehement love, for which hell is not punishment but purification. The wisdom that inspires this vision is the wisdom of burning, boundless love. It is love that desires to save all but respects the dignity of freedom to reject love.

The vision of Gehenna as the purifying fire of uncreated love is how hell looks from within illumination and glorification. It frees purification from all trace of fear and terror. It is one of Saint Isaac's most precious insights into wisdom, but it should not be assumed it makes sense outside the wisdom that gave rise to it. The Gehenna texts were not included in the collection of Homilies translated into Greek, and were rediscovered only recently. The tradition tends to conceal its heart in times that are not yet ready to assimilate love's mysteries, which, though hidden, were never peripheral.

The fire of love waits for a spark to spring into flame, concealing its beauty in the Holy of Holies. Holy love awaits the awakening of the heart so that the beauty of holiness is not profaned. Wisdom rests in the peace of the Name, abiding in the beauty of ineffable glory. Compulsion and fear have no place here, because where they intrude, glory is not blessing but a self–imposed curse. There are many mansions in between, many degrees of wisdom and love. But there is no middle ground between heaven and hell. The heart must choose: right glorification of God, or vain glorification and separation. Love of wisdom chooses love of God, and participation in that love, glorification of God by God, in God the Holy Trinity. For souls that are not yet ready, there are degrees of love imparting love through love. There are degrees of purification and illumination through love by love. Saint Isaac is not trying to impose an arbitrary opinion of Gehenna. He is transmitting the wisdom of love through love so we can see.

41.

In the 'Orthodox Faith,' Book 1:13, Saint John of Damascus teaches that the consubstantial and co-eternal Spirit proceeds from the Father and abides in the Son. The Spirit does not proceed from the Son, although he can be said to be the Spirit of the Son, because he is bestowed upon us through the Son. Maximus had taught that the Spirit proceeds from the Father alone, but acknowledged that in the West, some said that the Spirit proceeds from the Father through the Son, meaning the Spirit is bestowed through the Son.

The Spirit's eternal procession from the Father to abide or rest in the Son, is a crucial insight of Orthodox wisdom. There is an eternal presence of the Spirit in the Son because the Spirit proceeds from the Father to abide eternally in the Son. The Son is the Wisdom, and *Logos*, of the Father, in whom the Spirit rests. The co-inherence of the divine persons interpenetrates without confusion, an indivisible abiding of the Spirit in the Son, as well as the Son in the Father, that anchors Christian wisdom in the ineffable oneness of all three persons beyond modalism and tri-theism.

The wisdom of the Spirit co-inheres with the wisdom of the Son, in the Father of all wisdom, a mystical Trinity of wisdom, without transgressing the ineffability of the ineffable. Both monism and dualism are transcended, but so is reification. 'Three' signifies not number but perfect completeness, a crucial insight for wisdom. It is not that the Trinity is derived from number theory but that Triune completeness transcends number.

Wisdom as uncreated energy is also tri-hypostatic and triune, grounded in the ineffable openness and uncreated presence of God. Saint John of Damascus' troparia transform these dogmas into doxology, Scripture into poetry, images into chant, that has nurtured Orthodox Tradition ever since. Wisdom is nourished by his Odes, so that the glory of the Name is hallowed in prophecy and prayer. Wisdom is communicated in wondrous poetry, preserving the Name from profane objectification. Wisdom mysteries are transmitted intact, creating all things new.

42.

Abiding eternally in the Son, the Spirit of Truth guides us into the whole truth that gives life to the love of wisdom and the Name. Wisdom is the indivisible truth that makes us free. It is not conceptual in itself, though its ineffability can be expressed conceptually. It is not a conceptual system but a living tradition that the Fathers interpret. Saint Gregory Palamas is transmitting the tradition he discerns in Evagrius and Macarius, Diadochus and Maximus, when he refers to Basil and Denis, who speak of an infallible circular movement of the *nous* in the illumined heart. To turn is to return from outward dissipation into vision of God in the midst. The heart returns to itself so that through an infallible circular motion, centred on God in the midst, it is freed from delusion and ascends to God.

The turning of the *nous* is direct self-recollection that is no longer centred upon the self-centred self, but God. It transcends the selfish self, freeing self-love, *philautia,* to release into love of God. It is through the purifying uncreated 'I AM' in the midst that God is seen and glorified. It is through the Name revealing God in the midst that wisdom awakens and releases delusion. It is in the glory of the hallowed Name that the Kingdom comes and God's will is done. Saint Gregory Palamas interprets the whole tradition when he insists that turning illumines infallibly, and that uncreated light frees the heart of delusion.

Stillness, *hesychia,* is grounded in self-recollected vision of God seeing God, the union of seer and seen. Fruit of the return of the *nous* to God's vision of God, through God, in the inmost heart, stillness liberates the heart, says Palamas, from toil and anxious care. Presence is spontaneous when wisdom awakens to ineffable openness. The Spirit, who eternally proceeds from the Father to abide in the Son, discerns the wondrous oneness of the Father and the Son, sharing with wisdom what is seen.

43.

Christ says that if we believe in him and trust in his Name, we shall not only do what he does, but shall do even greater things, because he goes to the Father. [37] The Paraclete comes to do greater things, gathering us into the truth of the whole. It is not that Christ is surpassed but that his amplitude expands. So it is good that Christ goes forth from concepts to raise us to truth. The fallen mind turns icons into idols, so he leaves. In Emmaus, he disappears. In Galilee, he ascends. His Kingdom is not of this world. God cannot be objectified. Christ goes away that the Spirit may come, revealing him in the midst, everywhere and always. The narrows are opened, the shallows are deepened whenever the Name is hallowed and the Kingdom comes.

It is good Christ goes away out of all our versions of him, and that the Spirit of Truth comes to guide us into a more wholesome truth. The Spirit is freedom not compulsion, so it is good that omnipotence, by going away, refrains from preventing us from abusing freedom. Wisdom's commission of transmission is in fallible hands, marked by incompleteness. But Wisdom's mission is to impart the infallible encircling truth of Holy Trinity that sees incompleteness as witness to expanding completeness.

Christ walks away from 'powers' of manipulation and control, when he glorifies God on a cross of wild love. The wisdom of this love is what glorifies God, curing the narrows of terror and fear. It does not terrorize fear driven terror, knowing it is only a struggle to survive. He died abandoned, failing to found what fear wants. He trusts love. He goes, trusting everything to love. The Spirit guides us into the truth of love. All sins are forgiven when love loves much. Love forgives and forgiveness loves. The Spirit imparts the wisdom of love. Love is the glory of the saving Name.

---

[37] See John 14:12.

44.

Wisdom inspires the prophecy that elders impart to awaken prayer of the heart, hallowing the Name. Wisdom is concealed in the legacy of glory that angels unveil, glorification in the Name. At once hypostatic and energetic, it is by the uncreated act of grace that wisdom is loved and known. The Eucharist makes all who partake of Christ into divine human sacraments, incarnating the hallowed Name. Trinitarian wisdom incarnates without ceasing as mystery and living sacrament.

Christ is the key to wisdom mysteries whose glory is without bounds. He is what we shall be, so we look to him to reveal who we are becoming. He goes away to free us from confusing at centre the uncreated and created. He departs to deliver us from confusing 'me' with 'I AM.' He dies to free icons from idols, including ideology. Trinitarian wisdom is invisible indivisibility imparting ineffable inseparability.

The culture of wisdom is a culture of free gift. It cannot be bought. Uncreated grace is lost when we cling to it, found when we give it away. We give away our own to receive what is his, just as he gave away his own to give us what is his. If we cling to what is our own, we will lose what is his.

Transcending past and future, 'I AM' saves. If I give myself away, I am his. The flame of the Name passes from elders to disciples like a tongue of fire. Love loves the beloved not itself. The Spirit and the bride, his beloved wisdom, say, 'Come!' The Spirit comes to free us from fear, fear for our survival, our security, and our safety. Above all, the Paraclete comes to heal the unconscious terror that underlies and determines fear. Where the Spirit is, here is freedom.

Prophecy trusts the Spirit to transmit wisdom in the Word that names the Name. Prayer trusts the Spirit to intercede with sighs too deep for words. Wonder beholds what wisdom sees and is struck dumb with awe. Stillness is uncreated wonder beholding the glory of 'I AM.'

45.

Wisdom imparts 'wholeness,' *catholicity*, to every perception, turning confusion into communion and separation into union, so that translucence is transparent to glory in every moment. 'Wholeness' is mystery not external universality, wisdom not institutional conformity. For wisdom, the mutual interpenetration, *perichoresis*, of the uncreated and the created in Christ means that opposites do not oppose. In the *Logos*, opposites do not obstruct one another, but mutually embrace one another. Wisdom sees mutual interpenetration as 'wholeness,' arising as the mutual simultaneous embrace in which opposites mutually abide. Wisdom's vision sees all round and all at once, as it were, transcending in the *Logos* the constraints of conventional logic. In Christ, mutual exclusion of extremes gives way to mutual arising and abiding.

Wisdom in Christ is free of all fixated views, so indivisible communion is free of confusion, and differentiation is no impediment to union. There is no obstructive opposition between the spiritual and the sensible in Christ, so nothing impedes the love of God in those whose hearts are overwhelmed by love. It is not that 'either-or' gives way to 'both-and' alone, but 'neither-nor' as well. Everything is glory, mirroring glory in Christ glorified, which wisdom discerns as the glory of the age to come.

Crowned vision sees the gold in everything, and embraces the jewel in everything, so that wherever wisdom turns, lead turns to gold and stones are jewels. There is no denigration in wisdom's vision, and so no enmity, no violence. There is no isolation or confusion in Christ, in whom wisdom is uncreated light, enlightening the world. War between the spiritual and the sensible becomes peace in Christ, in whom wholeness is luminous and serene. To turn into wisdom is to see with Christ's single wholesome 'eye' and to abide in the glory of his presence. Glory reflects glory everywhere, here, in the oneness of his translucence. Violence voided, terror melts in tears of joy. Fears dissolve into the bright presence of 'I AM,' whose glory supports, contains and consummates all things. Wisdom transmits the Name, whose glory is bright wholeness.

46.

Wisdom discerns what Saint Diadochus calls 'love's glory' at the heart of the Name, revealing love at the heart of the unfolding of glorification. Until 'love's glory' is seen, no one can be of benefit to others; no one can even be of benefit to themselves. The seer of 'love's glory' leaps into the ocean of love that glorifies God, in God, through God. Confusion unravels and separation shatters in the uncreated light of the unveiled 'Face' of Glory. The 'eye' of the heart opens and glory interpenetrates all in all, seeing into the glory of 'I AM.' The seeing is sudden, all at once, but assimilation takes time, to the extent there is still time, now that all is eternally now.

If the Lord's Prayer is the way, then we hallow the Name. We give glory to God in his Name. We put our whole-hearted trust in the capacity of the Name to save. The Spirit is hallowing the Name eternally, so prayer in the Spirit is unceasing. The Spirit beholds the Son in the radiant sphere of the Father's Name, 'I AM,' sharing seer and seen with seers who die now to all that death destroys. God's 'Face' is seen in the place of the Name. Confusion falls away. Separation disappears. The pearl of great price is found. There are many metaphors for this, but the opening transcends them all.

Once the 'eye' of the heart awakes, everything reveals the glory of God in Christ glorified. There is no trace of doubt in glory, or wavering in glorification. It is just that we fall back into doubt whenever we lose heart. We hesitate and dither again, until glory clarifies doubt and seeing cuts through separation. Elders do not see themselves as proficient, but as beginners, or even as not having begun to turn and see. This keeps them supple and humble, receptive to uncreated grace and the Glory of the 'Face.'

Elders do not grumble at separation. They see the Name move mountains of separation without turning a hair. What can separate God's Name from God? What can separate wisdom from God? What is there to grumble at, now that separation has no foothold and storms of fear are stilled. True, glory is unfathomable, but it is at peace with its depths.

47.

A secular age may be a spiritual wilderness, but the desert is not degenerate as long as it hallows the Name. Many are afraid that illumination is impossible in a fast food age, forgetting that when the Name saves, glory is glory, just as in ancient times. The cultivation of the Name is what a culture of wisdom always does, wedding an earthly heaven to a heavenly earth. A secular age is like a fish that denies the sea it cannot see, or a bird that says air does not exist as it soars. The sciences only need to turn and see the glory they overlook, to become homes for wisdom, but they can never know as science what only wisdom sees.

It is for wisdom to be wisdom, not science. Science laboratories are not oratories, and were never meant to be. Wisdom sees the sea of glory and ascribes it to God. Science is not looking for God and so overlooks seas of glory wherever it turns. Wisdom steps back, seeing who sees.

The 'Philokalia' sits on the shelf, unread even in Church circles, until a pilgrim comes and sings a song of the Name. The love of beauty that gives the 'Philokalia' its name, undoes confusion in the hallowed Name. The 'eye' of the heart awakens the moment wisdom sees through the delusion of separation. For wisdom, glory is no rumour of beauty round the next corner, but uncreated light unveiling light in the midst. Neither of the East nor of the West, Christ glorified transmits the Name in glory, 'I AM who I AM.' 'Before Abraham was, I AM.'

Turning that is not yet seeing is difficult. Seeing that spontaneously turns is light and bright. To persevere with the former is excruciating suffering. To practice the latter is illumination as in a mirror, obscurely. Glory is face to face, knowing as it is known, but is lost when the delusion of separation sets in again and time and space return. We live between the three 'times' of turning, seeing and glory, the eschatologies of purification, illumination and glorification. What looks like inconsistency on a flat surface, makes clear sense in anagogical ascent.

48.

Negative asceticism polishes the mirror in the hope of seeing the light of glory. Illumination sees no trace of obscuration in uncreated light, so leaves the mirror to be a mirror, and glorification to see glory is direct and needs no mirror, so puts all mirrors away, until time is back and space separates. In time, mirrors are back until the next time that time is timeless in the hallowed Name. Glorification is not profaned. It descends and ascends, in the Holy of Holies, beyond our control. Illumination stands steady to catch us when we fall back into time. It holds us until the next time timeless glory descends to abolish time. The more seeking seeks to grasp glory, the further away glory seems.

The injunction to turn and see imparts the *praxis* of *theoria,* not a grip on glory. Illumination turns to see and sees to turn, without ambition to grasp glory, which drives glory away. Glory comes when it comes, and blows where it wills, free, as God is free, from all will to power. But once glory comes, illumination sees that its centre of gravity is glory. It remembers it is most itself when it is living beyond itself. It recalls it is most at home not in itself but in glory. Illumination marked by glory is humble. It does not presume. It knows the Holy of Holies belongs to God, and is not at the beck and call of men.

Illumination is not afraid of self-emptying *kenosis,* and does not seek to avoid the void in the midst. It knows the void in the midst is God, and that God is self-emptying *kenosis,* free of fear that seeks to avoid the void. Illumination is sustained by the *praxis* of *theoria,* seeing nothing created in the midst, giving glory to God, by hallowing the Name. Glorification is God's blessing of *theoria,* raising resurrection to ascension and so to glorification itself, glorification by God in his Name. Fear is afraid to let go of fear, fearing to fall from glory with no way of staying the fall. Glory lets fear fall away, knowing that glory is the realm that frees glory from fear, that glory gives glory to God in everything, and everything gives glory to God. Fear is afraid to lose control, whereas glory ascribes glory to God saying, 'Thy Kingdom come! Thy will be done!'

49.

The Spirit comes to help us in our weakness when we fall back into fear, interceding for the salvation of all in the midst. The Spirit's prayer in the heart is unceasing, praying '*Abba,* Father!' with sighs too deep for words. Freedom from the passions of fear no longer falls back into fear because it is freedom in Christ, dead to terror and alive to God in the midst. The Spirit who raised Jesus from the dead raises us in him, making us children of light in his Name. Children of glory are no longer in bondage to fear, because in the midst of terror, the Name frees terror to rise, saving terror from terror. The Spirit bears witness with our spirit that 'I AM' by grace is witness to 'I AM who I AM,' 'gods by grace' bearing witness to true God from true God. It is the glory of 'I AM' that saves fear from fear, coming to us as the glory of the age to come.

Illumination awaits glorification, knowing the freedom of glory of filiation in God longs to be made more fully known. The first fruits of the Spirit groan as illumination yearns for glorification. Prayer of the Spirit in the heart searches out what transcends our capacities: 'I AM' knows 'I AM' through 'I AM,' God the Holy Trinity. The Spirit intercedes by hallowing, glory by harrowing the hells of terror. In everything, glory communicates love through love, glory through glory. If God is for glory, what is against glory once fear falls away?

Nothing can separate love from love, glory from glory, in Christ glorified. No 'powers' of fear or terror can separate what God has joined. No confusion can confuse what communion unites, or separate what union heals. There is now no separation for what God has indivisibly joined, no disintegration for what integral wisdom has inseparably healed. Glory is un-objectified as indivisibility, ungraspable as inseparability. The Holy of Holies is not profaned, though glorification is shared by wisdom. The radiance of glory is peace and joy in the light of ineffable completeness. The Name has been with us from the beginning, and comes to save us as the glory of our final destiny. The Spirit comes to be our Pentecost with tongues of flame, consuming fear in flames of fire.

50.

The inheritance of the saints in light gives thanks for illumination whilst it awaits the inheritance of the saints in glory, as wisdom makes it known. All things hold together in wisdom, which holds the secret of their completeness. God imparts the irreproachable and blameless holiness of the Holy of Holies to the saints in his Name. It does not belong to them in themselves but to God, but it is truly theirs in God through his Name. God is blessed in his Name, and his Name blesses with blameless hallowing. Love's destiny of glory chooses to bless in love all who are chosen in Christ to be hallowed in God's Name, chosen before the foundation of the world to turn and see God in the midst. In fact, all are chosen, because 'God became man,' but not all choose to be chosen for 'man to become God.'

The destiny of love is a destiny of wisdom. The destiny of grace is a destiny of glory, as forgiveness undoes falls. Wisdom sees deeply into the insights that glory alone knows, the mysteries of completeness that only glory sees. The ineffable openness of wisdom is key to the presence of oneness in the Name. The destiny of glory is open to wisdom as the radiance of the Name. Completeness is not in time but completes all times in the timeless scope of wisdom. Glory is not in time but completes incompleteness in time in the light of timeless completeness. Love's destiny of glory is not in time but completes our incompleteness in the timeless glory of the age to come.

Glorification happens when our incompleteness meets completeness in timeless recognition. 'I AM' is seen as recognition of God in the midst. Remembrance of God is unceasing in the Spirit's prayer, interceding for the salvation of all. We are created for glorification. The Spirit seals the heart with truth, pledging glory to give glory to God 'now,' so that glory will be timeless glorification of God 'then.' Glorification holds steady in this critical tension, never letting the extremes tear apart what God has joined. It is the Father of glory who sends the Spirit of wisdom that reveals the glory of the Son. It is the Spirit who unveils the glory of Christ glorified as glorification.

51.

Wisdom is not confused with our perceptions, neither is wisdom separate from them. These subtle discernments are not the product of reason but of revelation of God in the heart. Wisdom does not stand aloof from perception, but also does not dissolve into perception as delusion. Perceptions arise but wisdom stands steadfast as remembrance of God in the midst. Wisdom does not seek elsewhere, just because the light looks brighter elsewhere. Seeing sees as seeing is seen, where turning turns. Here, where wisdom was lost, wisdom is found. Turning turns to see. The 'eye' of the heart opens. Wisdom sees glory, not as this or that, but as uncreated light. 'I AM' is not this nor that, nor both nor neither, here where glory unveils the mysteries of the Name.

Glorification is participation in the glory of Christ glorified, transcending the mysteries of resurrection as purification, and ascension as illumination. Disempowered 'powers' are subject to Christ, King in his Kingdom of wisdom and glory. All 'powers' in the age to come, are subject to him. 'Powers' in him are a 'footstool' to his 'throne of glory,' according to the ancient symbolism of Temple wisdom. Metaphor clothes speech with imagery, giving language power to transmit wisdom in the Name. Spiritual wisdom needs its poetry if it is to reveal the mysteries of glory and the Holy of Holies.

Chariot vision sees what the Cherubic Hymn sings, mysteries of glorification hidden from the beginning in the Holy of Holies. Christ glorified is enthroned on the right hand of the Father in the Holy of Holies. Wisdom discerns Christ glorified, and opens these mysteries to us to make them our own. We have no words for any of this, so the Spirit comes to our help in our bewilderment. Glory pervades everything, purifying confusion. Glory is pure presence ineffably open to wise oneness. No definitions adequately define this. No perceptions adequately discern this. The Spirit shares his insight with wisdom, unveiling the glory of the Son, through whom the glory of the Father is loved and known.

52.

Wisdom cuts through conceptual grip and leaps over separation. To practice *metanoia* as a means to acquire *theoria*, is to be stuck in separation, always one thought away from illumination. Thought can think conceptual inseparability, without breaking through separation. Thought is confusion that thinks separation wherever it turns. Thought is separation, which wisdom cuts through. Wisdom heals confusion and separation in realms of integral completeness. Wisdom sees completeness encompassing everything in the Son, of one substance with the Father of all completeness, from whom completeness proceeds with the Spirit's eternal abiding in the Son. Thought cannot penetrate the completeness of the Holy Trinity, but wisdom generously shares her vision of completeness, without usurping the ineffable completeness of God.

Christ glorified accomplishes glorification from the throne of glory, penetrating everywhere as glory in all, encompassing all in glory. Glory pervades all in a union of infinite co-inherence, *perichoresis,* mutual doxological interpenetration of the uncreated and the created without confusion. Glory frees union of interference and communion of obstruction. The uncreated does not interfere with the created in union, nor do they obstruct one another in communion. Wisdom discerns the mutual effacement of the uncreated and the created as profound self-emptying *kenosis,* glory manifest in the world but not of the world.

Glorification in Christ glorified sees glory pervading all in all, without interference from 'powers' of confusion, and without obstruction from 'powers' of separation. Glory has no degrees from God's side, because God is God and glory is glory, although there are degrees in the assimilation of glory from our side, glory purifying us, illumining us, and deifying us according to our measure and capacity. Glory is holistically divine-human, meaning that glorification steps back from interfering 'powers' of confusion and obstructing 'powers' of separation. The truth of this holistic wholeness is truly ineffable completeness.

53.

Christ in glory still asks, 'Who do you say that I am?' But the scope of this question rises as pedagogical resurrection ascends through anagogical ascension to the ineffable openness of glory as mystagogical glorification. Who is he as 'I AM,' revealed in glory, embracing all in glory without interference from confusion or obstruction from separation? Who is he as 'HE WHO IS: I AM?' Since he is who we shall be, can we say who we shall be, if 'I AM' in glory is ineffable? But we can say that we shall be as he is, and since he is in glory, we are obliged to consider mystagogical glorification. We can no longer ignore love's glory as we used to do. We cannot overlook deification, *theosis,* as we would perhaps prefer to do. We cannot stay in the narrows and shallows of fear, if love invites us to rise to love, and glory calls us to ascend to glorification, to the point of total self-emptying *kenosis.*

Glory reflects glory, from glory to glory, oneness in oneness, oneness in all, all in one oneness, all oneness in all. Doxological oneness is ineffable presence, revealed in glory as ineffable openness. It is discerned by wisdom as integral glorification, Orthodoxy raised and ascended in Christ into the glory and completeness it really is, but tries to avoid when wisdom is shunned. Wisdom has always known doxological Orthodoxy, and desires to unveil it to all. The prophet Elijah under-estimated the number in Israel who remembered God in his Name. He was told he was not alone. Many are saved on the day of the Name. The Spirit is poured out on all. The young prophesy, the old dream dreams and youths see visions. The Spirit opens Pentecost to all, unveiling glory in the Name. All who call upon the Name are saved. [38] The Name unveils Christ glorified as glorification of all in the Name. The scope of this glory is already expanding openness, unveiling new depths of presence and oneness in the Name. Who can say what it shall be? Wisdom knows that it is always an unveiling of who he is, 'HE WHO IS: I AM, before Abraham was.'

---

[38] See Joel 2: 28-32. Acts 2: 14-47.

54.

The mysteries of glory in Christ glorified are universal and personal, free of interference from confusion and obstruction by separation. 'Powers' of confusion can interfere, and 'powers' of separation can obstruct glorification if turning is shallow and incomplete, or if seeing is narrowed down to blind belief, bereft of wisdom, deaf to glory in the Name. Purification is narrowed when it is reduced to puritan prejudice, and illumination is watered down to shallow changes of opinion that fall short of transformation of heart. 'Powers' retain power over narrow and shallow religion, until wisdom is heeded. They recede to the extent that glory purifies and illumines religion. Glorification calls for the holy work of prophecy and prayer, which frees the heart from interference from confusion, and obstruction by separation. It stems from Christ glorified, as the Orthodoxy of glorification, grounded in illumination and purification through the Name.

Mutual reciprocal abiding of the uncreated and the created in Christ glorified, is a mutual reciprocal containment without interference from confusion, and a mutual reciprocal interpenetration without obstruction from separation. It embraces a mutual reciprocal inclusion free of interference from confusion, and a mutual reciprocal wholeness without obstruction from separation. The inclusion embraces all so that the wholeness heals all. The simultaneous interdependence of each in all and all in each, means that each includes all and all are wholly present in each, as well as all, without confusion or separation. Inclusion is integral and wholeness is personal in the mysteries of glory in union and communion.

Reciprocal mutual co-inherence means that glory is in each and all without interference from confusion or obstruction from separation. It is the radiant uncreated light of glory embracing all in each and each in all. The glory of Christ glorified shines forth in each and all. Completeness is simultaneous presence and primordial oneness in the ineffable openness of glory. Completeness is one in all and all in one as glory in the midst. The Name unveils the glory to wisdom in Christ, who shares it with one and all.

55.

Wisdom is primordial in scope and profound in depth, releasing bonds and dissolving fixations. Christ in our midst is a two-edged sword severing confusion to free separation. Glorification, beyond every contrived fabrication, gives glory to God. Wisdom infuses perception, without confusion with perception, being light in the world but not of it, glory in the midst but not confined by it. Glory has boundless capacity to permeate time and space with wondrous love. Christ unveils the Name 'I AM' to transmit wisdom. The Spirit descends to open the 'eye' of the heart. Saints turn and see God in the midst. The root of transmission is not magic words or miraculous powers. It is revelation of God in his Name.

Ineffable capacity and spontaneous potential unite in the wondrous openness of wisdom. The turning is crucial. Turning cuts through the delusions of confusion. Seeing releases the seizures and unties the knots of separation. Turning severs confusion to restore union. Seeing moves mountains of separation, to abide in unobstructed communion. Discernment frees union from interference from confusion. Wisdom liberates communion from obstruction by separation.

The Word reveals God in his Name. Christ would not be who he is if he were not 'I AM.' Hesychasm would not be a tradition of wisdom if 'I AM' was not uncreated light illumining the world. Glorification would not be the completeness of purification and illumination if the revelation of the Name in glory were not wisdom's key to Holy Orthodoxy.

Wisdom sees right through to the heart of freedom by surrendering whole-heartedly to the glory of the Name in the age to come. This bears witness to the Kingdom come and the mystery of the Holy of Holies. 'Powers' submit to the power of turning and seeing. The axial point of turning is uncreated light in the midst. The pivot is Christ, who is unveiling God's Name in the midst. The Name saves, which is what the name 'Jesus' means. Glorification draws on great freedom and great peace. The Holy Spirit comes with power, praying Christ's prayer for the salvation of all. Christ is in our midst. His wisdom stands steadfast.

56.

The wisdom injunctions at the heart of Hesychasm are: 'Turn and see.' Turning, *teshuvah,* is *metanoia,* that turns the inmost heart from addiction to the created, to freedom born of the uncreated in the midst. Seeing, *theoria,* is vision of God in uncreated light, 'I AM that I AM,' seer and seen in the midst. If we turn, 'powers' submit. If we see, 'powers' unravel. This is the medicine of immortality that cures addictive passions. This is the Holy Grail that is the fulfilment of all that we seek. Seeing is not visual perceiving, and yet wisdom infuses every perception with light from light. All the senses become really spiritual, once glorification begins to unfold the secrets of *theosis.* Deification unveils things as they are. Purification and illumination are not yet definitive. They unveil things as they seem along the way.

Desert wisdom has always centred on revelation of God in the heart. It has always listened to the still small voice unveiling the Name in the midst. It loves stillness because it hears the gentle whisper in the sanctuary. Since ancient times, wisdom in the wilderness has been a living witness to direct awakening, transcending indirect preoccupation with ways and means. Saint Antony went into the desert to know himself, discovering true knowledge of God. When he was followed into the desert, he resolved the doubts of seekers, because he had penetrated right through to the depths. Wisdom frees the heart from dithering, opening dissipation up to serenity and purity of heart. The desert insists that purity of heart is crucial for wisdom, but at the same time, wisdom is essential for purity of heart. Wisdom mothers purity of heart.

Elders do not cultivate a cult of themselves, surrounded by flattering disciples. They are doing their job when their disciples can safely function as elders, passing on without reserve what they have received without self-interest. When elders are in no hurry, it is because maturation in glorification is no small thing. Incompleteness is not yet balanced, but subject to extremes. It is wisdom that imparts completeness to incompleteness, beyond one-sided extremes.

57.

Unfathomable wisdom relies solely on the saving Name, not on clever innovations or sophisticated interpretations. Contrived contortions are no substitute for genuine wisdom. Glorification tempers and refines the heart so that turning freely turns and seeing freely sees. Glory purifies the heart by fire, tongues of flame inspiring an unceasing Pentecost of the heart. Glorification is the Name in act, actualizing mutual reciprocal co-inherence in glory in every dimension. Words and images serve transmission. They are not the quintessence of the way. Wisdom is uncreated creative energy, not psychic power. The transmission is in the Spirit through the Word. It is not something controlled by power hungry gurus, eager to sell 'power' to gain 'power.' Wisdom is not bought or sold. It flourishes in a culture of mutual love and respect, which is a culture of gift.

Wholeness has no boundaries. Completeness has no favourites. Wisdom shares her gifts with generosity, overflowing with divine abundance. The benevolence of wisdom is seen, and then believed. Administration in the Early Church was the task of bishops, priests and deacons, whereas elders imparted the Word that unveiled the Name in wisdom. Of course, clergy were often also elders, but their respective functions were not confused. Not all clergy functioned as elders, and not all elders were clergy. Not all clergy functioned as prophets, but elders revered prophecy as the inspiration of pure prayer.

Wisdom binds and looses from generation to generation, crystallizing dissipations and freeing fixations moment by moment. Patched robed solitaries bound and loosed the dolorous wounds of their times, ascribing all glory to God. Remembrance of God was their concern, not clever theories, *theoria* not theoretical speculations. They entered with wisdom into the Holy of Holies of the awakened heart, returning with the seal of wisdom to impart what they received. Informed opinion can be valuable in secular circles, but in the desert, wisdom not opinion is what counts. Christ glorified generates glorification, not sophistication, in the desert, nurturing wisdom that transmits the Name.

58.

Recognition frees immediacy to die, rise, ascend and glorify as only God can do. Christ includes us in his timeless immediacy, which mediates immediately in every dimension. We die, rise, ascend and experience glorification in his glory, partaking of his timeless immediacy. Wisdom penetrates right through to immediacy, free of interference from confusion and obstruction from separation. 'Powers' of confusion cannot interfere with wisdom. 'Powers' of separation cannot obstruct the glory of the Name. The Word unveiling Presence swallows up all trace of confusion and separation. The circulation of glory round the hallowed Name is infallible, freeing truth from delusion as it moves like a 'Chariot Throne' or sings like a 'Cherubic Hymn.'

Saint Antony transmitted wisdom in the desert that uncovered knowledge of God, at the heart of self-knowledge, without confusing the self with God. Saint Cuthbert communicated the power of the Name as wondrous healing, long after his many healings in the north were forgotten. The desert still lives from wisdom when it transmits the Name, as Archimandrite Sophrony bore witness in our time. "Now, O my Christ, in Thee and by Thee...NOW, I AM." [39]

Seeing turns towards God in the midst, whereas delusion turns away. Who is I AM? Who do we say he is, Christ in the midst? The question of 'I AM' is crucial for desert wisdom from the beginning. It is not the only way to voice wisdom, but it is immediate and direct. The fullness of the stature of Christ is transmitted as Christ glorified. Glorification is this mature fullness, reflecting as in a mirror the glory of the Name. The unveiled face of glory is revelation of the uncreated Face, the light of whose Countenance blesses all who hallow the Name.

---

[39] Archimandrite Sophrony *We Shall See Him As He Is*. 1988 p 234.

59.

Clear and free, seeing clears vision of confusion and frees wisdom of separation. Contrived concepts obscure the mysteries. Blind thoughts cloud the Spirit of Truth. When the blind persist in leading the blind, wisdom is exiled and returns to heaven from whence she came. Wisdom transcends conventional religion and sectarian narrowness. Glorification is not dragged back into the shallows and narrows of religion. Wisdom is never trapped in the narrows or condemned to the shallows, but frees into ineffable openness and descends into unfathomable depths. Wisdom is unpredictable as it binds what needs binding and looses what needs to be loosed. Glory transcends glory as we die, rise, ascend and glorify God in Christ glorified, ascending from glory to glory. But ascent is not 'superior,' inviting smug pride. It sees things as they are, and is really quite ordinary, once seeing is the norm and glory the air it breathes.

Glorification gives glory back to God in his Name, delivering glory from vanity to restore glory to the Name. Glory is like gold extracted from the lead of vainglory. It is gold hallowing the Name like a halo, glory glorifying the Name like a crown. Glory no longer falls short like vainglory does, but clarifies everything so that it rises and ascends as ineffable openness. Vainglory makes all efforts vain, because it is vanity going after vanity in vain. Seeing this, glory does not despair but ascribes glory to God, remembering God in his Name. The Spirit transmits glorification as the truth of the whole, handing on what before we could not bear to transcend or include. The Spirit comes to help us in our incompleteness, freeing us to live in the uncreated light of completeness.

Wisdom transmits light through light, glory through glory, as we ascend in Christ from illumination to glorification. Wisdom never lost the pearl of great price, or neglected the treasure of glory in the familiar field. But blind fear loses it and neglects the treasure of glory, afraid to lose control. Glory is love reaching down into the prisons of fear to free love from fear. Love hallows the Name to free love to heal terror. Love ascribes glory to God to free fear for wise love.

60.

The integrity of Christian wisdom is Christ, not the narrow and shallow versions of Christ that religion produces when it rejects wisdom. The integrity of desert wisdom is Christ glorified in the midst, inspiring glorification of God in the Spirit that unfolds glorification through God, in God. The integrity of integral Orthodox Christian wisdom is the integrity of God the Holy Trinity.

Wisdom is integral when it lives the integral uncreated creative energy of the Name as glory, glorifying the Father, through the Son, in the Holy Spirit. Integral glory is integral self-emptying *kenosis,* each divine person emptying self of self, inspired by love's glorification of the other, in mutual reciprocal glorification that never falls apart. The integrity of Christ glorified is the integrity of mutual reciprocal glorification by the Father of the Son in the Spirit, which answers the mutual reciprocal glorification of the Father by the Son in the Spirit. The integrity of glory in God holds steady between the Father and the Son, inspiring us, like the Spirit, to abide eternally in the Son.

The integrity of Christian wisdom is receptive to wisdom wherever wisdom is to be found. We see this when Jesus responds to the wisdom of Enoch, John responds to Temple wisdom in Jerusalem, Paul to Greek wisdom in Corinth, Clement and Origen in response to many traditions of wisdom in Alexandria, and the Fathers from Gregory of Nyssa to Denys and Maximus, to the different traditions of wisdom in Athens as well as Jerusalem.

The desert is heir to many traditions of wisdom, whose integrity is guaranteed by the integrity of glory in Christ glorified, which is the integrity of glory and *kenosis* in God the Holy Trinity. The integrity of Christian wisdom is Christ, but he welcomes wisdom wherever wisdom is to be found. He does the same in every age, opening the tradition to ineffable opening openness, whose integrity is assured. He is this integrity in his person, because Christian wisdom is the uncreated creative expression of his person, not some external conceptual system outside him. He is this integrity in 'I AM,' his ineffable *HYPOSTASIS,* and so in the Holy Name of God. He transmits his integrity in his Name, and the integral wisdom of glory in glorification.

61.

The integrity of Orthodox Christian wisdom differs from the integrity of other wisdom traditions, but this does not invalidate it or them. There are ineffable mysteries that are unique to Christ, just as there are ineffable elements that are unique to each of the other mystical traditions. Wisdom is not a universal metaphysics that stands above the traditions, reducing Christ to a peripheral phenomenon. The integrity of Christian wisdom is Christ, in whom wisdom from many wisdom traditions has been integrated over the centuries without loss of Christian integrity.

Living in a global world, we are now more aware of other traditions of wisdom, each of which has its own integrity, each of which is unique in different ways. Mature Orthodox Christian wisdom handles this global awareness with integrity, without confusion and without division, resonating with all wisdom in its own unique way. It is wisdom that is integral, not opinion, because opinions not only differ, but collide, conflict, and clash in all sorts of ways. Wisdom holds steady in Christ, neither seduced into confusion, nor deluded by division. Opinions are divided, but the integrity of Christian wisdom holds steady, free of interference from confusion and disintegration from division.

Wisdom is the state of *theoria* that sees God in the midst with God's 'eye' of the heart. It transcends form even as it utilizes form to express its ineffable insight. When the Fathers encountered wisdom in Plotinus, Christian wisdom was at home with what cohered with it, and so well able to baptize Hellenism without loss of Christian integrity. Many things were transcended, but wisdom from Athens was included with wisdom from Jerusalem, going back to the wisdom of the first Temple, including Apocalyptic as well as Pythagorian traditions drawn from the Temple. The subtlety and complexity of Patristic synthesis taxes even the most learned scholars. Desert wisdom focuses instead on the timeless integrity of the Name, Christ in the midst, and wisdom's discernment of glory at the heart of glorification. Grateful to the scholars, but concerned with living transmission, the desert hallows the Name so that glorification anchors purification and illumination in the integrity of Christ glorified.

62.

Wisdom sees the descent of glory as a new heaven and a new earth, a New Jerusalem, where God indwells each, and all indwell God, a Holy City, adorned with glory like a bride. Wisdom sees the glory of completeness at the beginning to be one with the glory of completeness at the end, the *Alpha* and the *Omega* of the Name. The 'overcoming' between the beginning and the end is seen in the Spirit as mutual reciprocal glorification of angels and saints, a Holy City of brilliant jewels, resplendent with crystalline glory, jasper, sapphire, chalcedony, emerald, sardonyx, carnelian, chrysolite, beryl, topaz, chrysoprase, jacinth and amethyst. Gates of pearl and streets of gold are lit by the glory of uncreated not created light, and wisdom flows forth from the throne as living water. Here, wisdom is a tree of life for the healing of all, and all those who have the Name on their forehead see the glory of the unveiled Face. [40]

Wisdom's vision of angels and saints in glory sees the heavens as a heaven of jewels, each jewel reflecting the glory of each, and all reflecting the glory of all. The infinity of this infinity of glory is wisdom's vision of glorification on earth as in the jewelled heavens. Since each is the reflection of glory in all, the glory of all is reflected in each. Mutual reciprocal glorification of all in each, and each in all, is also envisioned as a jewelled city, glory of all in each and each in all. The interdependence of each and all is seen as doxological co-inherence, *perichoresis,* where glory in each includes glory in all, beyond all interference from confusion or obstruction from separation. Glory is infinite as infinite glorification, once the 'powers' of confusion no longer interfere, and the 'powers' of separation no longer obstruct. Glorification reflects a boundless infinity of glory in each and all, imparting completeness of glory to all in each, reflected as completeness of glory embracing each and all.

---

[40] See Revelation 21:1-22:5.

63.

Glorification unveils ineffable glory in the Father, communicated as an expanding openness of glory in the Son, embraced as completeness of glory in the Holy Spirit. The way of glorification in Christ glorified is profound, veiled by symbolism and unveiled in silence. Scripture offers the symbols, wisdom the silence. Seers see through the symbols to the glory they veil, but are normally silent. The opening to openness is ineffable. Yet many saints have spoken nonetheless, unable, like Saint Silouan, to quench the Spirit or stifle prophecy. Others have felt obliged to speak, because their silence was being widely misunderstood. At a time when it is widely assumed Christ has no wisdom, the desert may be obliged to speak. Silence is read as assent. If there seems to be no Christian wisdom, little wonder many look elsewhere.

For some Orthodox, all talk of wisdom is heretical, and only ethnic loyalties and religious conventions can be trusted. For New Age seekers, this confirms their conclusion that Christianity is without wisdom. In such times, silence is read as agreement that both are right, and that Christ has no wisdom to offer, and the desert is bereft of wonder. So what do seers go into the wilderness to see? If Christ is not wisdom, why turn and see? If Christ is not glorified, what does wisdom see?

When the desert reluctantly but finally speaks, it does not profane the ineffable, preferring speech that encircles the ineffable as poetry or chant. It is mild in tone but fierce as fire, consumes confusion, sings to inspire. The way of glorification in Christ glorified discerns an infinity of glory in the Father, unveiled as ineffable openness of glory in the Son, and as a healing completeness of glory in the Holy Spirit. Mystagogical glorification in God descends to meet anagogical glorification of God in ascent. Heaven descends to answer earth's anagogical ascent as *theoria,* and pedagogical ascent as *metanoia.* Pedagogical turning weds anagogical seeing to enter the mysteries of mystagogical *theosis.* If Christ is without wisdom, Christianity is flat, narrow and shallow. There is neither ascent nor descent. But if wisdom opens the 'eye' of the heart, the desert sings.

64.

The remembrance of God is sustained by glorification of God, through God, in God, which is purification by fire, illumination through light, and glorification in glory. The trajectory of glory passes from a body of purity, born of turning, to a body of light, born of seeing, to a body of glory, born of glorification. In fact, it is not a question of three bodies, but of three spiritual stations in the spiritual refinement of one and the same body as it is purified, illumined and glorified. Glorification of God, through God, in God, purifies, illumines and deifies the whole Adam, body, soul and spirit.

Seers of God by grace, whose spiritual bodies are resurrected in Christ in purification, ascended with Christ in illumination, and glorified with Christ in glorification, experience deification as the deification of all in each, and each in all, calling for a body of translucence capable of reflecting glory like a heavenly jewel. Seers see the Son of Man in throne vision as embodied in rainbow light. The body of translucence is a body of rainbow light, luminous and glorious, like that of angels. The rainbow spectrum becomes visible on the cusp between uncreated light and uncreated glory, reflecting the whole spectrum of light like a body of rainbow light, a body of translucence. Primordially pure, the body of light is infused with glory, uncreated creative energy. Glory is like sunlight that shines on a pure and transparent crystal. The light refracts as rainbow light all round, but without light, the crystal is not translucent.

Remembrance of God is not perception of an external phenomenon, nor is it perception of a subjective phenomenon. It is recognition of God in his Name, beyond inner and outer phenomena. Remembrance of God refracts uncreated light as rainbow light when uncreated glory shines through the crystal of our primordial purity. It is not that we start seeing rainbows, anymore that saints see halos, but that symbols like the rainbow or the halo refract glory, so that seeing can see what seeing means. Symbols enable the ineffable to become articulate, giving pure energy voice and form. The body of light serves the saint, whose glorified life is a life of love, embracing each and all.

65.

Glorification is not constructed by us, but deconstructs us so that we become children of God by grace. The uncreated creative energy of glory can purify, illumine, and deify us, and through us, all that there is, once the obstacles of confusion and separation are disempowered. Transmission of the Name enables the uncreated energy of light to illumine us, and the uncreated energy of glory to deify us, but rites of Baptism and Chrismation can cure us only if the medicine of the remembrance of God is taken too. The injunction to turn and see reminds us that, without purification and illumination, rites of initiation are like medicine. Potentially effective, when applied, their power is unproven if the medicine is not taken.

Wisdom has the capacity, through the saving Name, to move mountains of separation and oceans of confusion at a stroke. Neglect has the capacity to shut the door on wisdom and the Name, so that mountains of separation and oceans of confusion remain. Glory is uncreated, so void of created characteristics, like uncreated light. Light and glory have great capacity to save and heal, but if we neglect wisdom, it is as if the Name had never been revealed. Inoperative religion cannot heal, but can do enormous harm when it is reduced to warring ideologies, each out for the kill. We cannot blame anyone but ourselves if religion is reduced in this way, yet religion is widely blamed, calling for wisdom to set things straight.

From the standpoint of glorification, purification and illumination are not stages in a temporal process, but energies of timeless presence. The completeness of glory shines forth directly from the Name, discerned by wisdom in the Holy of Holies. All extremism falls away when wisdom discerns glory. Glory is the completeness of *praxis* and *theoria,* so glorification is actually the foundation of purification and illumination, complete from the beginning. But this is hidden when time re-imposes succession, and purification and illumination are once more seen as stages on the way. It is distanced to the degree that incompleteness obscures completeness and external blessing replaces the purity, light and glory of the way.

66.

To depart in peace is to enter into rest in glory, and to enter into rest is to abide with the Spirit in the Son, on the inside of God the Holy Trinity. Oneness in spirit with the Son, in the Spirit, does not come and go as passing states of mind do. It is inherent in God in our midst and the Spirit abides therein. We are from God through the Son, and in him, we are returning. To abide, with the Spirit, in him, is to rest in peace, timeless in the glory of the Name. To abide in him is to die before we die, living Baptism as death in him, and resurrection in his timeless life. Life in Christ is timeless abiding in the oneness of the Father and the Son, which the Spirit does eternally, and we do in the Spirit, never wavering from the centre of all centres where all centres coincide. Angels and saints, without exception, are centred in the Name, with wisdom, experiencing glorification.

Before illumination, purification is seen as the accumulation of merit. Illumination sees purification as the *praxis* of *theoria*. Glorification sees both *theoria* and *praxis* as the uncreated activity of glory purifying and illumining the heart. Since wisdom must use concepts to communicate, there is always the possibility that concepts will usurp wisdom, which wisdom handles by shattering or melting conceptual opacity to let glory through. Fixed stages melt and shatter too, along with all conceptual fixation. Glory is timeless presence and spontaneous oneness in the ineffable openness of freedom, and incompleteness is the veil that unveils as well as veils completeness.

Gnomic literature bears witness to wisdom, not opinions about wisdom, but at the same time does not presume to usurp wisdom. It points to where wisdom is to be found, rather than talk about what others have said about wisdom. It is not opinion but wisdom that unveils the saving Name. Christ is the wisdom of God present in the midst. The words are fallible, provisional and inadequate. It is not the words but their meaning that opens the heart to the remembrance of God.

67.

Glory crowns the wisdom of the Name. The glory of Christ glorified never forsakes the wise hallowing of the revelatory Name. The Spirit crowns our spirit with a halo of truth that never withers. Hallowing flowers as saving completeness coming to heal our incompleteness in every moment. The experience of glorification is Cosmic Liturgy, hallowing the Name, revealing the completeness of Christ glorified in the course of a primordial Cherubic circular movement around God at centre. At the same time, glorification in the Spirit proceeds with the Spirit from the Father to abide eternally in the Son, his final rest. 'I AM' is the refuge of all who, in the Spirit, invoke the Name. Here, in 'I AM,' the Spirit abides. Here, as 'I AM,' the Spirit glorifies the Name. The Spirit is no stranger to the glory of the Name.

Love's glory understands love, because Christ glorified is indeed this perfecting love, communicating perfecting love as glorification. The Spirit loves the Son, inspiring love of the Son as love of wisdom, primordial philosophy, that loves wisdom with myth's love of symbols as well as religion's love of mysteries. Such love inspires spiritual filiation in 'I AM,' praying, *'Abba! Father!'* in the guileless Spirit, hallowing the Name. Wisdom turns and sees. Attention understands, praying, *'HALLELU YAH!'* The heart is a temple of the Name, the place of grace where the glory of wisdom is unveiled, and the seal of glory marked with the sign of the cross. Glory clothes angels and saints, sprinkling them with wisdom so that faces shine. Grace frees and glory, freely given, glorifies all who are hallowed by it.

Fear persecutes love and gratitude, but persecution cannot penetrate through to wisdom. Fear is stupid and does not realize that its machinations trap fear itself not love, leaving 'I AM' untouched. 'I AM' is at the end what 'I AM' is at the beginning, but in between there is time for 'powers' to inject confusion and separation. Interference and obstruction intervene until 'powers' are overcome. Wisdom overwhelms 'powers' in the glory of the timeless Name. Glory crowns 'I AM,' King in the Kingdom of God. 'I AM' reigns, here in the midst, hallowed and hallowing.

68.

Wisdom is light to the 'eye' of the heart, joy to the soul that awakens. Glory is generous in its nourishment of the fruits of glorification. Holiness is beautiful in the saints, and love of this beauty is love of wisdom. Glory can be rigorous but mercy is prior, preferring to cure terror with kindness than terrorize terror, which drives terror into more and more terror. Wisdom is wiser than fear, and imparts the completeness of glory to incompleteness, to cure fear with wise love. Wisdom leaves footprints of light for faith to follow, showing fear that love can be trusted. Temple wisdom knew that the Most High is seen by seers and known by knowers, for wisdom is loved and known by seers in the City of God.

The desert imparts temple wisdom through the Name, opening the Holy of Holies to hearts thirsty for right glorification. The Father of glory generates the Word of glory, in whom the Spirit of glory abides eternally in the Holy of Holies. Remembrance of God in his Name, as in the ancient invocation, 'HALLELU YAH!' glorifies God to undo fall from glory, strong in the power that overcomes 'powers' of confusion and separation. Seers open their hearts to the remembrance of God, watchful and vigilant, in case interference or obstruction begin to intrude. Love's glory hallows their lives as they ascribe glory through glory. Glory resurrects them to primordial purity so as to ascend with them to illumination. But glory does not stop at ascension. It descends from heaven like a bride, glorifying each and all. It descends even to the depths of hell, to raise the dead to life.

The secrets of glory remain hidden even in an age of transparency, because wisdom calls for seers to see and without seeing, glory remains veiled. Wisdom texts are accessible everywhere as never before, but the 'eye' of wisdom is not so easily for sale. Always on free offer, it remains a gift of the Spirit and a Charism of Grace, persistently overlooked in commercial worlds. Seers receive wisdom's 'eye,' when they give glory back to God, the glory that had fallen short. Wisdom empties us of self-obsession. It costs everything. Wisdom is loved and known in a desert culture of gift, generous and kind at the heart of the Name.

69.

Illumination ascends as union with Christ in ascension, whereas glorification descends in union with Christ in glorification, his descending bride. Glory's descent is from within, for glory is more inward to us than we are to ourselves. The union of the Father and the Son is accessible both as glory welling up from the deeps, and as glory descending from above, meeting where the Name unites heaven above with earth below, emptying hells beneath. Here in the midst, 'I AM is I AM,' consuming confusion to heal division, but enthroned off centre we are 'THOU' to God's 'I.' Prophecy bears witness that, 'THOU art my beloved son, by grace,' once we are no longer usurping God in the midst.

The Spirit abides in the Word that names the Name, one glory discerned in oneness by wisdom, where heavens coincide at centre, and glory unites with glory where all centres coincide. The seventh heaven is right here, where glory from above meets glory from the deeps, consuming confusion to heal separation. The nuptial union of 'THOU ART' with 'I AM' lies at the heart of the mysteries of the Song of Songs. Love's glory lies at the heart of wisdom and the Name, ascribing glory to God for everything. Glory falls short whenever vainglory substitutes something created in place of God in the midst. More radically, glory falls short whenever glory known is substituted for the glory to come, which transcends all we have known or can know.

Glory soars way beyond our grasp, leaving us baffled by its dance of veiling and unveiling. *Kabod, doxa, gloria* eludes our grasp, veiling unveiling from profaning. The ascent and descent are a *parousia* of glory, an advent coming that ever eludes curious scrutiny. The glory is of such abundance that it dazzles, again and again, calling abiding out into emigration, and emigration back into abiding. We are most ourselves when we are his, and we are poured out utterly into his outpouring love. The ebb and the flow of glory inspires unceasing prayer in the heart, ineffable but revelatory.

70.

There is a catholicity of love and a wholeness of glory that is wholly free of self-interest, being Christ in glory unveiled in glorification. The unattainable excess of glory spills out to embrace each and all, so that the experience of glorification is guaranteed and sealed. Always personal, glorification is nevertheless valid for each and all. Wisdom discerns glory in the Name, but increasingly is seen as folly in an age that neglects wisdom. As the folly of the cross, wisdom is unveiled in the guise of folly, turning the folly of rejection into its opposite. From Parsifal to Prince Myshkin, the fool proves wiser than conventional sophistry, holding the space for glory to be revealed.

Wisdom stands in awe before the wondrous glory revealed everywhere and in everything. Seer and seen are one in glory, one in each heavenly jewel and in all jewelled heavens, inspiring awed reticence in the sage. A jewelled wisdom was transmitted by the Greek Fathers to the Latins, by Denys and Maximus to Bonaventure and Eckhart, inviting us to turn and see. A rigorous critique of Gnosticism bequeathed key insights to the Cappadocian Fathers, and gave to Origen his vision of the spiritual senses in glorification. The transfiguration of inner vision is also a transfiguration of all the senses, glory turning every perception outside in and inside out.

For wisdom, glory is beautiful and loves beauty in each and all. Vision is light seeing light, glory seeing glory, not knowing how. Glory is everywhere and in everything, seeing glory everywhere and in everything, glory revealing glory to glory in each and all. Illumination beholds the light that illumines it, which helped the Fathers see in Christ the insight that glorification beholds the glory that illumines glorification. Glory, simple and luminous, flows through all things. It is not that light of glory is only present when it is seen. Rather, we are present only because, in light of glory, we are seen. Wisdom loves wisdom, now as then, but opinions that are incompatible with wisdom, conditioned by culture and convention, fall away.

71.

Love's glory is ecstatic, raising self-love out of self-interested vainglory into resurrected love that gives all glory to God. Purified love is disinterested, like God, illumined love is ascended love, infused with dispassionate freedom, whereas glorified love is ecstatic love, one with the glory of Christ glorified, love that lifts the self out of itself into love's glories, love that ascribes all glory to God. Glory crowns self-emptying love, adorning it with jewels of glorification, each of which overcomes confusion and separation in spiritual warfare for the crown. Right glorification purifies, illumines and glorifies love so that self-love is resurrected, ascended and glorified with Christ. The crown of true glory completes the Covenant of the Name as right glorifying love. The victory of love's glory is love that seeks not its own, giving glory in all through all to God.

The Name is imparted by the Word, opening wisdom's 'eye' of the heart in the Spirit, transmitting eternal life from the Father, the fruit of whose peace restores souls to freedom. Glory takes captive the captivity of confusion, freeing souls to follow in the footprints of light. Glorification graces hearts with love, grounding the way of wisdom on the rock of the Name. Wisdom enlightens the 'eye,' anoints the face with glory, restores paradise in the midst, and blesses every perception with fragrant remembrance of God. The Name interprets the beauty of glory, communicating the truth of love.

Wisdom is holy and without blemish, hallowing all who hallow the Holy Name. Right hallowing is right glorification of the Name of God, enchanting the heart with hallowing chants. Wisdom clothes the sun of illumination with the glory of uncreated creative glorification, ineffable openness unveiling the timeless presence of uncreated oneness, glory abiding in the Father through the Son. The Spirit proceeds from the Father to abide in the Son, inspiring our spirit to abide in the Son, giving glory to the Father. The Spirit knows the mysteries of glory from within, and transmits them in wisdom through the Name. 'I AM' mirrors glory by unveiling our face, so confusion is consumed. 'I AM' refracts glory by revealing God's Face, so separation is subsumed.

72.

Glory crowns wisdom, releasing glory from vanity in every perception, as it creatively creates all things new. Glory does not stray from wisdom's crown as it hallows the Name, unveiling glory in the Holy of Holies. Glory's crown is peace, blessing wisdom's work of peace, which begins with peace, in the Name, and in this peace, prays for the peace of each and all. The crown of wisdom work is peace, always already present in Christ as his peace, which passes all understanding. Peace is shattered when 'powers' interfere with it and obstruct it in subtle realms, the interface between the uncreated and the created. The fruit of wisdom work is peace, not as the world gives, but as God gives through his Son, discerned by the Spirit as the harvest of spiritual intercession. It is the work of glorification, which is not a reward for good behaviour, but a work of costly love on the front line of spiritual warfare. It is the work of glory descending to hell to empty hell of violence, to uproot violence by the root, undoing delusion and division.

Glory crowns wisdom with peace, not false peace such as the world gives, but sound peace, such as the Name reveals. Round, sound peace is the primordial ground of love of enemies, which is not shallow sentiment but the indivisible state of timeless peace that transmits peace even before it speaks. This is the serenity of which Saint Isaac speaks, the peace at the heart of stillness that transcends conceptual grip. It is this peace that makes peace upstream from war, attending the roots of violence beyond violence. The blessing of this peace is ineffable.

Glory crowns desert wisdom with peace in ways that remain hid with Christ in God, inaccessible to curious scrutiny. The Spirit intercedes for peace as the inspiration behind its unceasing prayer of the heart. It is the Spirit's prayer, not verbal prayer, which does not cease. It is the Spirit that interprets this prayer of tongues, tongues of fire consuming confusion and separation. It is the Spirit that discerns glory at the heart of love and opens the mysteries of glorification, whose crown is peace.

73.

The theological exegesis of the first Eucharist on Holy Thursday, the Crucifixion on Good Friday, the Descent into Hell on Holy Saturday, and the Resurrection of Christ at Holy Pascha, lies beyond the scope of one called to intercede in the desert. But unselfish love, which inspires glorification, falls within the scope and concern of desert intercession. The love of enemies that inspired Christ to be a curse for our sake and made to be sin for us, lies at the heart of the mysteries of intercession. The love that inspired Paul to pray in the Holy Spirit that he be cursed and cut off for the sake of his brethren, if his kinsmen are not saved, even though he knows nothing can separate him from the love of God in Christ, inspires love at the heart of glorification. The love that drove Moses to pray that he be blotted out of the book of life, if the sin of Israel's idolatry was not forgiven, is this same love, revealed in Christ. Such love chooses separation, to overcome separation. The vow to sacrifice one's own salvation for the salvation of others, is an expression of Christ-like self-emptying love. It lies at the heart of glorification. [41]

Saint Silouan was inspired to pray for the salvation of all, and to keep his mind in hell without despair, which together inspire prayer for all, and self-condemnation to hell that all may be saved. A lover's prayer for a beloved can reveal this same love, which freely loves to the point of separation, if only separation can be overcome by love. The heart of the mystery is love's love of the freedom of the beloved, even to the point of love's complete self-emptying. Love would be condemned to eternal self-contradiction if it did not love as Christ loved, and pray as Paul and Moses prayed. Love would not be love, if it did not hope and pray for the salvation of all. Love is obliged to hope for the salvation of all, and to love the beloved's freedom, even if it chooses to be lost eternally. If love were to withhold either love, the desert would be deprived of the love that pierces the heart and inspires love's intercession for all.

---

[41]   Galatians 3:13; Romans 9:3 and 8:39; Exodus 32:32.

74.

The sin against the Holy Spirit is separation that demonizes love, the separation that condemns to hell the love that overcomes separation. It is the inverse of Christ's love that freely condemns itself to separation if only love could overcome separation. The freedom of the beloved is loved to the point of complete self-emptying. God's free love freely acknowledges its limit, which is our freedom to reject it. True synergy demands this. It means God's omnipotence is not omnipotent. There is no limit to love's mercy, but love runs up against the freedom to choose to remain closed to love forever. It is possible to demonize grace out of ignorance, but it is also possible to demonize grace as demons do. Demons repel and demonize grace, or they would be angels. So love is condemned to suffer as it intercedes for the salvation of all, and to suffer when love is frustrated by the demonization of love. Can divine love outwit the demonization of love? Can the opposition of divine love and human freedom be overcome? They are eternally overcome in the love that knows no limit. They are eternally reconciled in the wisdom that discerns love's glory as hope.

Glorification is the holy work of glorification of God, through God, right at the heart of these difficulties, these *aporia*. It is prayer in the Spirit at the heart of the conjunction of love and freedom. It is intercession for all who suffer separation out of despair, despair that separates separation from any hope of overcoming separation. It is prayer for all who in ignorance, or delusion, sin against the Holy Spirit. Demonization is rife, and it often does not know what it is doing. So who will pray for those who demonize love? Who will pray for those who despair of all hope of overcoming separation, for those who let separation separate them from all hope of deliverance from separation? At the heart of these hells, separation is closed to love, inseparably bound to separation against all love or hope. Glorification is one spirit, one indivisible activity, with the love that never despairs. It prays for all out of love for all, and hopes beyond hope that all shall be saved. There are no limits to such love from God's side, and love's prayer undoes all limit from ours, wooing freedom at the heart of separation. Glorification is love's prayer for all in all.

75.

In the Odes of Solomon, Christ says, "I opened the gates that were shut; and I broke in pieces the bars of iron. My fetters grew hot and melted before me, and nothing seemed to me to be shut, because I was the opening of everything." [42] He also says his prayer was his love, releasing the prisoner's bonds. Such prayer, inspired by the Spirit, inspires intercession in the desert in the spirit of liberating openness. Ineffable openness is eternally open to love's openness to love, eternally overcoming separation at the heart of separation. Eternal oneness is eternally one with love's overcoming of separation at the heart of separation. Uncreated presence is eternally present at the heart of separation, overcoming separation. So when love assumes separation to overcome separation, separation dissolves. When oneness assumes confusion to cure confusion, confusion is released. When presence assumes absence to undo absence, absence transmutes into ever present completeness.

In troubled times, when elders are few and far between, prophecy introduces the Name directly, rather than as a mode of devotion to elders, which can be abused. 'I AM' is Christ in the midst, and devotion to him is safe from abuse when no one usurps him. 'I AM' is primordially pure, present everywhere, and permeating all things. There is no projection of an objectified subject, object or inter-subjective 'me,' 'it' or 'us' in 'I AM,' so all basis for abuse is consumed. Christ's humility cannot be compromised, which wisdom sees as way, truth and life, curing vainglory and pride. The glory of the Name is not something to be attained, but the uncreated light of 'I AM,' which is the uncreated completeness of the age to come. Its presence is 'I AM: HE WHO IS, WHO WAS, WHO IS TO COME,' not an objectified deity or an objectified subjectivity, subject to confusion and separation. 'I AM' is the opening of everything to ineffable, un-objectified openness.

---

[42]   Odes of Solomon xvii 8-10 Tr. J A Emerton, Apocryphal Old Testament, Ed. Sparks Oxford 1984.

76.

The glory of the Name is prior to the arising of elemental energies, the fire of earth, the fire of water, the fire of fire, the fire of air and the ethereal fire, and so prior to the separation of subject and object. Everything comes from 'I AM,' but 'I AM' has no beginning. 'Before Abraham was, I AM.' The Name purifies everything but itself requires no purification. Wisdom illumines everything but itself requires no illumination.

When wisdom is neglected, *praxis* is cut off from *theoria,* and is reduced to ascetic labour that seeks to be worthy of *theoria* as merited reward. For wisdom, the *praxis* of *theoria* is the way truth is lived, because 'I AM' is way, truth and life. For glory, glorification is right glorifying *praxis* of 'whole-eyed' *theoria.* This 'Orthodox' *praxis* of 'Catholic' *theoria* is the realization of the body of glory, the prophetic word that embodies glory, and pure prayer that assimilates the mind to the Mind of Christ glorified, which is the Mind of Scripture, the Mind of the Fathers and the Mind of the apostles, prophets and saints. This Mind of glory is 'Orthodox' and 'Catholic' in the original and primordial sense, which reveals 'right glorification' in full 'accordance with the wholeness' of the whole.

Glorification no longer handles passions as poisonous enemies that require future purification or transformation, but as glory releasing poisonous enmity into glory as pure energy, glory that spontaneously gives glory to God. The vanity of poisonous passions is liberated by the Name into glory, so vainglory is no longer vainglory but radiant glorification of God. The key to right glorification is the remembrance of God in his Name. The key to wholeness is 'whole eyed' seeing that turns and beholds God in the midst. It is this that reveals the body of light, which glory unveils as the body of glory. Glory releases the passion of anger, for example, into lucid clarity, and self-love into compassion, releasing energy from interference from confusion and obstruction by separation. Glory crowns wisdom in the kingdom of the Holy of Holies. Glory releases all that arises in the ineffable openness of the hallowed Name.

77.

The offering of the prophet is the ascending word that names the Name, bringing illumination, and of the priest the descending glory that crowns wisdom, glorification. The Name is sealed until wisdom opens the seal in the heights, as illumination, and the glory is veiled until the Spirit awakens the heart in the depths, as glorification. The Name and wisdom meet in the Holy of Holies, hidden with Christ in the Father, in whom the Spirit reclines eternally, one breath, one inspiration, one life. The uncreated light of the Name is everywhere present, in the Spirit, inspiring prophecy, fulfilled in the Anaphora of glory that crowns wisdom, inspiring priesthood, in the Eucharist. Prayer fulfils the offering of the prophet in prayer of the Name, and the offering of the priest in prayer of the heart. The prophet-priest prays the prayer of the Name in the heart as the remembrance of God in glory, uniting ascent and descent, illumination and glorification. Ascent and descent unite as one divine-human energy, consuming confusion and separation.

The Name and wisdom are one in an ineffable mystery of union and communion at the heart of ascent and descent. Transcending purification and illumination as way or means, glorification lives the union of Name and wisdom, not as confusion or separation, but as communion in Christ glorified. Beyond all ways and means, union of Name and wisdom crowns all ways and means with jewel-studded glory. The jewels are the particular unions and the gold is the radiant communion that crowns wisdom with the Name. Jewels are glorified stones and gold is glorified lead, but for glory, purification and illumination are instantaneous revelations of glory. Glory cuts through confusion and leaps over separation, freeing the jewels from interference and the gold from obstruction. Glory sees everything as wisdom, whilst wisdom sees everything as glory. This wondrous secret remains hidden, with Christ, whose glory remains veiled, until God is seen in the midst, through the Name.

78.

Glorification is transfiguration of transparent translucence. Everything is a crown of wisdom in the Name. Wisdom sees the body is transparent, the soul is translucent and the spirit is transfigured in the uncreated light of the glory of Christ glorified. Purification unveils transparency, illumination translucence, and glorification transfiguration, though in transfiguration, transparent translucence is instantaneous. Glory is sudden, from a temporal point of view, and timeless, for eternity. The age to come is always now, for wisdom and the Name. We live in time, but completeness of glory is timeless. There has always been a critical tension between time and the timeless. The antinomy is irreducible. The dilemma is irresolvable, from below. Indivisibility is effortless, from above. We live divine humanly, as timeless and in time.

The Name is the supreme path to liberation. Wisdom is the uncreated light that illumines apostles, prophets and saints. The wisdom of the Name is the universal *logos,* which inspires Scripture and the Fathers. 'I AM' cannot be objectified, being ineffable and incomprehensible. The 'eye' of the heart really sees that there is nothing created to see in the midst. Seeing God in his Name is seeing, by grace, with wisdom's eye of omniscience. It sees the omnipresence of glory. It does not make seers into 'know-alls', because information is not wisdom. The completeness of glory frees hearts from the stress of effort and the strain of struggle, replacing them with uncreated grace and healthy synergy.

Wisdom knows that the scope of Christ glorified infinitely transcends the many versions of pre-modern Christendom, modern Christianity and post-modern Christianness, which, in different ways, have attempted to approximate to him, but it does not follow that the scope of any version of Christianity is destined to close the gap. The boundaries are there, on the relative plane, even though wisdom discerns Christ way beyond them. As wisdom, Christ is all wisdom, and the scope of wisdom transcends all formulations and expressions in this or any age. The integrity of Patristic wisdom holds steady, anchored in the Name.

79.

The glory of the Name liberates elder and disciple into ineffable openness, with infinite capacity to cure the plethora of pathological parodies of eldership that threaten to subvert the transmission of wisdom and the Name. Genuine transmission has various viruses to contend with, many of which substitute the word that unveils the Name with relative opinions on relative matters, that have nothing whatever to do with spiritual transmission. Many kinds of pathological subservience usurp genuine obedience, and many forms of pathological abuse parody genuine transmission of the Name.

Wisdom is essential to discern the difference between parody and tradition, but we should not despair, for every age has had its Simon, who presumes to buy and sell the Spirit to gain power, but tradition has survived. [43] Power and money is not the only parody. In monasticism, there is power and status in the community, power and flattery, and many varieties of power and vanity that subvert the tradition with parodies. In the desert, elders would often flee deeper and deeper into the wilderness, but found that it was wisdom, not geography, that cured the virus. The remedy lay in the remembrance of God and hallowing the Name, together with confession of thoughts, humble fellowship and holy humour.

Wisdom not only shows up fallibilities and flaws but reveals the Name that heals them. After all, it is Christ, not a fallible teacher, who is the way, which is why the tradition looks to him, not gurus, and abides in him, like the Spirit, in timeless freedom. In a healthy culture of humility and openness, the pathologies are acknowledged and diagnosed, remedied and cured. It is no surprise that a secular culture has difficulties sustaining wisdom, given wisdom's apparent fragility in the face of overwhelming 'powers.' But appearances are deceptive. Wisdom is timeless overwhelming of all 'powers.'

---

[43] See Act 8: 9-25.

80.

Wisdom is infinitely generous and of boundless capacity to embrace our incompleteness with the glory of her completeness. But the human receptacle differs in its capacity to reflect the uncreated light of wisdom. Capacity for glory is rarer than capacity for light, and capacity for light rarer than capacity for limpid purity, but glory is the key to a balanced encompassing of the mysteries of the Name. For this reason, Christian wisdom looks to Christ's capacity, as the Son, which it is the capacity of the Spirit to reveal, to unveil the ineffable capacity of the Father, rather than the capacity of human receptacles to discern the balanced completeness of the glory of the Name. So although the way is said to unfold as purification, illumination and glorification, it is glorification that reveals completeness, always already present in purification and illumination. It is glorification that reveals things as they actually are.

Wisdom is ahead of us, discerning the glory to come, not just what our incomplete capacity is capable of including. The gift of wisdom inspires prophecy that says, 'Come and see! Come up higher! There is more to this than meets the eye. Permit the Spirit to open the 'single eye.' Awaken to the body of light. Awaken to the glory of the age to come. Turn and see the completeness of glory in the Name. We may be flawed, we may be fallible, but wisdom is neither in the hallowed Name. For completeness, all is always very good, for in the Spirit, evil releases into good. In the Name, delusion is no more.'

Wisdom's gift sees ahead, and so is able to discern our destiny of glory. When we disdain wisdom, we no longer see ahead, and so see only what is right in front of our noses, and we overlook the glory that is present even there. Those who insist that wisdom is heresy are blind, and the ditch for them is all there is. If the blind were humble, there would be grounds for hope. But if pride is blind, there is no way out of the ditch. Wisdom sees and weeps, interceding in the Spirit for the blind to see. But wisdom is kind, and does not impose. Wisdom is gentle, and waits for us to turn and see. The 'converted' are sometimes the last to turn, the last to see. But wisdom prays for all, that all may see.

81.

Wisdom discerns the way of glory in the Name, that is always already the timeless completeness of 'I AM.' The way of glory is Christ glorified, and he is even now the completeness that wisdom knows and loves, beyond all ways and means. Glory cuts through confusion that sets cause apart from effect, means apart from end. Glory leaps over separation that seeks to overcome confusion and separation by adopting ways and means.

The way of glory sees things differently from all ways that cling to means, and so separate way from truth, and truth from life. Ways that cling to means live as if Christ was not yet glorified, not yet the way of truth and life. Ways that cling to ways as well as means live as if Christ is not yet ascended, and so no ascension is yet in view. Ways that cling compulsively to ways and means live as if Christ is not yet risen, and resurrection is out of the question for us too.

Separation separates way from truth and truth from life, clinging to ways and means. Wisdom sees through separation to the glory that dissolves it, extinguishing confusion instantaneously. Wisdom sees the way of glory in Christ glorified, always already present in the glory of completeness, always already present in the oneness of the glory of 'I AM.'

Wisdom sees Christ in glory beyond all means and ends. Wisdom sees Christ resurrected and ascended, beyond cause and effect. Wisdom sees in glory that 'I AM' is from 'I AM,' in 'I AM,' beyond all ways and means. Wisdom abides in the glory of the Holy Trinity, beyond all means and ends.

The Spirit proceeds from the Father to abide in the Son, completeness which wisdom discerns as her eternal home. Wisdom abides here at centre where the Spirit abides, replete with completeness. She abides here at centre where all centres coincide, imparting completeness to incompleteness. She abides here in glory, beyond all ways and means, where completeness embraces incompleteness as intrinsic to her dynamic expression.

82.

The wisdom of the death of Christ lies in the Word that is not a word, which is the revelation of the Name, which is not a name, in the silence, *hesychia,* of death and burial, the silence of the death of God. Death is death, here, and speech falls silent. The Word is immortal, revealing the Name, which is immortal, but here, on the cross, he dies, is taken down and buried. Glory descends to die so that death ascends to glory. Words are silenced when speech passes beyond speech, and the temple veil is torn from top to bottom. But the last word before silence was the cry, 'My God, my God, why hast thou forsaken me?' Flowing forth from silence, blood and water pour from the pierced side, and wisdom beholds the silence of this piercing as her own silent piercing, her discernment of love's glory. The glory of this love silently undoes separation at the point of extreme separation, so that wisdom's blood and water flow forth. The veil is rent so separation is no more.

The pierced heart is wisdom's outpouring in the mysteries, water and blood, Baptism and Eucharist, initiation and union, illumination and glorification. The *kairos* of glory completes chronological times and reveals completeness in timeless silence, beyond all words and names. The *kairos* of 'I AM' saves, piercing in the midst, beyond all ways and times. The 'body' of glory is the 'bride' of 'I AM,' the 'Amen' of synergy with the hallowed Name. Quantitative time, *chronos,* is shattered by qualitative time, *kairos,* which is the timeless presence of glory now, a deposit or pledge of glory to come.

Christ died for all so all are dead to death and alive to the glory of resurrection, ascension and glorification in the Kingdom come. He shatters separation, so all are dead to separation in the age to come. He extinguishes confusion, so all are dead to confusion in realms of glory. Time is no longer our own, but Christ's, just as being is no longer our own, but God's, the inter-being, well being and eternal being of Christ in us. Christ's time is not our time, and his being in not our being, yet in wisdom we are his. His time is ours in the Name, his being is ours in wisdom. The glory of Christ glorified is grace and truth to all who are obedient to the glory of self-emptying love. Glorification is this *kenosis,* this 'Amen!'

83.

The wisdom of Christ glorified is a wisdom of veiled hiddenness at the heart of revelation. The veiling protects the unveiling from profane scrutiny. The wisdom of the cross provokes scandal and contradiction in that the seeming folly of hiddenness is deemed wiser than sophisticated sophistry. The wisdom of veiled hiddenness discerns and yet protects the destiny of glorification. It uncovers the hidden depths of the Son's generation from the Father, discerned by the Spirit, who abides in him eternally. The Spirit proceeds from the Father to abide in the Son, so when wisdom becomes one spirit with the Spirit to search out a dwelling place for wisdom, its home is the glory of the Father's indwelling of the Son.

Christ is wisdom's home of glory, who is home of our glorification too. The Father vests us in the glory that belongs to God alone, and it is the glory of his Name that is our home of glory in the Name. Wisdom's orientation is glory, but grace is not abused. Glory never violates divine ineffability or human freedom, but calls for graced synergy. It is the Spirit who imparts wisdom to discern the grace of glorification. Without this gift of the Spirit, we would not understand the glory of grace. Those who say wisdom is heretical do not understand what they are saying. Not only do they not understand the function of wisdom, they do not understand grace or glory either. It is wisdom's function to discern grace and glory, and neglect of wisdom deprives grace and glory of what discerns them.

Patristic wisdom is indispensible to all who seek to interpret the wisdom of Scripture and the wisdom of Christ glorified. The wisdom of the cross is crucial for all three. There is no confusion between uncreated wisdom and created intelligence or intellectual acumen. To confuse them is sophistry. There is nothing wrong with intelligence; it is sophisticated confusion that leads astray. Natural intelligence cannot see or hear uncreated wisdom. It is God who sees and it is God who is seen in *theoria*. Uncreated wisdom is always folly to all who do not turn and see. Genuine wisdom is *theoria* awakened by genuine *metanoia,* quickening seers of God, making us like him, when we see him as he is.

84.

The ineffable openness of glory is hidden until the glory of Christ is seen. The hiddenness of glory on the face of Moses is transcended only when the uncreated light of glory is seen and acknowledged. The temporal gospel unveils it in time and the eternal gospel unveils it in timeless presence, and so in ineffable openness. Uncreated light is unveiled as the radiance of uncreated love, and uncreated love as the glory of ineffable openness. The saints do not preach themselves but Christ, and him glorified, as timeless presence, uncreated oneness and ineffable openness. Transfigured openness of glory is the consummation of the ineffable union of purifying transparent presence and luminous translucent oneness.

The earthen vessel is flawed and fragile in different ways, but this does not invalidate the transfigured openness of glory, or its roots in transparent translucence. We ascribe the abundance to God, not ourselves, because our weakness is obvious. The limitations of the receptacle bear witness to the openness of the glory, proving it is the glory not the receptacle that is glorious. Christ in glory is revealed in the Spirit to be ineffable openness, transfiguring all who are transparent and translucent in him. We no longer know him after the flesh, but in resurrection that purifies us, ascension that illumines us and glorification which glorifies us. Crucified for all, he is risen for all, ascended through all, glorified in all. All this he offers to the Father in all and for all.

Love's glory is unveiled precisely where it is most veiled, overcoming separation precisely where separation overwhelms. The hiddenness of glory in ineffable openness reveals completeness in incompleteness, inseparability in separation, indivisibility in division. The cross and glory are inseparably one in this oneness. Hiddenness and revelation are indivisibly one in this oneness. Humble hiddenness and wondrous openness co-inhere in glorious oneness. The oneness of the unveiled face of glory is wondrous openness. The Father of glory generates great openness in the Son, imparted through the Spirit as he abides in the Son, proceeding from the Father to ensure this abiding. We abide in his abiding.

85.

Wisdom discerns the glory of the Name, and discovers it is self-emptying love. The glory of Christ glorified is kind, unselfish love. Glory is not something that makes someone special, seductively separating someone from others. Glory is not something special at all, and so provides no grounds for jealousy or pride. Glory is not self-love, which springs from confusion between oneself and God. Vainglory is boastful, arrogant and rude. Vainglory always insists on its own way, and is easily irritable and resentful. Vainglory is envious and overjoyed when things go wrong for the one it envies. Glory cures vainglory of vanity by consuming the confusion at the heart of vanity. Glory empties vainglory of pride by overcoming separation wherever love turns. Unselfish love bears all things, believes all things, hopes all things, and endures all things.

Wisdom discerns the glory of the Name to be self-emptying love that has no end. Prophecies pass away. Even prayers cease, but the prayer that is unceasing is the prayer of the Spirit in the awakened heart, which is unceasing love. Love intercedes for all, that all shall be saved, because the energy of the Name is love, desiring that all shall be saved. The Name is saving. Saving is what the Name does, so self-love finds nothing to get hold of. Prayers pass away, but love's unceasing prayer for all does not. Such love never ends. Prophecies and prayers are imperfect, so pass away when the perfect completeness of love's glory comes.

The Apostle Paul imparts wisdom to the perfect by unveiling love's glory. He reveals glorification to illumination by unveiling love's glory face to face. Illumination does see, but as in a glass darkly. Wisdom sees glory face to face as self-emptying love. Wisdom knows glory as glory is fully known. Illumination knows in part, but glorification is love, love that knows completeness, as completeness can alone be completely known, not as sophistry, but as unselfish love. Wisdom discerns love to be wholly worthy of trust. Even hope gives way to love, for love abides at the heart of love between the Father and the Son. The Spirit proceeds from the Father to abide in the Son, that we too may abide where love abides, where love's glory is self-emptying love.

86.

Wisdom is Christ, whose wisdom is his Father's wisdom, the wisdom of God. Christ lays no claim to be sufficient unto himself, humanly speaking. His Covenant of the Name is Spirit that gives life. The face of law was veiled, the face of temporal gospel is unveiled in part, whereas the face of eternal gospel is unveiled, so that sclerosis of heart is healed. It is the Name that removes the veil. It is wisdom that turns and sees. When turning turns to 'I AM' and sees, the veils are removed. The Spirit knows 'WHO HE IS.' Wisdom sees 'HE WHO IS,' and knows that 'I AM' saves. Where the Spirit is unveiling the Face of 'I AM,' freedom reigns. Wisdom beholds the unveiled Face of 'I AM,' whose glory is the image of God transforming us from glory to glory, into greater and greater likeness to God. Wisdom discerns in 'I AM' the glory that glorifies all who ascribe all glory to God.

Wisdom commends herself as Christ's wisdom, which is veiled until the 'eye' of the heart is opened. The spiritually blind have not yet seen the uncreated light of the eternal gospel of glory, because the 'eye' of their hearts is still blind. Wisdom is not personal opinion. Wisdom is vision of God in his Name. Wisdom sees Jesus is 'I AM.' Wisdom is witness that uncreated light shines to illumine the heart, and that light is uncreated glory in the unveiled Face of 'I AM.' Wisdom is witness that it is the glory of God that vision sees, unveiled in the Face of 'I AM.'

Wisdom also knows we have these treasures in earthen vessels, so that we are a living witness that glory is God's, not our own. Our lives are not our own, but God's. The glory is not our own, but God's, so glorification extinguishes all that is not God's in us. All is to the glory of God, here, where the Name is hallowed and the Kingdom is God's. The eternal weight of glory is discerned by wisdom and imparted as the eternal gospel of glory in the Name. The temporal gospel absorbs what it can within the limits of time, separated by past and future. The eternal gospel opens to the timeless presence of oneness and ineffable openness of glory in the Name. It deepens our awareness of what hallowing means, and opens us more deeply to the Name through wisdom.

87.

When Orthodox Synods seek to curb what they see as the excesses of sophiological speculation and monastic devotion to the Name, they can sometimes leave an impression that wisdom and the Name are somehow suspect, even heretical by default. On the other hand, were Orthodox Tradition to despise wisdom and quench all love of the Name, it would deprive itself of all connection to its mysteries, which might leave ethnic religion intact, but destroy all basis for purification, illumination and glorification in the Name. It would deprive Orthodox Tradition of its heart, which ethnic religion might not notice, but the desert would experience as destruction of all that it loves. Love of wisdom and love of the Name are not universally seen to be the heart of the Orthodox Tradition, but the Hagiorite Tome is clear that they are the living heart of Hesychasm. Desert Wisdom and stillness are contested, but this is nothing new, for they have been signs of contradiction in every age.

When Desert Tradition insists on love of wisdom and the Name, refusing to confuse excess with the wholeness of the original, it holds open the sacred space for wisdom to discern the glory of the Name. It lets the Spirit impart wisdom, inspired by its mutual reciprocal abiding in the Son, which unveils revelation of the Father in his Kingdom. Without this, ethnic cohesion can survive, but not Orthodox Tradition.

The Synods do not intend to despise wisdom or quench the Spirit that inspires living transmission of the Name. They seek to preserve Orthodoxy from extremism, not to stifle it at source. But to cure the excesses of extremism, wisdom is required, and the communion that frees union in the Name. So the Synods need to draw on wisdom and the Name, in order to heal the excesses of extremism, which may occasionally threaten to subvert wisdom and the Name. In the last analysis, it is wisdom that cures sophistry and the Name that cures idolatry. It is Desert tradition that has the remedies to cure occasional excesses, which may sometimes arise on the periphery of wisdom and the Name. It was Synods that canonized the Hagiorite Tome, so it is no surprise that Synods were convoked at a time when wisdom and the Name were attracting opinionated extremes.

88.

Glory is ineffable in everything and everything is ineffable in glory. The Name is consuming fire of glory in the midst. Confusion and separation burn, leaving union and communion unconsumed. Wisdom begins with a burning bush, with the ineffable mysteries of the Mother of God. By the end, we come full circle, renewed anew at the end, as in the beginning. The Name is God's self-revelation in the midst, revealing where God is to be found. Glorification comes full circle, extinguishing at centre all that is not glorification of God. The Name turns us round so seeing sees. Purification restores the primordial awakened state of grace, so that illumination renews all things in vision of uncreated light. The Name turns us back so glory unveils the mysteries of the Holy of Holies. As in the beginning, so at the end, glory rounds all round with glory, embracing all that has arisen in between.

Wisdom sees glorification as grace of uncreated presence communicating glory as deifying oneness, inspired by the Spirit's eternal abiding in the Son. The Spirit proceeds from the Father, to abide in the Son, unveiling the love of the Father for the mutual indwelling of the Spirit and the Son. Glory is ineffably present everywhere, embracing the glorified as ineffable openness. Love's glory is shared with wisdom. Wisdom shares it in the Name.

Life unfolds like a prayer rope of twelve centuries, beginning with the Name. It is love's wondrous presence and holy wisdom embracing mysteries of glory, and the completeness of glory in wise stillness. Wisdom steps back into wise wonder unveiling the wonders of wisdom. She is the wisdom of prophecy and prayer. Coming full circle, her completeness is once again the wisdom of glory and the Name, but it has embraced everything in between. It sees completeness in the incompleteness of all that lies between. It sees perfection in wisdom's embrace of flawed imperfection, as it embraces separation to cure separation. Wisdom embraces incompleteness, to raise incompleteness. She descends to incompleteness to ascend to completeness. She eventually sees incompleteness as integral to an unfolding revelation of the wisdom of completeness.

89.

Completeness of glory is ineffable openness revealed in the mutual glorification of the Father and the Son, union in the Name as luminous oneness, unveiled in the glory of this union before the foundation of the world, and communion in wisdom, mirroring the glorious presence of the Spirit in the Son. Nothing wavers from glory anywhere, when it is centred in God the Holy Trinity, where glory is ineffably complete. Christ does not seek his own glory but ascribes all glory to the Father, veiling yet unveiling that this is also true of the Father and the Spirit. Each is hidden in himself, revealed in the other, unknown to us in himself, known only through the other. Glory is seen in signs, in Saint John's Gospel, but the vision of Christ glorified remains hidden until after he is risen and ascended. It is consummated in the remembrance of God in his Name, humanly in the death of Jesus, divinely in the revelation of glory. Love's glory is the Cross, the extremity of love's human ascent and divine descent from glory to glory.

Love's glory is revealed in the hour of glorification, which is the Cross, when his own received him not. Love comes to save, not to condemn. The Spirit is witness to this love at the nodes, which are everywhere. The Spirit sees the ultimate unveiling precisely at the nodal point of the veiling of the glory of love. The light of love unveils the depths of hell, the rejection of love. There is no dialogue here, where love's glory meets no interlocutor. Christ imparts eternal life by opening hearts to the glory of 'I AM,' which is the heart of the reciprocal indwelling of the Father and the Son, and the heart of the reciprocal indwelling of the Spirit and the Son. The Paraclete beholds the pierced heart to be the unveiling and the veiling of wisdom, the unveiling of the Name, and the veiling that protects the Name from being taken in vain.

The pierced heart is the womb of the Spirit, the poverty that offers God true glorification, *doxazein,* in the sphere of glory between the Father and the Son, which is unveiled also between the Spirit and the Son. Glorification is the gift of wisdom flowing from Christ's pierced heart, opening hearts to God's ineffable openness of glory.

90.

The Paraclete opens hearts to glory with tongues of flame, which reveals the Spirit's glorification of the Father in the Son. The Spirit eternally proceeds from the Father to abide in the Son, revealing the glory of self-emptying love. The Spirit does not seek his own glory, but the glory of the Father in the glory of the Son, which is the glory of reciprocal indwelling and abiding.

Christ goes away so that the Spirit can come, as the Spirit of truth, to guide glorification into all truth. All truth is whole truth, divine human truth, mirroring truth of Holy Trinity. It is the Spirit who discerns that the poverty of the Son gives all glory to the Father, and that this poverty is none other than the completeness of his glorification of God as God, which embraces all incompleteness. It is the Spirit who reveals that God's answering glorification of Christ, in whom we are all glorified, is the completeness of Holy Trinity.

It is the Spirit who searches out the ineffable depths of openness in the oneness of light and presence of glory in the Name. There would be no mysteries of light or glory if the Spirit did not open them through wisdom and the Name. It is the timeless Pentecost of the Paraclete who unveils them in tongues of flame. It is the Spirit's unceasing prayer of the Name in the heart which sustains revelation in prophecy and prayer. The Holy Spirit is key to the wisdom of Christ crucified, consuming confusion and dissolving division. The fall from glory is undone when 'powers' of confusion no longer interfere, and 'powers' of separation no longer obstruct union and communion in the Name.

Wisdom chooses us in Christ before the foundation of the world. Love's glory is our destiny, which is glorification by the glory of grace, giving glory back as glorification to praise the glory of grace. Wisdom is glory, freely giving glory away to the glorified, as the glory of uncreated grace pouring out grace with immeasurable abundance. Love's glory is ineffable openness, illumined by the uncreated oneness of the Father and the Son, glorified in the abiding presence of the Spirit in the Son. The Holy Trinity is mutual reciprocal glorification of God, through God, in God, transmitting wisdom in glory, through glory, to all, hallowing the Name.

91.

Jesus transmits wisdom to Mary Magdalene in resurrection, as 'Touch me not,' purifying sense perception of confusion. He transmits wisdom in ascension, as 'Touch me not,' illumining the *nous* in the heart to heal separation. He transmits wisdom in glorification, as 'Touch me not,' to glorify the whole Adam and to deify all things in the Name.

Mary Magdalene was the first to see Christ risen, the first to bear witness to the resurrection, and so was apostle to the apostles on the first Sunday of *Pascha*. She awakens to noetic vision of Christ resurrected, ascended and glorified in her heart, and so was a prophet to seers in the age to come. She is resurrected with Christ resurrected, ascended with Christ ascended and glorified with Christ glorified and so her prophecy inspires prayer that prays the Spirit's unceasing prayer for all, interceding for all with unutterable groans and sighs, crying, '*Abba!* Father!'

The wisdom of Mary Magdalene's prophecy and prayer, taught by the Spirit of truth, hallows the Name here on earth, as it does eternally in heaven. If patriarchal ages had difficulty assimilating her wisdom, perhaps in our time, the time has at last come for the Spirit of truth to guide us into her truth, a truth we were unable to bear before.

Christ appeared first to her because she loved much. The Gospels bear witness to her love, so that she becomes a humble icon of the love that is stronger than death, as the Song of Songs puts it. Her love is the first to bear witness to the resurrection, and so is *Amma* to all who bear witness to resurrection, including all the apostles, prophets and saints. The last, with the other two Marys, to remain at the foot of the cross, she is the first to arrive at the tomb, the first to awaken to the resurrection that awakens all to resurrection. She loved much, and such love overcomes all obstacles, all 'powers' of confusion and division, transmitting a wisdom that mysteriously shines forth from the Bridal Chamber of the Holy of Holies.

'Touch me not,' is not 'no,' for love, but 'yes,' the 'yes' of resurrection, the 'yes' of ascension, the 'yes' of glorification, the 'yes' that transmits deification.

92.

The Father blesses us in the Son by pouring out his Spirit of truth, who eternally abides in the Son. The Spirit of truth imparts wisdom, which enlightens the 'eyes' of the heart, revealing God in our midst through his Name.

The mystery of love's glory is revealed by the Spirit in the Son, unveiling the radiance of love as ineffable openness of glory, revealed through the presence of bright oneness, in the hallowing glory of the Name.

The priority of the 'only-begotten Son' is never overtaken, nor is our growth into the fullness of his stature inverted into a usurpation of him. We are reborn in him, not confused with him. We are one spirit with him, infused by the Spirit, not confused. Divisive separation between the uncreated and the created is indeed overcome, but not at the price of a monistic swoon. Glory transcends monism as well as dualism in the mysteries of the Holy Trinity.

Wisdom is our home, because wisdom is first home to God, who unveils wisdom as icon of ineffable depths of glory, precisely where wisdom is already icon of ineffable heights of glory.

For the wisdom of the Holy of Holies, ascent is completed by descent, resurrection and ascension by glorification, which descends to embrace every last dark corner of hell and unite it to heaven.

The heights and the depths are one, one ineffable but unconfused openness, and the oneness is love's glorious completeness always already present as the destiny of love's glory from the beginning.

The perfection of wisdom is hid in completeness that embraces incompleteness as intrinsic to ineffable completeness, not as clever formula, but by costly love. Love's glory is revealed in ineffable completeness that embraces incompleteness, freeing it to embrace completeness.

93.

Glorification is ineffable, but is always much more than obedience to regulations, more than verbal assent, more than ways or means that have not yet turned, not yet seen the glory of ineffable love, ways and means that stop short of love's glory, hallowing the Name. The beyond of love's glory has always already gone beyond all mysteries that might claim to go beyond it.

The glorification of God's Name, as in the ancient un-translated invocation, '*HALLELU YAH,*' is inexhaustible. The glory of the Kingdom to come is always already present in wisdom songs, the hymns and doxologies that are scattered all over the New Testament.

All wisdom and all glory are present in this ineffable presence, present as wisdom transmitting wisdom through wisdom songs. Even the nothingness of pure nihilism is overcome when Christ is no longer just the object of love's glory, but its subject, its ground, and its inner principle. Nothing is actually outside this glory, or left out of this ineffable love.

The completeness of this glory of love defines us, because it reveals the Name, key to wisdom and glory.

The decisive recognition of God in his Name directly introduces love's glory as completeness.

Ineffable openness weds oneness and presence in consummate completeness, unveiled in the glory of the Name.

The consummation of this completeness embraces the expanding scope of ineffable glory.

The completeness of wisdom discerns the implications of love's glory.

94.

The Spirit unveils God to wisdom, imparting recognition of God in the midst. The Spirit is himself the wisdom that sees and the glory that is seen, abiding eternally in the Son, where generation and procession meet. The Father is love's glory poured out into the Son, meeting the Spirit as love's glory abiding in the Son, who is love's glory returning to the Father.

Wisdom is not sophistry, but love's glory lived and loved and known in the transfigured heart. God loves us in his Son, and God is loved in his Son, but it is the Spirit who proceeds from God to abide as love's glory in the Son, and who abides in the Son to restore us to God.

There is no argument between the Spirit and the Son, no envy, no rivalry or jealousy that separates God from God. In Christ, one died for all, so all are already dead to all that is not of God, all that separates us from God, all that confuses us with God and obstructs our union with him. Wisdom does not nullify difference or union, but preserves both in her embrace of both, as communion.

The *fiat* of wisdom does not conjure up the truth to which it offers consent, but assents to the truth of love's glory that the Spirit reveals. The *fiat* of wisdom is the *fiat* of the Cross, which baptizes us into Christ's death, resurrection, ascension and glorification. The mysteries of love's glory all pour forth from his pierced side, making us sons by grace in the only Son.

The Spirit prays, '*ABBA,* beloved Father,' in our midst. Love's glory abolishes confusion and separation, here at centre, unveiling the translucent destiny of illumination in the original transparency of purification, grounding transfiguration's glorification in transparent purity and luminous translucence.

Wisdom abides in glory and glory in wisdom, hallowing the Name in us, hallowing us in the Name. Wisdom lives for glory and glory for wisdom, in the image of God, the Spirit for the Son, the Son for the Father, the Father for the Spirit and the Son. Between God and God, love's glory glorifies God.

95.

The openness of the Father and the Son, veiled in the glory of the age to come, is one spirit with the openness of the Spirit in the Son, unveiled even now in the midst. It is indivisible openness, *parrhesia,* veiled in the glory of the Holy of Holies, revealed in glory to wisdom through the Name. The veiled face does see the glory but not as the unveiled face sees. When glorification sees openly what illumination sees veiled, the uncreated light of the glory of God is unveiled to wisdom.

The reason wisdom is loved is that she is witness to revelation of the Name, for without her, the veils remain closed. Wisdom, however, belongs to God, as glory does, so there is nothing here about which anyone can boast. Openness empties us of vainglory to fill us with right glorification, releasing vanity into vanity, so that glory is free to be glory of the hallowed Name. Glory ascribes glory to the uncreated, not to the created, in the Name, unveiling mysteries of the deification of creation through uncreated grace. Wisdom inhales glory so confusion and separation are no more, releasing abundant oneness and abounding openness of glory in the Name.

Abounding openness is abundant peace here where, in Christ, the separate becomes inseparable, and the interference and obstruction of the 'powers' is overcome. Overflowing openness, in the Spirit, embraces all who were far off, addressing 'I AM' as God's 'THOU,' in each and all. Wisdom trusts what the Name reveals, the hope of glory already unveiled and proleptically present in the abundant oneness and abounding openness of glory. The revelation of glory to wisdom, in the Name, frees glory to open glory to glory, in liberating openness.

Prophecy communicates completeness by embracing incompleteness. Prayer is then a wordless, patient sigh, releasing everything into liberating completeness. The Spirit intercedes for all with wordless sighs, releasing all in all. The Father holds nothing back, so when the Spirit cries, *'Abba'* Father, love's glory is wisdom's home. Love's glory is consummate completeness, poured out, by the Spirit, through the Son, to embrace incompleteness with abounding openness.

198

96.

Illumination sees one heaven of glory in wisdom's ascent, whereas glorification unfolds seven heavens of glory in wisdom's decent, harrowing seven hells of vainglory in wisdom's hallowing of the Name. The poetry of 'seven' should not be mistaken for conventional mathematics, or schematic constructions imposed on chaotic experience. Desert wisdom long ago absorbed the same Temple wisdom as Pythagoras, for which 'seven' is a symbol of completeness. Glorification is unfolding completeness, enfolding hells of incompleteness into heavens of expanding completeness. Wisdom's poetry of 'seven' comes into play to do justice to the enlightened scope of ineffable opening glory, hallowing the Name by harrowing hells of confusion and separation. Love's glory has this enlightening scope, which is wisdom's descent from heaven to hell on Holy Saturday, and includes resurrection, ascension and glorification in its blessed unfolding.

Clement's 'Stromateis' unfolds as seven books and seven stages of wisdom, in the tradition of Temple Wisdom, Apocalyptic and Hermetic mysteries, as well as the wisdom of Pythagoras. The symbolism of 'seven' is an example of Clement's ineffable language of the ineffable. Clement is consciously and deliberately both saying and not saying what cannot be said. He is not inappropriately divulging the mystery of the Holy of Holies at the heart of the Name, but he is communicating wisdom, which Paul calls manifold, and Clement calls variegated, even kaleidoscopic. He says he is 'obscure' for good reason, not because he is incapable of clarity.

The logic of Clement's mystagogy is neither a linear nor a lateral logic, but transcends both, to abide with the Spirit in the *Logos*. It is wisdom logic, that sees the *logoi* from within the *Logos*, a 'logic' of *theoria* that opens out into the wisdom of consummate completeness, *anakephalaiosis*, recapitulating the 'sevens' of wisdom in Christ. The poetry of 'seven' gives Clement ways to hand on the wisdom of the Apocalypse of John, and of Jesus, the wisdom of Enoch and the first Temple, so that Patristic wisdom is heir to the wisdom of the ancients as it unveils the glory of the age to come.

97.

The Name is the alpha of original destiny and the omega of consummate glory made one. Glorification in the Name lives this oneness as ineffable openness, made present by hallowing the Name so that the Kingdom comes. The 'single eye' sees the body as light, as glory, when the glory of 'I AM' is revealed. This glory is hidden with Christ in God, so that, in glorification, it is revealed with Christ in glory. Opening to this anticipates the Kingdom in the hallowed Name. Openness to this is the Kingdom come and God's will done. Openness to this reflects the glory of 'I AM,' but reflection, being direct, beholds the glory of the Name. *Theoria* sees. The light of the temporal gospel beholds this in time. The light of the eternal gospel beholds it unveiled in the Holy of Holies. The unveiled face beholds the glory of 'I AM.' We all behold this glory when we turn to 'I AM,' and the veil of the heart is pierced. The eye of Spirit, proceeding from the Father to behold the glory of the Son, bears witness to the eternal gospel, which sees the glory of 'I AM.'

Glorification is the glory of illumination ascending to the glory of Christ glorified, from glory to glory. The unveiled face beholds the image or icon of the glory of God in the face of Christ. Where the Spirit of 'I AM' is unveiled, there is always freedom, liberation and release from glory to glory. This proleptic anticipation of the Kingdom is wisdom's gift, but the critical tension holds steady in wisdom's embrace, because our incompleteness in time never usurps God's timeless completeness. Unconditioned hope is intrinsic to unconditioned love. Trust trusts love's glory as the love that unconditionally hopes. Future glory is present in the unveiled Name, giving trust, hope and love their glorious beauty. Wisdom does not extinguish the tension, but holds completeness steady in the midst of incompleteness.

Wisdom is always from glory to glory, well able to receive and interpret the glory given in the beginning, and the glory given at the end, together with the veils and unveilings in between. The Spirit comes to impart the wisdom of the ineffable, discerning the ineffable, and bearing witness to the ineffable with the help of ineffable symbols, in prophecy and prayer.

98.

Wisdom is folly to all who ignore the Spirit and refuse to let the Name unveil God in the midst. Wisdom remains hidden in realms where the 'powers' of confusion and separation rule unchallenged. God is usurped in the midst. Christ is crucified in every perception that is oblivious to the remembrance of God. The 'powers' would not crucify the Lord of glory if confusion no longer interfered. The 'powers' would recognize God in his Name and wisdom as God's seer, if they were not obstructing wisdom by imposing separation. Spiritual pride lays claim to wisdom on the basis of confusion, and vainglory presumes to own wisdom in isolated absolute knowledge, without undoing separation. Sound wisdom is folly to vainglory and pride.

The wisdom of the cross puts confusion and separation to death, unveiling the cruciform heart of form in glory, and the cruciform heart of the formless in the Name. The hammer of wisdom nails confusion and separation to the cross of love, unveiling the formless form of the Name. The circular movement of love is closed to vainglory and pride. Love's glory is closed to the 'powers' of closure, but open to glory, unveiling him as we are, unveiling us as he is.

Completeness is God's, not ours. Our incompleteness reminds us we are fallible and fall short of glory. Completeness is impossible for incompleteness, possible for illumination, and actual for wisdom discerning glory. Glorification lives the tension and unevenness between these 'ages,' without collapsing one into the other or dividing one from the other. The impossible actuality of wisdom is precious beyond words. Only wisdom can handle wisdom, which is why wisdom points beyond itself to Holy Trinity, not absolute isolation. Wisdom humbly acknowledges that the powerlessness of love overcomes the 'powers' of interference and obstruction, not puffed up sophistry. Wisdom is ever mindful of parodies that fail to hit the mark. Humble kindness sees more deeply than clever scrutiny. Wisdom tenderly unveils glory, in the gentle love that hallows the Name.

99.

Wisdom is joy, great joy. It is not the ephemeral elation that passes like a cloud, but the joy that underlies peace, present in the love that just loves. Unconditioned joy rejoices even in sorrow, even unto death. Joy weeps with the weeping, and laughs with the laughing, rejoicing in the glory of the Name. The power of joy is not a will to power. It infuses tribulation with the glory of the Name. In moments of abandonment, joy may not be felt, but is still present as the Name is present, upstream from feelings that come and go.

Great joy rejoices at forgiveness, awakening wisdom songs in heaven. Joy feasts when the prodigal returns, and leaves joy in the air, joy that lets none perish if trust trusts joy. Great joy is present, though veiled, even in the cry from the cross, 'My God, my God, why hast thou forsaken me?' There is no moment of extreme suffering that is abandoned by joy, that joy cannot love. Joy never turns away, so turning can always turn back to joy, whatever the conditions. Suffering is light when love loves, revealing joy in the midst of love, even in suffering.

Joy abides where the poor are blessed, and mourning, hunger and thirst are all states of ineffable, blessed openness. Joy frees all conditioned states to liberate into un-conditioning. Love's Cross at the heart of joy is the glory of love, the love that trusts joy beyond conditioning, and trusts trust without conditioning. Joy is the joy of all, rejoicing with all who rejoice, turning pain to joy. Love's embrace of suffering releases pain into pure joy. It frees pain to release into ineffable, glorious joy.

Christ is joy, turning pain to pure joy, which is the uncreated creative energy of resurrection, ascension, and glorification. Impossible for conditioning, these mysteries of glory are possible only when the unconditioned transcends conditioning, when wisdom discerns glory at the heart of the Name.

Suffering bears fruit as glory, renewing wisdom that renews the world through love. Completeness comes when Christ perfects love in us through our 'yes' to love, our 'Amen' to glory, our 'yes' to joy that makes love able to suffer without despair.

100.

The way of the Name may be narrow, but those that find it discover it is ineffable openness. The circle of twelve 'Centuries' began with the Name as a consuming fire. Confusion and division burn, so that union and communion rise unconsumed, like the burning bush in the desert, and wisdom's mystery of the Mother of God. The Name is God's self-revelation in our midst. The two-edged sword severs soul from spirit in the midst, releasing confusion into glorious openness. We begin where God is to be found, unveiled in the Name. We turn back, only to be turned right round, discovering the Holy of Holies to be right here where we are, unveiled in the primordial awakened state of grace in uncreated light. We end where we begin, but the Name is ever new, always able to make things new. There is nothing stale or weary about glory, nothing senile or decrepit about wisdom. Religions may age, but not wisdom, which renews them again and again.

'Wisdom Songs' began with *Logos* that names the Name, and ends when wisdom unfolds the glory of the Name as glorification, on the basis of purification and illumination. The way of the Name comes full circle when it returns to where it always begins, which is the glory of the Name before the beginning and after the end. The Name is Alpha and Omega, beginning and end, and all that passes between is the glory of hallowing. There is no end to glorification, which begins here in this life, but whose life is eternal. Christ is in our midst now, but he is as he shall always be, and we shall be as he is.

Love's glory in the Name not only bears suffering but bears witness to the suffering borne by the Son eternally, to the glory of the Father, borne also by the Spirit abiding eternally in the Son. When the Son suffers, pain rises from glory to glory. When the Son bears the suffering, it liberates. When the Son bears our pain, glory frees glory from vanity, to be glory in God to God. Love's glory in the saints abides here in the midst of the Father and the Son, glorifying the Father through the Son, with the Spirit's unceasing prayer in the heart, which is wisdom's glorification of the Name.

www.ingramcontent.com/pod-product-compliance
Lightning Source LLC
Chambersburg PA
CBHW021052090426
42738CB00006B/307

9 780983 586746